SEVEN CONSTRUCTIVIST METHODS FOR THE FOR THE SECONDARY CLASSROOM

A Planning Guide
for Invisible Teaching℠

Ina Claire Gabler, Ph.D.
Educational Consultant and Writer

Michael Schroeder, Ph.D.
Professor, Augustana College

Boston | New York | San Francisco
Mexico City | Montreal | Toronto | London | Madrid | Munich | Paris
Hong Kong | Singapore | Tokyo | Cape Town | Sydney

Series Editor: *Traci Mueller*
Series Editorial Assistant: *Erica Tromblay*
Marketing Manager: *Amy Cronin Jordan*
Production Editor: *Marissa Falco*
Composition Buyer: *Linda Cox*
Manufacturing Buyer: *Andrew Turso*
Cover Administrator: *Kristina Mose-Libon*
Electronic Composition: *Modern Graphics, Inc.*

For related titles and support materials, visit our online catalog at www.ablongman.com.

Between the time Website information is gathered and then published, it is not unusual for some sites to have closed. Also, the transcription of URLs can result in unintended typographical errors. The publisher would appreciate notification where these errors occur so that they may be corrected in subsequent editions.

Library of Congress Cataloging-in-Publication Data

Gabler, Ina Claire,
    Seven Constructivist Methods for the Secondary Classroom: A Planning Guide for
    Invisible Teaching / Ina Claire Gabler, Michael Schroeder.
        p. cm.
    Includes bibliographical references (p.) and index.
    ISBN 0-205-36056-4 (pbk. : alk. paper)
      1. Effective teaching. 2. Constructivism (Education)   I. Schroeder, Michael
    II. Title.

LB1025.3 .G32 2003
371.102—dc21

2002074617

Printed in the United States of America

10 9 8 7 6 5 4 3 2 1   07 06 05 04 03 02

#499427449

To Dave, for his devotion
ICG

To Sue, Nick, and Andy, with love
MS

■ CONTENTS ■

Section B BrushUp 35

It's said that it takes a village to raise a child. In a similar vein, we have learned that it takes a community of sorts to produce a book. We could not have written and published *Seven Constructivist Methods for the Secondary Classroom: A Planning Guide for Invisible Teaching* without the help of other professionals from the beginning to the end of the process.

We therefore wish to extend our sincere appreciation to all those who gave their best efforts on our behalf. Our editor, Traci Mueller, has extended her support and enthusiasm right from the start. Her sound advice helped us make important decisions throughout the revision process. Ms. Mueller's assistant, Erica Tromblay, was efficient, sincere, and always helpful.

We also extend our sincere thanks to the following colleagues for their incisive professional advice.

Randy Hengst, Augustana College, Rock Island, Illinois

Chuck Hyser, Augustana College, Rock Island, Illinois

Jack Garrett, Augustana College, Rock Island, Illinois

Melissa McBain, Augustana College, Rock Island, Illinois

Mary Ellen Verona, Maryland Virtual High School

We also appreciate the reviews of our early drafts from Jill Suzanne Bennin and Joanna Kluever. Many of the excellent suggestions went into the final draft.

Mike Schroeder would like to extend his thanks to Charles Weller, Orrin Gould, and George Kieffer of the University of Illinois at Urbana-Champaign for their impact on his professional development, an influence that can be found among these pages.

Thanks also to Deb Nelson and Angel Duncombe for their technical assistance.

We would like to express a special word of appreciation to David Curtis for his invaluable technical assistance as well as other areas of expertise throughout the entire process of this book.

We are grateful to all these people for their time, effort, and support.

THE LEARNING ENVIRONMENT

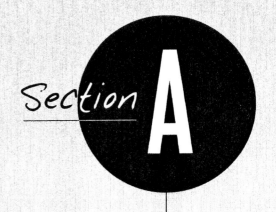

Section A

Overview

Welcome to Seven Constructivist Methods: A Planning Guide for Invisible Teaching. In this section, we give a global view of constructivism as ideology and practice in Module One, "What Is a Constructivist Approach?" In Module Two, Part 1 "Resocializing," we attempt to integrate the underpinnings of a student-centered, constructivist approach. We demonstrate how Maslow's Needs Hierarchy and Bloom's Taxonomy can work together in developing your students' cognitive abilities in a nonthreatening learning environment. We also invite you to consider various ways in which you can resocialize both yourself and your students from traditional to constructivist practices. Module Two, Part 2, "Classroom Management," provides many suggestions for a constructivist approach to discipline and engaging students in the learning process.

What Is a Constructivist Approach?

Human beings have always longed for magic. All through time—from the mythologies of ancient Greece to the snake oil of nineteenth-century America—people have looked to powers greater than their own to help them cope with life's endless challenges. Yet, magicians know better than anyone else that magic is a human construct.

Seasoned teachers know that magic in the classroom is the moment when a resistant student risks *trying* for the first time; when a frustrated student suddenly gains clarity; when a group of students, once passive learners, take initiative and work fruitfully on a problem-solving project.

How does a teacher work such breakthroughs? Seven Constructivist Methods: A Planning Guide for Invisible Teaching addresses that question for the professional teacher. Fledgling and seasoned teachers have different professional needs, but there's one thing they both have in common. The danger of growing stale, of succumbing to routine, otherwise known as *burnout.* How does the fledgling teacher cope with the overwhelming tasks as well as the excitement of juggling all the demands within and apart from teaching itself while still learning the craft and art of the professional? How does the veteran teacher maintain that younger enthusiasm and zest after eight, fifteen, or twenty years and more?

We believe that our constructivist methods help both groups of teachers. For the novice, these methods and techniques provide clear, structured, yet flexible guide-posts. If you're a seasoned professional, constructivist methods can help restore your sense of discovery. If you're already working with student-centered approaches, these cohesive instructional strategies and practical ideas can enhance your talents further and enrich your classroom for both you and your students.

The *constructivist* perspective on learning holds particular relevance for teachers in all subjects at all levels and will be the governing practice within this inservice guide. In some respects, the origins of constructivism may be traced to the perspectives on the learner described by John Dewey, Jean Piaget, and Lev Vygotsky over the first half of the twentieth century.

Dewey placed great emphasis on connecting to students' "capacities, interests, and habits" through the establishment of interactive, student-centered "learning communities" within the classroom (Dewey, 1934). Piaget articulated a developmental perspective on constructivism as he investigated the influence of experience on how children learn in various settings. Piaget's later research and writing (1965–1980) focused especially on learning as a dynamic, multidimensional, nonlinear process involving stages of disequilibrium, that is, consideration of existing ideas that contradict, expand, or are different from new information, and subsequent construction of new cognitive structures (Fosnot, 1996). Vy-

gotsky placed even greater emphasis on the importance of a social context as learners actively construct knowledge. Vygotsky (1931/1978) asserted that knowledge cannot be imposed by adults, that the creation of productive new cognitive structures within learners is best facilitated in an interactive setting in which learners have some degree of control over the nature and direction of discussions and activities and help each other learn.

Learning, from the constructivist perspective, is best promoted through an active process emphasizing purposeful interaction and the use of knowledge in real situations, otherwise known as *authentic learning.* We believe that much about this constructivist perspective is conveyed through an ancient Chinese proverb:

> *I hear and I forget.*
> *I see and I remember.*
> *I do and I understand.*

The implications of the constructivist perspective and associated research on students, teachers, and classrooms are nothing short of revolutionary. We hope that this perspective challenges you to think about the processes of teaching and learning in new ways. In describing this perspective in more detail, we believe that a constructivist teacher is one who recognizes the following:

- Learners of any age make sense of new experiences by relating them to their own previous experiences. Making ideas understandable from a learner's point of view is not merely a motivational ploy or nice when possible, but *essential* for deep learning.

- Memorization of facts and reproducing information on tests is not the path to developing deep, flexible understanding of any subject. Although it may be necessary to memorize certain facts as part of a learning experience, deeper learning involves cognitive restructuring on the part of the student. We believe that a teacher's most important role is as a "stage setter" and facilitator of this active learning process.

- Learning is something that a learner does, not something that is done to the learner. Because meaningful learning involves active cognitive restructuring, students must be involved in the learning process, making their own inferences and experiencing and resolving cognitive dissonance (i.e., struggling with new ideas that contradict or differ from existing beliefs).

- Effective teaching involves continual probing of the nature of student understanding, "getting into students' heads" to the greatest extent possible.

- Deeper understanding includes gaining insights into the connections between disciplines and knowledge of the ways of thinking within them.

- Superficial, *encapsulated* information is the result of teaching that emphasizes *covering* content rather than building student understanding through active student experiences both within the classroom and in the world at large.

- Continual reflection on practice (i.e., thinking carefully about what we're doing and why) is a vital part of effective teaching, an activity that promotes the learning of students and the empowerment of teachers as professionals.

Each method and technique we suggest in this guide will reflect constructivist beliefs. If you've never or rarely attempted a constructivist, student-centered approach in your classroom, early efforts along these lines might create cognitive dissonance, a clash with present beliefs or practices, within you as a teacher. We ourselves experienced this dissonance when we each began to consider shifting from the model of teacher-as-dispenser-of-information to the model of teacher-as-facilitator-of-critical-thinking. But it didn't take long to be convinced. During our earlier years as secondary teachers of inner-city and mainstream students, we began to experiment with student-centered methods. Our students often worked on projects tailored to their interests and participated in open-ended discussions. They researched and created products (magazines, videos, original experiments, etc.) for real audiences or real applications as *authentic learning*. The higher our expectations, the harder our students worked. Engaged in their original efforts, they sometimes pleaded to remain behind when the bell rang. This kind of student reaction is every teacher's dream come true.

So, if we catch ourselves blaming our students for their apathy or supposed "inability to learn," we may need to plan with a *more,* not less, challenging approach that relates to the students' interests. Our Resocializing module includes a suggested plan for helping your students—and you—orient to such a constructivist setting. The results may amaze you as well as your students.

In using *Invisible Teaching,* you'll discover that a constructivist classroom will feature the following:

- *Assessment through performance,* with a wide range of suggested assessment methods

- *Curricula that emphasize depth over breadth* and big ideas

- *Teacher as guide/facilitator/coach;* student as worker/ independent thinker

- *Interaction,* with value placed on teacher- and student-generated questions, and consistent use of methods that promote student–student interaction

- *Variety of teaching methods* utilized, even within a single class period

- *Engagement of students* in subject matter, with students becoming historians, writers, scientists, mathematicians, and so on

In these ways, the techniques and constructivist methods in this inservice guide help you as an innovative teacher to enhance your classroom as an *active* place.

The constructivist learning perspective has a direct connection to you as a product of our current educational system. All of us, owing to our past experiences *as students,* consciously or unconsciously develop assumptions about teaching and about students as passive listeners, assumptions that may not change as a result of experiences in education courses or as veteran teachers. If some students fail to thrive, we often succumb to our assumptions and blame the students, their background, and so on. One of our major goals in this professional training program will be to help you recognize and reconsider some of your possible beliefs regarding teaching that may unintentionally foster a passive student role and even boredom. If you are already attempting to develop your students' critical-thinking potential as active learners, this program may further develop your own ideas and practices. Like many professionals, you may straddle both fences. If so, *Invisible Teaching* can provide direction to enhance your talents with a student-centered approach.

To sum up our ideas so far, we believe that two areas need to be integrated in order to shift students from the familiar role of listeners to that of active learners: *affect* and *constructivist methods.* By affect we mean state of mind and state of being, the student's belief in self-empowerment. By methods we mean instructional templates for lessons that encourage students to *construct meaning,* to be critical thinkers, to be independent learners, with the teacher as an informed mentor, facilitator, and co-learner.

Our constructivist methods use Bloom's Taxonomy (1956) as a guide for cognitive growth. Bloom's approach moves from low cognitive skills such as *naming, defining,* and *applying* to high cognitive skills such as *analysis, synthesis,* and *evaluation.* Using this hierarchy, though not always in a linear fashion, creates comfort when students explore new and complex ideas, challenging learners when they are ready to take a *leap* rather than intimidating them too early and making them feel "stupid." In addition, we describe the importance of affect or state of mind in our discussion of Abraham Maslow's Needs Hierarchy in Module Two, "Resocializing." This module suggests how to integrate Bloom's Taxonomy and Maslow's Needs Hierarchy with constructivism. In this way, we're carrying out our belief that *affect is the gateway and critical thinking the pathway to meaningful learning.*

In addition to methods, we provide a gallery of techniques that you can use creatively with all the methods.

Because methods and techniques are often confused with each other, we'll briefly clarify the difference here. A method is a blueprint or template, a cohesive instructional strategy. For example, each method, such as the Exploratory Discussion or Inductive Concept method, contains specific features or characteristics that we call *method markers*. A technique, on the other hand, is a specific practice or procedure that can be employed with any method. Examples of techniques are role-playing, questioning, personalizing, concept mapping, peer-group interaction, and so on. We pay special attention to questioning techniques, which we consider to be the underpinning of all methods. Each method is designed either to be used as the cohesive template for a single lesson or to be combined into a combo lesson; that is, minisegments of two or more methods can be integrated into one lesson to meet your instructional intentions most effectively.

A dominant feature of *Invisible Teaching* is its modular format; the modules are divided into three parts: Section A, *The Learning Environment, BrushUp,* and *Constructivist Methods.* Section A, *The Learning Environment,* attempts to give you a global perspective on constructivism as practice as well as ideology. As the name suggests, Section B, *BrushUp,* presents familiar aspects of planning, some of which you may use more than others. *BrushUp* may also introduce you to some new ideas that can expand your repertoire of planning and teaching practices. In addition, *BrushUp* establishes a common planning template with Core Components for workshop participants. Our seven methods are described in Section C, *Constructivist Methods,* complete with sample lessons and tips for technology. The modules build on one another, yet they're autonomous, permitting flexible, nonlinear use according to need or interest.

For standards in sample lessons we refer to the Interstate New Teacher Assessment and Support Consortium (INTASC). The INTASC Standards (see Appendix) govern teacher training and as such are appropriate for an inservice workshop. The INTASC Standards have also influenced content foci and social learning goals in specific subject areas. Both the INTASC and subject-area standards emphasize a constructivist, affective approach to learning. INTASC Standards therefore apply to all subject areas and provide a uniform standard for teachers of all subjects, novice or experienced, in this training program.

As standardized testing increasingly becomes a national measure of achievement, educators may question if a constructivist approach, which emphasizes the process of learning, can result in enough "right answers" on national multiple-choice exams. The answer is yes. A constructivist classroom encourages quality learning rather than rote repetition. Memorization—of definitions, numerical operations, important dates, lines in a play, and so on—has an important place in learning. However, retention serves as the foundation for higher cognitive levels rather than as the ultimate goal. Research has shown that constructivist teaching, which emphasizes critical thinking in authentic contexts, produces results on standardized tests that are at least equal to those of traditional teaching (Wiggins & McTighue, 1998). In addition, other assessments that examine conceptual understanding and critical-thinking skills reflect superior results for constructivist-taught students over traditionally taught students (Newmann, 1997). Two of our methods are especially designed to meet the demands of a syllabus with information overload: the Directed Discussion and the Interactive Presentation methods in Modules 9 and 12, respectively.

In addition, our methods and techniques can help you teach more effectively with technology. See our "Fishy Mystery" scenario in Section C, *Overview of Constructivist Methods.*

We are sharing these methods with you as a way of helping you to expand your teaching repertoire, not promoting them as anything absolute. We hope that you will apply your own successes in the classroom and adapt some or all of the method templates to your own ideas, talents, and your students' learning needs, even taking risks as you experiment, making the methods your own. As for ourselves—former secondary teachers and now teacher educators—we keep relearning that a constructivist approach enables all students as well as teachers to cross new thresholds of learning and thinking.

Which brings us back to magic.

When you combine positive affect—that is, the students' belief in their ability to learn—with constructivist methods that foster independent thinking and awaken a love of learning from early childhood, be prepared for breakthroughs. A resistant student takes his first plunge. A confused student discovers an elusive principle herself. Groups of once-bored students apply themselves with newfound motivation.

A rabbit may not appear out of thin air. However, the challenges and motivation in a constructivist learning environment can take your classroom as a place of engaged minds and spirit beyond what you may now think is possible.

REFERENCES

Bloom, B. (ed.). (1956). *Taxonomy of educational objectives, handbook I: Cognitive domain.* New York: David McKay.

Dewey, J. (1934). *Art as experience.* New York: Minton & Balch.

Fosnot, C. (Ed.). (1996). *Constructivism: Theory, perspectives, and practice.* New York: Teachers College Press.

Newmann, F. N., & Associates (1997). *Authentic achievement: Restructuring schools for intellectual quality.* San Francisco: Jossey-Bass.

Vygotsky, L. S. (1931/1978). *The mind and society: The development of higher psychological processes.* Cambridge, MA: Harvard University Press.

Wiggins, G., & McTighe, J. (1998). *Understanding by design.* Alexandria, VA: Association for Supervision and Curriculum Development.

A

Module Two

Resocializing

PART I
The Importance of Change

■ OVERVIEW

change **Change** changE cHange **chAnge**
chaNge **chanGe** Change

Ain't nothin'
like puffin'
on a pipe,
settlin' in,
feelin' that the world's just right.
Hmm mmm!
comfy & cozy &
keepin' out nosy
pokes
trying to stoke
up trouble, double
talkin', fast walkin'
through my mind,
sayin',
"Times a' changin',
Sam.
Just listen
to that man."
Invasion
of a kind.
But I'm stayin'
just the way
I
am.
Yes, siree.
I'm fine with me.
Ain't no hurry
to rise up out of my nice
stuffed chair
and hit cold air
to cross the street
just to meet
a stranger.
© 2001 Ina Claire Gabler

Change. We fight it. We find all kinds of reasons for it to be unnecessary. We justify things as they are merely because they always have been so.

Why do we resist change?

We can offer many reasons. Take the verse "Change" for example. We all like to feel comfortable. Staying with the familiar gives us the sense that we fit into the world in a defined place. New ideas may challenge our perceptions of things and because of that, new ideas may make us feel insecure, wobbly on our legs, uncomfortably *strange.* We're not sure how to proceed when we become uncertain of *the rules.* The longer we stick with the familiar without challenging ourselves to discover new pathways, the more likely that we will become rigid and stale. This is when we risk blaming our students when they lack zest for learning.

This module is devoted to the importance of change. We invite you now to reflect on the role you play as a teacher and the part you encourage your students to take in their learning.

■ GOALS

We hope to encourage you to reflect on your assumptions about teaching. This reflection includes comparing traditional practices with constructivist ones in the following areas:

- Awareness of a wide range of your students' needs
- The importance of the classroom setting
- The nature of the teacher's response to students
- Teacher and student roles
- Materials versus methods
- Meta-awareness
- Modeling peer-group learning

■ FOCAL POINTS AND DISCUSSIONS

If you are willing to weather uncertainty in the process of changing, if you embrace the spirit of discovery and growth at whatever age you may be, then the more likely you will be the type of teacher who is ever youthful, ready to try new things all through your teaching career. This aspiration has a rough road at times. Many students have a negative attitude toward school. Often they have not succeeded in the traditional-style classroom. Some students lack a home environment that fosters study. Low self-esteem, anger, and boredom are frequent consequences of the broken contract between our schools and the students they are meant to enrich.

With self-initiated and motivated students, almost any teaching mode will harvest bounty. Of course, this statement raises the question of standards, the goals and criteria by which we work toward success in school. But for now, let's assume that success means doing well on exams and maintaining a stake in being an engaged student. With at-risk or bored students who do not excel, however, the challenge to be an innovative teacher is a trumpet call. But even motivated students are entitled to *take joy* in learning through creative teaching.

We believe that *every human being wants to learn.*

If our students appear flat, uninterested, if they don't seem to care about grades, or if they don't appear motivated to challenge themselves or able to think critically, we as teachers have not found the way to reach those particular students. Shoveling on more of the same teaching approach—teacher talk and question–answer dialogue that seeks "right" answers much like an oral quiz—may not be the way to stir your students' interest. We need to discover what their frames of reference are and relate our subject to that, and we need to find methods of *actively engaging* our students with what we know is valuable in our subject area so that the students *experience* the value for themselves, rather than listen to our claims and take our word for it. In other words, we need to use our intelligence and imagination in fresh ways.

Which brings us back to the importance of change: change in the student role, change in the teacher role, change in the very concept of what constitutes *learning* and *teaching.* If your students have been socialized over the years to take a passive role, they need to be resocialized to take an active role. That means that you may want to reflect on your concept of the teacher's role. If you assume that the teacher takes the limelight as the *dispenser of knowledge* (Cuban, 1996; Freedman, 1992; Johnson & Johnson, 1989; Kyle et al., 1996; Putnam, 1997; Slavin, 1995), that role dovetails with a passive student role. To be on the cutting edge as a constructivist, hands-on teacher who facilitates active learning—critical thinking and problem solving—you may need to reconsider your assumption about the teacher's role as it applies to yourself.

With these points in mind, let's turn to the elements that change a traditional classroom into a constructivist one.

Focal Point 1 Maslow's Needs Hierarchy

Teacher and student roles interact to shape the classroom environment. These roles, in turn, are bound up with your students' and your own needs. Needs and change are interrelated. In his book *Motivation and Personality,* Abraham Maslow (1987) describes a hierarchy of human needs that now bears his name. If you sincerely want to help your students change their self-perceptions from passive listeners to active learners, then Maslow's Needs Hierarchy is an important guide. We've summarized the hierarchy in the following discussion. As you consider each need, think of how it could apply to resocializing your students as constructivist learners—and resocializing yourself as a constructivist teacher.

Discussion 1 Maslow's Needs Hierarchy

WISDOM IS ALWAYS NEWS

[T]he individual is an integrated, organized whole . . . it means the whole individual is motivated rather than just a part. . . . [S]atisfaction comes to the whole individual and not just to part of him. Food satisfies John Smith's hunger and not his stomach's hunger.

—Abraham H. Maslow (1987, p. 3)

A Foundation of Needs

How do we as educators motivate the "whole" person within the four walls of a classroom? What triggers a teacher's motivation to be the focal point or to be a facilitator? What triggers a student's motivation to persist with a task in pursuit of excellence through the wax and wane of interest? If Maslow is right, then the answer lies in the gratification of values and needs for both teacher and student as human beings. According to Maslow, these needs occur in the following hierarchy:

1. Basic physiological needs: These range from physical hunger, shelter, sex, and sleep to the need for activity. There is an endless range of physical survival needs, which could include the need for sensory stimulation.

2. Safety needs: Like physiological needs, safety needs have a wide range according to the individual. Examples of safety needs are security; stability; protection; freedom from fear, anxiety, and chaos; structure; law; and so on. (p. 18).

3. Belonging and love needs: This needs center involves mutual affection with friends, spouse, family, and community members. If an individual is not able to establish such affection relationships, the results can be destructive: disorientation, isolation, and the like. Gangs satisfy the need to belong as do various training and self-help groups.

4. Self-esteem needs: Self-respect and esteem for others fall into this needs center. The first tier includes desire for competence, strength, achievement, and mastery as well as independence and freedom. The second tier includes the desire for high reputation, recognition, appreciation, dignity, and so on. Satisfaction of these needs results in self-confidence and a sense of worth, capability, and being useful in the world.

5. Self-actualization needs: In Maslow's words, "What humans *can* be, they *must* be" (p. 22). Self-actualization is the need for fulfillment in one's own terms, according to one's gifts and abilities. It is the desire to increasingly become what we have the potential to be. On this level, one achieves *by choice* as singer, writer, carpenter, athlete, teacher, hot-rod racer, or at any pursuit that manifests one's individual talents.

Although he describes these basic needs as emerging in a hierarchy, that is, the gratification of a lower need (e.g., physiological needs) permits the expression of a higher need (e.g., safety needs), Maslow emphasizes that these needs are not linear. For example, a student's act of persisting in a writing task for school may express safety and esteem needs (maintaining a high average and staying in an advanced class), love needs (earning parental and teacher approval), and self-actualization (desiring to become a professional writer one day).

The Importance of Affect

The common denominator of the needs in Maslow's hierarchy is affect. *Affect,* the noun, refers to feelings, a state of mind, state of being, and so on. The affect of your students in your classroom significantly influences the quality of learning. Chances are that as a student, you yourself were turned on to learning for its own sake in those classes in which you experienced positive affect.

Examples of Maslow's Needs in the Classroom

Let's explore Maslow's hierarchy in terms of your students' attitude or affect in *your* classroom.

1. Basic physiological needs: Applied to classroom learning, this need level ranges from your students' being well-fed and well-slept to being physically comfortable with the seating arrangement, room temperature, lighting, and so on so that they can concentrate. If you notice students who frequently sleep in your class or who are chronically irritable, some of their physiological needs may be deprived. This shortfall may result from such things as a student working too much at a job, neglect at home, or substance abuse. Referring such students to a guidance counselor or a school breakfast program or calling parents may help.

2. Safety needs: The feeling of safety is absolutely crucial in a constructivist classroom. In this instance, safety translates into a nonjudgmental atmosphere that welcomes all responses. No boom or disapproval should fall on students who give "wrong" answers in earnest. Instead, the constructivist teacher seeks to guide insight into appropriate schemata, meaning, parcels of information, or concepts with specific characteristics such as *tree* or *war*. As for those students who clown and toss out silly answers to win laughs, let them know you expect them to take the lesson seriously—even, if appropriate, while acknowledging the humor. It is important to remember that at times there ARE right or wrong answers, or valid versus facile interpretations, so **not** everything goes. But a

constructivist teacher emphasizes the *thought process* as an exploration that leads students to an appropriate schema with documented justifications. This matters. Many times, students give the "right" answer without meaningful understanding (Fosnot, 1989).

3. Belonging and love needs: Is it painful to remember your prepubescent and teenage years? For many of us, it was a time of self-doubts and with that feeling, the strong need for acceptance and belonging. This is the time of life when peer pressure reigns supreme. It makes sense that feeling safe to express ideas in your classroom ties in with a teenager's belonging and love needs. Nobody likes to feel diminished in a group, especially young people with tender egos. Love in this instance has a broad application, from your approval and peer approval to parental approval. The practice of affirming students' ideas and efforts to participate along with sending home even form letters of earned praise (e.g., for classwork, preparation, etc. as well as quality work) can help build positive affect in your classroom. This supportive approach is especially helpful for at-risk students (Lowan, 1990; Morris, 1991; Romano, 1987) and those insecure about their learning ability. These students need to build a new self-image that's compatible with school success. (It's important to be *consistent,* but not overly zealous or patronizing, with this type of positive reinforcement.) So we're talking about the interrelationship among social needs, self-esteem, and learning in your classroom.

4. Self-esteem needs: Self-esteem ties in with self-expectations. If a student has developed the self-concept of being an inadequate student over the years, then she will obviously not take the risks important for learning or exert much effort to engage in school. Helping this young person to change her self-image as a competent learner will slowly improve her positive self-esteem in your classroom. This positive affect will build upon itself if your setting is safe, affirming, and challenging without intimidation. The willingness to take risks and reach out for learning relates to the student's perception of self-empowerment (Weiner, 1972). For example, if a fourteen-year-old student with a low reading level believes it is "too late" for him to learn how to read and write according to his age, that student believes that self-empowerment is beyond his will, that his undeveloped literacy skills reflect his inborn inability to read and write well. In this case, you might try to find motivating reading materials (perhaps outside your subject area, depending on his interests) that ensure success for him at first, then increase the difficulty of the materials. In this way, the fourteen-year-old begins to see that he can, with motivation, learn, that his perseverance will eventually lead to success. We know this is harder than it sounds and that some students need far more than occasional encouragement.

As always, you will need patience, persistence, and *imagination.* Most of all, you will need faith in a student's ability to transcend disappointments in *learning how to learn*—her disappointments and yours. As more of your students develop positive self-esteem and increasingly take risks in the stimulation of a constructivist setting, they will grow in self-confidence as learners. Your own self-confidence in yourself as a teacher will also strengthen.

5. Self-actualization needs: You and your students both need this: the fulfillment of the goals that personally matter to each of you. For yourself, this may mean being an effective constructivist teacher whose approach integrates the social and learning needs of your students. Your self-actualization may include watching your students blossom or an at-risk student raising his hand for the first time. As for the students themselves, many of them may not yet know what they want to strive for. After years of boredom and failure to excel in a traditional school setting, many of them will be deadened to the joy of learning—for shouldn't learning be exciting? stimulating? gratifying? deepening?

EVERYBODY WANTS TO LEARN. If you make efforts to relate your subject to your students' world, if you create a safe environment in which positive affect and self-esteem can thrive, many of your students will rediscover the joy in learning that they once knew in kindergarten and first grade. That rediscovery is the beginning of their self-actualization. As these students awaken from slumber, both you and they will be amazed at how capable they are.

Of course, some, if not many, of your students will have a clear sense of what they want; they will be confident because they have enjoyed success in school. In this instance, your task will be to challenge them in new ways so that their imaginations and critical-thinking skills reach higher levels. They may also come to value learning more for its intrinsic value than for kudos and high GPAs.

Focal Point 2 The Setting

The *classroom setting* (otherwise called *setting*) refers to the overall learning environment. The environment, in turn, is comprised of two aspects. One is the *instructional mode* that fosters different teacher and student roles, from teacher-centered to student-centered. The other environmental aspect of the setting refers to the *physical configuration* of the room. The distinguishing feature of the setting is the *nature of teacher–student interaction.* Underlying all these elements is the teacher role as dispenser of knowledge versus facilitator.

Discussion 2 The Setting

In a teacher-centered setting, you would be at the center of the lesson, dispensing information, interpreting, analyzing, evaluating as if filling up your students' brains. In this setting, you might ask occasional questions, but they would be mostly at a low cognitive level, stressing right versus wrong with little if any expectation of your students engaging in a thinking process of their own. In the teacher-centered setting, your students assume a passive role as listeners, memorizers, and repeaters of information. The interaction pattern in the teacher-centered setting is mostly teacher–student (t–s), with some s–t at a mostly low cognitive level.

At the opposite end of the pole is the *student-centered* setting. In this learning environment, you expect your students to be independent learners, self-initiators. The student role in a student-centered setting is one of active learner, a problem solver, a seeker and finder, a learner learning how to learn, who knows that *mistakes* are an essential part of the learning process. In the student-centered classroom, your teacher role is that of a well-prepared facilitator, mentor, catalyst, someone who learns along with your students, especially in exploratory lessons in which the outcomes are not yet known. The interaction pattern in a student-centered setting is largely s–s with some s–t–s in the form of mentoring.

In the middle of this continuum is the *teacher-directed/student-focused* setting. As the setting name suggests, in this context you as the teacher *steer* your students, but at the same time, your students take an *active role,* engaging in critical thinking and even, for example, selecting topics and formulating questions for a unit that you design. In addition, you relate the lessons to your students' frames of reference. In this setting, the interaction pattern is a combination of t–s, t–s–t and s–s.

Conscious awareness of the differences among learning environments enables you to resocialize your students—along with yourself—from *this* kind of setting with *this* t–s interaction to *that* kind of setting and *that* kind of s–s interaction. Figure 2.1 encapsulates the features of these three settings.

Examples of Elements in the Setting

Several elements contribute to, *but do not ensure,* a student-centered or student-focused setting. Here's a list of the major elements.

EXAMPLE #1/PHYSICAL CONFIGURATIONS: HOW ARE THE DESKS ARRANGED?

a. *Open seating.* We suggest that on the first day of the school year your students sit in the conventional row configuration to which they're most ac-

Teacher-Centered	Teacher-Directed and Student-Focused	Student-Centered
• The teacher is the focal point. • The teacher controls all content, ideas, projects, performance criteria, etc. • Students must think mostly in the teacher's terms.	• The teacher selects the focal points but tries to relate information to the students' frames of reference. Teacher mostly facilitates. • Students' interpretations are encouraged and compared to an appropriate schema. • Students choose their unit or project topics within the teacher's prescription. • Some teachers permit students to envision their own topics with justification and teacher approval. • The teacher usually decides on standards of performance but may also encourage students to design their own with the teacher's approval.	• Students take initiative governed by the teacher's instructional Rationales. • Students conceive of appropriate topics and projects and work together in small groups as peer mentors, collaborators, or as individuals. • Students assign roles to themselves and one another. • The teacher is essentially a co-learner and resource person who makes clear what the Rationales are. • Performance criteria are usually determined by the teacher, but sophisticated students may determine even the criteria, with teacher approval, by which the teacher evaluates their work.

Figure 2.1   Teacher-Centered . . . Student-Centered Settings
© 2001 Ina Claire Gabler

customed. On that first day you can inform your students that on the next day the seats will be arranged in a circle or U-shape with one or two staggered rims. The configuration of the seats can be the impetus to begin meta-awareness (i.e., a global view, perception of the larger picture) and resocializing in the following ways.

The first time they are seated in an open configuration in your classroom, you might ask why they think you want them to sit this way and what the difference is in how they feel in this arrangement. Try arranging the desks in a circle, or a double horseshoe with seats in the second rim staggered in between spaces of the seats in the first rim so that every student has an unobstructed view. (See Figure 2.2 for a graphic representation of this seating arrangement.) In both these open configurations, you're free to stand and facilitate discussions as well as sit among the students as you choose—on the side, in the back, or in front. The open-seating configurations give every student an up-close feeling, right there in the midst of what's happening. There is no back of the room, only up-front **seats.**

b. *Peer-group seating.* Other times, the desks can be arranged in small-group clusters. We suggest three to five members to a group, with four being the optimal number for most activities. Dyads or pairs are also effective depending on your instructional intentions. Activity sheets with social roles are key for productive,

independent, peer-group learning (see Module 6, Parts One and Two).

c. *Rows.* This traditional configuration arranges students so that they all face you in the front of the room. Students in the back often feel removed from you up there at the podium. Some students, especially those who are not successful or engaged with your subject matter, intentionally sit in the back in order to hide out, a situation that only increases their alienation.

EXAMPLE #2/TEACHER AND STUDENT ROLES: ACTIVE VERSUS PASSIVE LEARNING

---

a. Awareness of the physical arrangement in the room and its influence on the learning atmosphere can lead into a discussion of teacher and student roles. Such discussions may be brief, a prelude to a lesson, and repeated for emphasis and a more in-depth meta-awareness in following lessons.

b. Some student responses may be silly and immature, others serious. The immature responses may be evidence that those students have been socialized to be passive listeners with little sense of responsibility for their own learning. They may feel threatened at first rather than positively challenged by the notion of an active student role. Immature responses mark the challenge of your resocializing.

EXAMPLE #3/ASKING QUESTIONS: PROMPTING CRITICAL THINKING

Using a global advance organizer (see Modules 4 and 12), inform your students that you will be asking questions more than lecturing or explaining. Otherwise, students may react in the following ways:

a. They may feel uneasy about making the necessary mind shift as quickly as you would like because they are accustomed to being passive and feel safe in that familiar role with prescribed behavior.

b. They may feel threatened by frequent questions, thinking that you are poking them for "right" answers. So it's a good idea to assure them that you're after the process of sharing ideas, that so-called mistakes are a necessary part of the thinking process and learning, that if they participate thoughtfully, it doesn't matter if they're right or wrong as individuals. At the end, they will arrive at justified conclusions as a team.

Now consider this. You might want to open a brief discussion about the value of asking and formulating questions. You might ask them "Why?" a lot (e.g., "Why do questions help you learn?," "Why is it important to think on your own?," etc.). You could also ask them how they feel at first about the technique of questioning. Some students may feel nervous about the new role you're asking them to take, and a discussion may help ease doubts about your motivation.

EXAMPLE #4/ESTABLISHING GUIDELINES: CREATING A SAFE ENVIRONMENT

Take a look at these examples.

Don't interrupt.

Never laugh at someone else's response. All smart people make mistakes when they're learning.

Don't mock or name-call.

Always be respectful, especially when you don't agree with someone else's viewpoint. Treat your classmates they way you want them to treat you.

You can also invite the students to codify their own guidelines for a safe learning setting. We have repeatedly found that this approach motivates students and gives them a stake in the classroom setting because it's *theirs.* To start them off, you could ask them something like, "What kind of peer behavior or guidelines would *you* need in our classroom to feel safe in open discussions?"

Now we'd like you to study Figure 2.3, which describes the continuum from a teacher-centered to a student-centered context. As you study Figure 2.3, reflect on these six questions. Use these questions as prompts to discuss your assumptions about teaching and learning with a colleague or with the entire group.

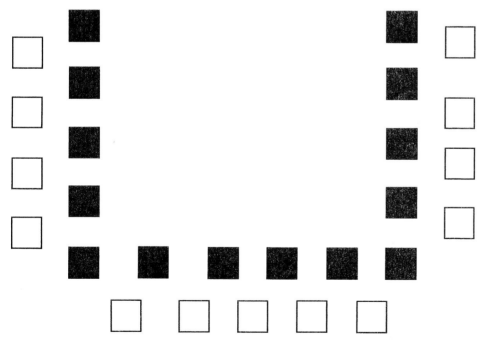

FIGURE 2.2 Staggered Horseshoe Seating
© 2001 Ina Claire Gabler

	Teacher-Centered	**Teacher-Directed and Student-Focused**	**Student-Centered**
Source of Initiation	Teacher-dispensed ideas	Teacher's and students' ideas	Students' ideas with teacher guidance
Content	Subject focused = right vs. wrong answers	Student focused = material related to students' frames of reference; thought process emphasized.	Student focused = material related to students' frames of reference; thought process emphasized.
Social Interaction	None or limited t–s	t–s as facilitation; t–s–s–t;	s–s; t–s as facilitation
Teacher's Role	Dispenser of knowledge	Informed facilitator, resource, and dispenser; prepares and guides students to think logically and critically; provides learning structure; encourages students' original insights with documented justifications	Informed facilitator, resource, and co-learner; prepares and guides students to think logically and critically; encourages students' original learning structures and insights with documented justifications

FIGURE 2.3 Classroom Settings
© 2001 Ina Claire Gabler

1. Which setting is what you and your students are most accustomed to?

2. Which setting is conducive to a constructivist approach? In what ways?

3. Which setting would be most comfortable to you at this moment? Why?

4. What are the advantages and disadvantages of each setting?

5. What beliefs about teaching and learning might you want to reconsider based on the features of the three classroom settings we have described? How do these beliefs relate to your role? to the students' role?

6. When would you employ each setting and why?

● Pause here to discuss these questions with colleagues before you continue.

Continuum

The teacher-directed/student-focused setting and the student-centered setting are not mutually exclusive. Instead, they can overlap each other on a continuum. The defining difference between these two settings is that in the teacher-directed setting, you as the teacher provide the learning structure(s), that is, a plan for learning or carrying out an activity, lesson, or project, prompts and

directions, Rationales, and so on. In the student-centered setting, you would define what the broad goals are, but the students would create their own learning structures best suited for carrying out those goals.

Both settings overlap in significant ways. For example, your students in both settings must formulate their own questions and tasks to direct the thinking process. Similarly, students in both settings obtain source materials in addition to the ones you provide, building the knowledge base itself and formulating concepts, principles, and unifying themes, adding materials as necessary. So the teacher-directed/student-focused setting is a precursor to the student-centered setting in which you become a co-learner for projects of new inquiry while also facilitating and guiding that inquiry.

Looks Can Deceive

A classroom setting may appear to be student-centered. Students may be arranged in small groups working together. The teacher may meet with individual students in quiet conferences. Yet, even you as the teacher may be deceived. If the lesson is designed so that you dictate what the students write and you emphasize right versus wrong answers rather than the thought process in order to arrive at understanding, then in fact such a setting is teacher-centered, not student-centered.

Conversely, students may sit in rows, and you may stand in front of the classroom. But the teacher-led discussion invites students to think independently and arrive at their understanding of facts and concepts, to generate original principles with documented justification, or to decide on their own unit topics and overarching questions. Such a setting is in fact student-focused or student-centered with you as facilitator.

Postdiscussion

Both the teacher-directed/student-focused and student-centered settings are fertile ground for a constructivist approach. These two settings may be alternately employed as your social and academic objectives would indicate. Is there a place for the teacher-centered approach? How could it be modified and integrated into a constructivist approach in a traditional school system? After you have mulled this over, see our Interactive Presentation Method in Module 12.

Keeping the ideas of your discussion about the various settings in mind, let's turn to a crucial component in the process of change in your classroom.

Focal Point 3   Teacher Response

Teacher response (or *response*) is the nature of teacher and student interaction. We believe that teacher response is the single most important factor that characterizes the classroom setting as teacher-centered, teacher-directed/student-focused, or student-centered (Atwell, 1987; Calkins, 1983; Meier, 1995; Michaels, 1987; Morris, 1991; Sperling & Freedman, 1987).

Discussion 3   Teacher Response

As the teacher, your *teacher response* is more significant for the encouragement of your students' active involvement in learning than whether the students sit in rows, a circle, or peer groups; whether they experience a fifty-minute lesson or an extended problem-solving project; or whether they use books or computer technology. It bears repeating that seemingly student-centered physical configurations and materials may camouflage a teacher-centered environment in which students must echo the teacher's viewpoints (Freedman, 1992; Sperling & Freedman, 1987). Consider these pointers.

- *Questions.* Do you ask real questions that invite the students' ideas and viewpoints with justifications? Or do you ask leading questions with embedded answers, the answers you want to hear? (See Module 5.)

- *Catalyst.* Do you encourage students to come up with their own justified solutions based on adequate preparation, materials, and guidelines? In other words, do

you facilitate? Or do you dictate what students "should" be thinking?

- *Process.* Do you emphasize the right answers as the end point? Or do you emphasize the thinking process, strewn with mistaken concepts, that ultimately leads students to appropriate schemata with in-depth understanding? Do you, in fact, spotlight the *necessity of misconceptions* as part of the learning process? Do you also insist on student justifications in their own words? Or are you satisfied with the rote repetition of standard definitions and thereby sacrifice intellectual rigor for the sound of fixed and "right" responses?

- *Affect.* As you pose questions and facilitate invention in the learning process, do you acknowledge the value of the students' *contributions* to building a logical development of a concept, of the answer to an inquiry question, and so on? Are mistakes received as a welcomed part of the learning process rather than as wrong answers? Do you sincerely appreciate your students' potential to learn and to strengthen their critical-thinking skills and *let them know that?* Is your classroom a safe environment, a team approach to learning whereby no one feels stupid and everyone feels valued?

To briefly sum up, teacher response is the key to a Maslowian classroom setting where positive affect nurtures the whole student toward independent, critical thinking (Boone & Hill, 1980). Your response, in turn, is influenced by your assumptions of the *teacher role and student role.*

Examples of Response

Here are some samples of teacher responses in a constructivist approach that help to create positive affect by making each respondent feel valued.

Example #1: This is an exploration. Don't worry about right or wrong answers. Every thoughtful response helps move things along.

Example #2 (collective praise after a series of responses): These have all been thoughtful comments that show you're getting at the heart of the matter.

Example #3 (in response to students disagreeing with each other): You're both helping us get a deeper understanding by challenging each other respectfully, in a thoughtful way. This is just what we want! Now, based on what Sandy and John have been saying, let's list the pros and cons and see where they lead us.

Example #4 (in response to a mistaken fact or concept): (a) A lot of people would agree with you about that, Jenny. Would you like to take a look at more of the

basic issues and see if you still take the same view? Or:
(b) *What makes you say that? (And after listening to the reason): (c) Okay. Your answer makes sense based on what you've just quoted from the journal. Now take a look at the fifth paragraph on page three. How does that compare or contrast with the information you just referred to?*

This type of respectful teacher response gives students a chance to arrive at more developed conclusions while inviting them to think things through more—not necessarily asking someone else to supply the desired answer and deprive the first respondent of the satisfaction of completing her thought process. As the teacher, you affirm rather than discount misconceptions as valued efforts while guiding students to more thought-out conclusions based on more information. Note how the last response asks the student to compare or contrast information, coaxing Jenny into critical thinking.

Now consider the teacher's intention with these responses.

> *Example #5 (a) Why do you say that the Mexicans were treated badly in the war, Jose? (b) [After Jose cites one or two documented reasons]: Okay, Jose, those are justified reasons. Now who else would like to give your view on those reasons, with evidence? (c) Who can add to what Jose and Lucretia have said? (d) Who thinks the Americans were justified and why? (e) Who agrees and why? (d) Who thinks the Americans were not justified and why? (etc.)*

> *Example #6. Who can sum up what Stan, Jesus, and Emily have said?*

> *Example #7. Who disagrees? Why? What's your evidence?*

> *Example #8. Why would a lot of people agree with Ruth even though most of you disagree with that view?*

In Examples 5–8, the teacher is bringing more students into the discussion with Redirected questions (see Module 5). This type of teacher response, inviting varied student responses on the same issue, enables the class to arrive at an appropriate schema with justifications, building on early, insufficient student answers while also affirming the students' participation. In this way, all responses are welcomed without your passing a value judgment. At the same time, you're facilitating a more comprehensive examination of an issue.

Focal Point 4 The Teacher Role

By *roles* we mean the teacher's and students' behaviors, practices, and responsibilities in the learning process

as complements and parallels to each other. The *teacher role* refers to the nature of interaction between you and your students. Do you tell them the facts, concepts, principles, and themes with only occasional opportunity for your students' critical thinking? Are you the focal point of the lesson? Or do you plan the activity sheets and other materials so that you facilitate your students' thinking process up Bloom's Taxonomy? In these ways, the teacher role shapes the setting and is bound up with the nature of teacher response.

Examples: The Teacher Role

Here are two scenarios depicting two types of teacher roles. A discussion follows each scenario. Note the characteristics of each teacher role depicted.

EXAMPLE #1/THE PERFORMER: SCENARIO #1

The curtain goes up and the spotlight shines. You're on, the star of the show, giving your heart and soul to the part. The audience listens and watches, enveloped in the dark, enraptured by your sterling performance. They laugh with you, cry with you. They applaud wildly and bring the house down. In short, you become the talk of the town.

You've earned it. After all, it isn't easy to learn all those lines, interpret the character's conflicting motivations, decide to emphasize this quality over that one so that the portrait does not succumb to stereotyping. You want to make sure that the audience comes away with a clear understanding of the character, one which you have honed to perfection and to critical acclaim. Your heartfelt desire is to touch hundreds more, maybe thousands of people with your in-depth characterization so that audiences go home ruminating on the brilliant insights you have given them. And even though you thrive on applause, your motives are sincere, for how could all those people grasp the character's complexity without you to show the way?

Discussion 4a The Performer

In Scenario #1, you have been posited in the role of a star performer. All eyes are on you. And in fact, you have a lot to offer. You've studied the part as it relates to the play's theme; you've mapped out the relationship of your character to all the other characters; and you've cultivated the fine art of acting so that your depiction is natural, earnest, even compelling. The audience is duly impressed by your mastery and bursts with applause. Yes, their admiration is your just dessert. And you have the satisfaction of knowing that you have given them your best and fashioned their understanding of an enigmatic character and a profound play, down to every word and subtle allusion.

So what's the problem? Nothing, as long as you're an actress on the stage. But let's briefly look at this performer model from the perspective of the teacher role.

Teacher as the Star

If you're the kind of teacher who performs in the spotlight of the classroom stage with your students as a captive and perhaps appreciative audience, *beware.* You may fall prey to the well-intended but misapplied *generosity factor.* Well-intended because after all, by preparing thoroughly, by bringing in a variety of creative materials, and by explaining so clearly what and why and how, by expounding upon the *if–thens* with articulated insights over which you so lovingly labored, you are giving generously from your mind and heart to your students. Their applause resounds in the form of all those right answers on the exam. Or, as is often the case, the students crash on the exam and leave you bewildered. Didn't you *cover the material* thoroughly? Didn't you *explain* so clearly to them? Wasn't your Hook a gem, in the full regalia of period costume? (See Module 3.) You give and give and they just don't get it. That's when the misapplied generosity factor insidiously turns into student blaming: *It's the students' fault, they just can't learn, they just don't care, don't listen,* and so on. As for those students who *got it,* their right answers gleaming on the exam, they're confirmation of your sterling performance and the value, for some students at least, of giving all you've got as the consummate teacher.

Such is a frequent outcome of the *teacher-centered role.* In the teacher-centered setting, the teacher is the *dispenser of information,* the *repository of knowledge and knowing,* the *mental mover* in the classroom. The signs are lecturing, the teacher's voice being the dominant sound in the classroom. The students are encouraged to concur with and repeat back what the teacher and text have said. Even if your students are captivated, what will they retain a week later? How have they developed critical-thinking skills as you entertain them?

Now let's take a look at another scenario that depicts a different teacher role.

EXAMPLE #2/THE DIRECTOR: SCENARIO #2

You assemble the performers for a discussion of each part in the play. Ostensibly, it's a comedy, but you perceive some darker threads in the writing, the potential for poignancy, even subtle satire—a delicious prospect, to direct such an unsuspectingly rich work! Eagerly, you open the discussion to the actors you will direct.

Now, you're bursting at the seams to tell them your interpretation of this theatrical gem. But you've learned from experience that when you force your interpretation on the actors, their inspiration, the stuff of a magical performance, is often missing. Yes, they will do a competent job because they're talented and you know your craft as a director. But you want more from them. You want them to shine.

So you don't spill the beans. You're all assembled bleary eyed in the early morning, with Styrofoam cups of coffee, seated at a wooden table on the stage of the empty theater. Everyone has a copy of the play with the notes you had asked them to write about their views on the characters, theme, implications, and so on. You sip your first taste of schlock coffee and begin.

Not with assertions, not with your opinions or goals about the play—all that's tucked in your mind and put aside. No, instead of spouting your own brilliant ideas, you open with an invitation: *Okay. Let's explore this work a bit, swap ideas. We'll go around the table. So, Vanessa, how do you feel about your character, Sarah?* You don't let Vanessa off with a word or two. You probe her a bit. Ask her to point to dialogue and action and author's directions to justify her interpretation, perhaps modify it a bit. Then you ask others how they viewed Vanessa's character and why. Compare and contrast, stir up the mental stew.

Do you agree, Dustin, that Sarah's a tough gal, a broad, so to speak?

Why? What does she say or do that makes you see things that way?

Okay, Dustin. Then why does your character Stan ignore her at first? Wouldn't he want to grab her attention?

What are some possible implications about Stan's motives in this scene? What's in the dialogue and situation that makes you say that?

In not much time, everyone's forgotten about the coffee because they're getting into it, big time, sinking their teeth in, chewing the script, making it theirs.

A funny thing happens—as you've finally learned it inevitably happens in such forums. Not only do the actors hit upon ideas that you did, arriving at interpretations based on their own spontaneous insights along with your questions that direct their observations, not only that, but they've hit on insights that you, the brilliant director, did not see. So now you're getting excited, too, because the dialogue and probing have opened up the play for everyone. Everyone has a stake in its interpretation. Sometimes you thrash it out as a group as to what to emphasize. And that's the most delicious morsel.

All this leads up to rehearsals, the process of bringing the characters to life. Now you all know what to aim for. And guess what? As the rehearsals take on a life of their own, more ideas—new character motives—come to light. So as you direct the performers, coaxing out subtleties, humor, irony, shaping unexpected satire, you all work together in the joy of creating an original and deep performance.

At curtain call the audience goes wild. They give a standing ovation. The performers take repeated bows. As you watch in the wings, you know you had an important part in a fine production that helped to bring out the best talent in the actors and that touched a lot of people—yourself included.

Discussion 4b The Director

In Scenario #2, you take on a different role, that of the director who elicits ideas and talents from the actors. Before the curtain rises on the first performance, you prompted, coaxed, challenged, asked for support of their interpretations, invited comparisons and contrasts, guiding and also clarifying. In this way, your actors felt confident of their perceptions and conclusions and made the characters and the entire play theirs. No one in the audience sees you or knows what your role has been in the outstanding production. Your influence has been invisible to the onlooker, invisible perhaps even to the actors you have skillfully guided to their finest level because you have served as the unobtrusive guide for their own thinking—as well as affirming their own spontaneous viewpoints. The spotlight is on them, and yet, without your reflective facilitation, without your skilled and subtle control that fostered their critical analyses, the performances would not have attained such heights.

Teacher as the Catalyst

The director's role in Scenario #2 is analogous to the teacher's role in the teacher-directed/student-focused or student-centered settings. For most of us teachers, this student-centered approach is potentially threatening at first. It seems to turn the classroom upside down. Students, who may lack the maturity of professional actors, appear to be in control, and the teacher appears to lack authority—every teacher's nightmare of chaos: an irretrievable loss of order, organization shattered as the students take over, no real learning—an unappealing prospect indeed.

But in fact, just the opposite is true in an effective student-centered or student-focused constructivist setting. Like the director, you must exercise control in a student-centered environment or the students simply will not follow the steps and procedures necessary for rigorous learning. With actors, the director simply lays out procedures and makes clear what is expected at a given time. With preteens and teens in a traditional school setting, you will need to establish rules and procedures and carry them out in a consistent manner.

As we've indicated earlier, at the beginning of the school year, it is often advisable to begin teaching in a way to which the students have been previously socialized, that is, in a conventional up-front-in-the-classroom manner. Little by little, as you win the students' respect and confidence, you resocialize the students—and at first yourself as well—to the teacher and student roles appropriate to a constructivist learning environment. (This stage should make full use of *meta-awareness,* discussed later on.)

As the guide, facilitator, or catalyst, you must be exceedingly prepared and exquisitely organized as well as flexible. *Invisible teaching* is proactive teaching and cannot succeed without well-thought-out planning. Thorough planning includes how to sequence the prompts (questions and tasks that guide a thought process) and materials, how to couple questions to content, how to define individual student roles in peer groups so that the students know how to proceed on their own (see Module 6).

Expressway versus Back Roads

You will plan for your students to reach a given destination via the expressway, and they will most likely take the back roads, enticed by scenic distractions. Only if you have planned well will you have a compass in your mind that will guide them to the desired town on those back roads. You can employ various techniques. Effective questioning refers them back to the substantive materials you've provided or to which they have access, directing them to forgotten prompts, giving support as they wade through frustration, providing confidence in their ability to arrive at the destination.

As you facilitate in this way, the students see that you clearly value their efforts to learn. In other words, as an *invisible teacher* you imbue your students with faith in their ability to learn by providing scaffolding or assistance in the thinking process. Guided in this way, your students will feel a personal victory as they employ facts to substantiate their insights, interpretations, comparisons and contrasts as critical thinkers. In short, invisible teaching is rigorous teaching.

Invisible Teaching

As the invisible teacher, you contradict the traditional norm. Like the director, you remain in the wings during the performance; your students take the spotlight. That shift from a traditional teacher-centered experience is not only your students' victory but yours as well. More and more, your students need you less and less as the year progresses. In this way, you give them a priceless gift: In a constructivist classroom, *students learn how to learn;* and they learn how to teach one another. The methods in this guidebook provide procedures and practices to help you achieve this outcome.

We do not mean to suggest that lecture has no place. Minilectures are useful to launch a unit or project and to summarize the midpoint in a lesson or the Culmination (see Module 3). In fact, one of the methods we promote is the Interactive Presentation, which includes segments of minilectures or mini-talks. Mini-talks with student input help provide clarity and cohesion. But as a dominant pedagogy, lecturing, for the most part, does not generate your students' original thinking, nor does it foster the *challenge and joy, the sense of personal accomplishment,* that accompany active learning with positive affect.

Focal Point 5 The Student Role

You can see from our description that the teacher role governs the *student role.* A teacher-centered setting results in a passive student role. This passivity translates into the students as listeners, imitators, with little if any sense of responsibility for and active engagement with their own learning. By contrast, in a student-focused or student-centered setting in which you as the teacher facilitate and guide, your students are active learners, increasing their responsibility for their own learning, planning the steps of learning, formulating questions, and so on, stimulated and eventually *empowered* as independent thinkers. Because our description of the teacher roles has already described the complementary student roles, we will now move on to the next focal point.

Focal Point 6 Materials and Methods

Materials and Methods (M&M) refers to the relationship between instructional tools, that is, devices and materials such as activity sheets, books, videos, overhead projector and computer technology (see Module 4) and active student learning. Materials in and of themselves—including dazzling software—do not govern active versus passive learning. Rather, instructional methods help to *implement* your instructional intention in a student-centered environment.

Discussion 6 Materials and Methods

M&M is the *heart* of the matter. The most dazzling materials in technology are only as effective as the instructional method (see Section C, *Constructivist Methods*). The method must be selected to employ the materials to full advantage; otherwise, focus, cohesion, and intellectual rigor are at risk. The newest technology can be used merely to carry out teacher-centered response. Relying on the materials to give direction is like relying on an airplane alone to get you where you want to

go. An airplane needs not only a compass but a map, not to mention a pilot.

On the other side of the coin, effective methods are compromised by inappropriate and shallow materials. As much thought must be given to selecting the content and level of substantive materials as to the method of instruction. A superficial text without in-depth supplementary materials or a software program that is more entertaining than instructional undermines an inductive method that seeks to strengthen critical-thinking skills.

Examples of Materials and Methods

We provide a range of examples of Materials in Figure 4.5 in Module 4. In addition, you can find a summary of our methods in the introduction to Section C, *Constructivist Methods.*

Focal Point 7 Meta-awareness

Meta-awareness is a concept that refers to knowledge of the thing itself—learning about the learning process, thinking about the steps of thinking, and so on. For example, your students' meta-awareness about the process of learning could involve awareness of the thinking process, moving from a knowledge base of facts to the higher levels of analysis, synthesis, and evaluation. As the teacher, you would introduce these concepts to your students, complete with the correct terms, and encourage them to consciously apply Bloom's Taxonomy (see Module 5) as a tool to develop and strengthen their learning skills. In other words, meta-awareness is a bird's-eye view that gives students conscious awareness. It lifts the veil between the practice and the underlying intention.

Discussion 7 Meta-awareness

Active versus Passive Learning

Meta-awareness is a useful key to resocializing your students—and yourself—about the virtues of active versus passive learning. Lifting the veil in this case involves awareness of various teacher and student roles and the classroom setting the roles create, along with the corresponding advantages and disadvantages. It also includes the importance of questions: (1) as prompts to guide thinking as students respond and (2) as tools to cultivate critical thinking as students themselves learn to formulate and sequence questions related to instructional materials according to Bloom's Taxonomy, just as you are in this course.

Giving your students meta-awareness is a bold step. It is the ultimate in invisible teaching; it is giving the spotlight away. But if you have your students' best interests at heart, the rewards are tremendous, for meta-awareness can heighten your students' motivation over time and turn bored students into active participants as they increasingly grow accustomed to and appreciate their empowerment as learners.

Remember Maslow

Above all, remember the importance of affect as the gateway to learning in a constructivist classroom. Without a safe, nonjudgmental environment in which everyone feels valued as a thinking person, only those students arriving at your door already confident will succeed. Try to incorporate Maslow's Needs Hierarchy, described earlier, remembering that every student is a whole person with an array of needs, not merely a cerebral repository of information. But don't go overboard! Beware of condescension or praising every response.

Examples of Meta-awareness
EXAMPLE #1/READING SKILLS

Yes, you want your students to understand the plot of Mark Twain's *Huckleberry Finn* and to discuss the controversial issues it raises. You also want them to realize that they're striving to develop their ability to interpret on a higher cognitive level. That means the students should try to analyze the various implications of Twain's characterizations and themes for today's society. In this way, your students are *consciously aware* that they are carrying out a thinking process that leads to evaluation and critical thinking, the higher cognitive levels that are beyond the mere knowledge base of details and events literally applied to a fixed historical context and not much more. This approach to reading can be applied to any subject.

EXAMPLE #2/THE LEARNING PROCESS

You might devote some time to an Exploratory or Reflective Discussion (see Modules 10 and 11, respectively) about teacher and student roles and about different methods of learning, both teacher- and student-centered. Similarly, you can introduce Bloom's Taxonomy and invite a discussion based on examples of each cognitive level. Consider these suggestions for follow-up.

Let students practice writing questions based on the taxonomy, related to instructional material, and posing those questions to their classmates.

The next level is to teach them how to evaluate their own questions, based on the responses of peers. Did the questioners succeed in guiding their classmates to a high

cognitive level of interpretation and evaluation?

Of course, students' evaluation of other students' responses depends on their own grasp of the given material. Again, an Exploratory or Reflective Discussion would help clarify the issues. In this way, students increasingly cultivate critical-thinking skills with growing awareness of the cognitive as well as academic intentions of the Rationale (see Module 3).

Focal Point 8 Modeling Peer-Group Learning

Modeling (see Module 4) is the act of demonstrating an individual behavior or procedure. It can mirror a cognitive process or social patterns back to the students. Modeling can therefore be used to socialize students as fruitful peer-group learners, focused thinkers, and persevering individual learners. As you model for your students or set up modeling situations with students who model procedures for their peers, you are also teaching yourself what is required of you as a facilitator along with what is required of your students as active participants in learning.

Discussion 8 Modeling Peer-Group Learning

Take a look at the following example of modeling peer-group learning. Notice that the students need to consider their social responsibilities as well as the learning activity.

EXAMPLE #1. SOCIALIZE YOUR STUDENTS TO WORK IN GROUPS

When you first establish peer-group work in your class, be sure to take one class period to introduce students to appropriate peer interaction. We suggest that you do this whether or not students have had group work in other classes. Your students may need to unlearn bad habits or examine, perhaps for the first time, the learning benefits of a student-centered setting. This is all part of building meta-awareness of being active learners.

ENLIST ONE OR TWO PEER GROUPS TO MODEL HOW YOU WANT YOUR STUDENTS TO INTERACT.

- Design a peer-group activity especially for modeling student–student (s–s) interactions, both social and academic. This modeling activity may double-dip as meaningful instruction. The activity sheet is crucial; it must specify social roles as well as directions for the task. (See Module 6, Part Two, "Activity Sheets.")

- The student demonstration that models desired behavior must include following the directions on the activity sheet, from assigning roles to attempting the task. You may coach the demonstration groups in advance to intentionally act out conflicts with rude behavior, then with respectful behavior, so that the class sees the difference in action. Invite recipients of aggressive and then kinder behavior to share their feelings. Discuss how feelings affect how they learn.

- Encourage reactions from the entire class at different points in the modeling enactments. Establish from the students why respectful interaction is important: improved group spirit, better learning, and so on.

- Based on the modeling, *guide the class to codify its own procedures* for group interaction.

ESTABLISH THE SPIRIT IN WHICH PEER-GROUP WORK TAKES PLACE: COOPERATIVE NOT COMPETITIVE. THIS EMPHASIS REQUIRES MORE THAN ONE OR TWO SENTENCES.

- Try an Exploratory or Reflective Discussion that identifies the advantages and disadvantages of competition and cooperation. Avoid giving points or grade credit for cooperating. This external motivation undermines the effort to encourage students to work as teammates for positive affective reasons (Michaels, 1987).

IF YOU WANT STUDENTS TO CRITIQUE EACH OTHER'S WORK, TRAIN THEM IN WHAT TO LOOK FOR AND HOW TO COMMENT. USE MODELING. THIS SHOULD TAKE ONE OR TWO CLASS PERIODS.

- Provide sample phrases on a handout: "That's a good idea because . . ."; "Maybe we can also say that . . ."; "Let's try to follow the instructions to keep on target . . ."; "I like your idea about X. But I think the teacher wants us to develop it more. Maybe we can do that together"; "Let's pay attention to each other more. We need to work as a team. Luvenia, say your idea again and this time we'll listen better"; and so on.

- Use modeling to practice the sample phrases so that the class sees how they can be effective. Again, you might want to briefly coach the demonstration groups in advance. Invite comments from onlookers.

Make the point that they will quickly figure out their own comments in different situations so that they maintain team spirit while they learn. The sample phrases are like training wheels to launch them.

The rehearsal is an investment with high returns on more fruitful and efficient group work in the future. Different types of group learning may require their own modeling for future lessons or projects. You may want to tell your students this.

EXAMPLE #2. DISCUSS ROLES IN PEER-GROUP LEARNING

Consider including a discussion on the teacher's and students' role in peer-group learning. Some pointers could be the following:

What are the students' responsibilities for their own learning?

What is the teacher's responsibility in a peer-group learning activity?

What are the advantages for the students?

How is an active student role different from a passive student role?

What are the implications for the students in an active or passive role?

In this way, you are facilitating your students' increasing meta-awareness of their part in quality learning. You're also expressing faith in their ability to learn.

Focal Point 9 **Thinking Process—Designing Heuristics**

As you can see in the example of modeling peer-group learning, an outcome of modeling and meta-awareness is often the codification of procedures that guides the students' critical-thinking skills up the ladder of Bloom's Taxonomy. A codified, step-by-step approach to digging up the deeper meanings or carrying out a process is called a *heuristic* (see Module 4).

Discussion 9 **Thinking Process—Designing Heuristics**

Really useful heuristics employ meta-awareness of the thinking process, whether for analyzing literature, historical events, a work of art, a science experiment, solutions for a math problem or sports strategies, musical techniques, and so on. In a constructivist classroom, students can create their own heuristics if you do some or all of the following:

- Model the thinking process for your students and ask them to spot the important elements.

- Require one group of students to write down its observations of another group's discussion, suggesting the behaviors to be noticed: defining, making connections, noticing repeating details, social behaviors that impede or further the group's discussion, and so on. Then the groups swap places and give each other feedback at the end of a completed cycle. This practice helps develop meta-awareness and thereby helps students to compile a heuristic for a given procedure or cognitive effort (Metzger, 1998).

- Encourage Exploratory or Reflective Discussions. Inject only broad questions or comments to suggest that students reexamine a metaphor, identify repeating words, reconsider from a different angle (without saying what that is), and so on. This approach can also help students to create codified steps in a thinking process appropriate to a given subject area. Obviously, there will be overlap in thinking processes for various subjects, and such double-dipping will strengthen your students' skills in learning how to learn independently.

- Provide pertinent information in addition to the textbook that your students don't know yet so the students can justify their approach with a documented knowledge base. (*Beware of just air between you and your students!*)

- Similarly, provide a particular example (e.g., require that students analyze a specific short story, a specific experiment, math problem, painting, football play, idioms in a foreign language, musical techniques, etc.) from which the students extrapolate the generic elements of analysis. Then require that they generalize a heuristic for that thinking strategy, procedure, and so on.

Example of a Heuristic

Students' learning how to learn is a process in which you do the following:

- *Reflect* with analysis of what worked, what didn't work, and why.
- *Replan* accordingly.
- *Retry* patiently.

This three-bullet strategy is an example of a procedural heuristic.

Focal Point 10 **Affect as the Gateway to Learning**

Call us sentimental, but we believe that *students' feelings count.* We're not saying there's a feel-good magic wand. There's not. Your students—and you—will definitely not change in a day or a week or a month. Resocializing takes time, patience, and imagination.

Discussion 10 **Affect as the Gateway to Learning**

When a lesson flops, try to resist blaming the students. Instead, reflect on how you might replan so that the lesson incorporates your students' world and engages them in a stimulating activity that carries out your instructional intention. Remember to reconsider the setting and the nature of your response. Have you been trying to stuff their minds with information? Or have you prepared materials and sequenced questions so that your students are guided to explore information, interrelate facts, think through concepts, and arrive at justified evaluations? Did you plan in a way that hooks into the students' interests or context?

Now consider this: Did the progression of the lesson enable the students to feel confident as they traveled from one cognitive level to another? Without student confidence, the most well-structured lesson falls flat. Again and again, we return to the importance of imagination. You can't pique your students' imagination unless you stretch your own. It takes imagination to effectively plan a motivating lesson or inquiry project.

This is where *Invisible Teaching* comes in. Our constructivist methods, anchored in Bloom's cognitive taxonomy and awareness of setting, help you to enliven any content in any subject—whether you teach in a school with a traditional time frame or in a block program. These methods and your eventual adaptations of them suited to your needs will serve you as a new or seasoned teacher.

Focal Point 11 **Resocializing Yourself**

It's time to have a fireside chat with yourself or with a colleague. You might benefit by examining your assumptions about effective teaching and the teacher's role. Why do you want to teach? If the reason is to be the entertainer in the spotlight, you might want to reconsider the value of that for your students in terms of their—and your own—self-actualization, based on Maslow's Needs Hierarchy.

Discussion 11 **Resocializing Yourself**

As you take your students step by step into the domain of constructivist learning, you are also training yourself along with them. For this reason, go slowly at first. Reflect on the outcomes. If you find yourself blaming the students, reconsider. Remember that everybody wants to learn. Instead of faulting your students, try planning the next lesson or project so that the students will be able to engage with the knowledge base, concepts, and themes in a way that relates to their frames of reference. Ask yourself, *Is my approach dry? The same old routine? Have I used my imagination?*

Have you brainstormed with an innovative colleague?

Find a Partner

Brainstorming with another teacher brings us to the next important practice. Try to find someone in your school who is innovative—regardless of the subject matter. The elements of the classroom setting matter more than the subject. There are a lot of creative, student-centered teachers who would be delighted to work with you. Not only would you learn from their experience but they also will pick up fresh ideas from you, as well as the methods you are learning in this constructivist program. Or you could work with a colleague who is about to experiment with a truly student-centered approach for the first time and eager to discuss new ideas.

■ ROUNDUP ■

Resocializing is the key to creating a vital, constructivist classroom. The elements of resocializing revolve around two major concepts. The first is Maslow's Needs Hierarchy, reminding us that our students are not just brains to be jammed with facts, but people, young people with a host of needs that must be respected for them to develop the courage to be independent and active learners. Students need to feel valued, just like you do.

The second concept is meta-awareness, which is crucial to having your students jump on board with you. Meta-awareness incorporates appreciation of the teacher and student roles in a constructivist learning experience and the importance of questioning, along with the setting. To aid the process of building meta-awareness, modeling social and learning behaviors—demonstrating how they are bound up with each other—gives the students a clear picture of what you expect from them.

Along with your students, you need to resocialize yourself. For you yourself may be a product of teacher-dominated instruction and are holding on to that schema with the best of intentions. If that worked for you when you were a student, perhaps you were among those who were motivated to achieve within a traditional school setting, with others supporting your efforts. Many, if not most, of your students may not fall into that category for

various reasons: They may be poor test-takers, they may have low self-esteem as a result of being low-tracked, they may not have adequate support at home, the subject may not be taught in a way that engages their interest. But they have the ability to excel, whatever they have achieved, or have not achieved, in a setting that reawakens their natural curiosity and love of learning. The nature of your response can either discourage your students from taking necessary risks in learning or encourage your students to reach beyond their grasp.

Will you be the innovative teacher who makes a difference? It's not easy. But you can do it. Your classroom can be vibrant with discovery—if you persevere with efforts to resocialize.

■ HANDS-ON PRACTICE ■

Acid Test: Analyze Two Classroom Scenarios

A Bit of Nitty Gritty. We invite you to explore two settings and two teacher–student roles by analyzing these two classroom scenes.

Directions

1. Jot down three to five significant details in each of the following scenarios. Describe each setting in terms of being
   a. Teacher-centered
   b. Teacher-directed/student-focused
   c. Student-centered

2. Refer to Maslow's Needs Hierarchy. In each scenario, *what* needs are being met? *Whose* needs are being met? <u>Justify</u> your interpretations.

SCENARIO #1: MS. SANTOS

Ms. Santos, a history teacher, organizes her thirty middle-school students into heterogeneous peer groups of four or five. Students are assigned textbook exercises about World War II as the behavioral objective/mastery task and do the assignment together. As they work, a hum of student interaction fills the room. Ms. Santos circulates from group to group. When she stops by each group, she enthusiastically praises students one-on-one for their right answers, then she refers the individual students who write wrong—or no—answers to the pages in the textbook where the right answers can be found. Ten minutes before the period ends, Ms. Santos convenes the class collectively. She reads each exercise question aloud and calls on individual students for the right answers; she motivates the students by entering an A in the grade book for each right answer. Proudly she demonstrates to the class a string of A's in her grade book, praising them for learning the material so well.

SCENARIO #2: MR. WASHINGTON

Mr. Washington, a history teacher, organizes his thirty middle-school students into topic groups of four or five. The students chose their topics from a list of twenty topics about World War II drawn up by Mr. Washington. In addition, the students generate their own subtopics by consulting school library sources and Web sources that Mr. Washington has alerted them to. Each topic group creates questions that it thinks are important for each subtopic based on the research. Mr. Washington consults with and advises each group or individual student who may need guidance. The Performance Objective is for each student to write an article on the subtopic of choice. The teacher also distributes a list of criteria for content and writing skills that each article and magazine must satisfy. The articles on subtopics are collected into topic magazines. This means that each group publishes a magazine. Collectively, these magazines cover World War II in significant scope and some depth.

Guidelines

If you are in a workshop setting, we encourage you to analyze these two scenarios in a peer group according to the following activity sheet. If you are reading this on your own, use the activity sheet yourself or with someone else in the program. In either case, note the design of the activity sheet for social roles and the academic task as a peer-group learning (PGL) experience (see Module 6).

ACTIVITY SHEET FOR SANTOS AND WASHINGTON SCENARIOS

Directions

Roles for task one

1. Time keeper: announces when five minutes are left.
2. Recorder: jots down the group's ideas on paper or a transparency.
3. Moderator: ensures that each person participates.
4. Prober: each group member will be a friendly prober of other group members' comments.

Roles for Task Two

1. Same roles as those for Task One.
2. Presenter: introduces the group's ideas in the class discussion.

Your Job

1. Task One (15 minutes): For each scenario, infer the following. Justify your views in terms of details from the scenarios.
   a. The teacher's belief about effective teaching
   b. The teacher's belief about the students' role as learners
   c. The resulting beliefs the students may have of themselves as learners

2. Task Two (20 minutes): Apply your analysis from Task One here.
   a. Discuss among yourselves how Maslow might analyze the teacher–student relationship in Ms. Santos's and Mr. Washington's classes. Explore from teacher and student angles. Suggested guidelines follow:

   Emotional and psychological safety needs: whose?

   Self-esteem and self-confidence needs: whose?

   Self-actualization: whose?

   b. Reflection: Offer two or more suggestions to one or both of these teachers so that their materials and methods better meet the Maslowian needs of some or all of their students while also striving for intellectual rigor. You may hypothesize different learning styles and confidence levels. *Justify your suggestion in terms of intellectual rigor as well as affect. Always ask yourself, "Why am I doing this?"*

3. (If appropriate): The workshop convenes for discussion of your ideas and to process this as a PGL experience.

REFERENCES

Atwell, N. (1987). *In the middle: Writing, reading and learning with adolescents.* New Hampshire: Boynton/Cook Publishers. Portsmouth, NH.

Boone, B., & Hill, A. (1980). If Maslow created a composition course: A new look at motivation in the classroom. ERIC, ED 191 053.

Calkins, L. (1983). *Lessons from a child: On the teaching and learning of writing.* New Hampshire: Heinemann Educational Books. Portsmouth, NH.

Cuban, L. (1996, October 9). Techno-reformers and classroom teachers. *Education Week on the Web.* (www.edweek.org/ew/vol-16/06Cuban.h16).

Fosnot, C. T. (1989). *Enquiring teachers enquiring learners: A constructivist approach for teaching.* New York: Teachers College Press.

Freedman, S. W. (1992). Outside-in and inside-out: Peer response groups in two ninth-grade classes. *Research in the Teaching of English, 26*(1), 71–107.

Johnson, D., & Johnson, R. (1989). *Cooperation and competition: Theory and research.* Edina, MN: Interaction Books.

Kyle, W., Jr., Schmitz, C., & Schmitz, E. (1996). *Electronic Journal of Science Education, 1*(2). (unr.edu/home page/jcannon/ejse/kyle.html).

Maslow, A. (1987). *Motivation and personality.* New York: Harper & Row, Publishers.

Meier, D. (1995). *The power of their ideas: Lessons for America from a small school in Harlem.* Boston, MA: Beacon Press.

Metzger, M. (1998, November). Teaching reading beyond the plot. *Phi Delta Kappan, 77*(3), 240–246, 256.

Michaels, S. (1987). Text and context: A new approach to the study of classroom writing. *Discourse Processes, 10,* 321–346.

Morris, C. (1991, March). Giving at-risk juniors intellectual independence: An experiment. *English Journal,* 37–41.

Putnam, J. (1997). *Cooperative learning in diverse classrooms.* Upper Saddle River, NJ: Merrill.

Slavin, R. (1995). *Cooperative learning: Theory, research, and practice.* Boston, MA: Allyn & Bacon.

Sperling, M., & Freedman, S. W. (1987). A good girl writes like a good girl: Written response to student writing. *Written Communication, 4,* 343–369.

Weiner, B. (1972). Attribution theory, achievement motivation, and the educational process. *Review of Educational Process, 42*(2), 203–215.

SUGGESTED READING

Bunce-Crim, M. (1991, September). What is a writing classroom? *Instructor,* 36–38.

Cleary, L. M. (1991). Affect and cognition in the writing processes of eleventh graders. *Written Communication, 8*(4), 473–507.

DiPardo, A., & Freedman, S. (1988). Peer response groups in the writing classroom: Theoretic foundations and new directions. *Review of Educational Research, 58*(2), 119–149.

Duckworth, K., & Lind, K. (1989). Curricular goals and motivating strategies with non-college-bound students in science and social studies. Eric ED 307 112.

Michaels, S. (1987). Text and context: A new approach to the study of classroom writing. *Discourse Processes, 10,* 321–346.

Pokay, P., & Blumenfeld, P. C. (1990). Predicting achievement early and late in the semester: The role of motivation and use of learning strategies. *Journal of Educational Psychology, 82*(1), 41–50.

Siu-Runyan, Y. (1991). Learning from students: An important aspect of classroom organization. *Language Arts, 68,* 100–107.

PART 2
Constructivist Classroom Management

Overview

Goals

Focal Points and Discussions:

How Can Effective Teaching Help Prevent Discipline Problems?

How Can You Involve Students in Establishing a Management System?

How Can Classroom Meetings Help Solve Problems That Do Arise?

How Can You Engage Parents as Learning Collaborators?

Roundup

■ OVERVIEW

In Part 1 of this module, we discussed the process of resocializing, which really amounts to challenging your students to buy into the creation of a constructivist learning community. In Part 2, we will pull together a set of suggestions and answer some final questions on how to establish and maintain such a community.

We hear a great deal about issues related to classroom management and discipline. In fact, classroom management has become a whole separate field within education in the minds of some. As you read through and perhaps experience our methods and techniques, it should be apparent that effective teaching must go far beyond *managing* students. Our approach to classroom management, which we would define as *the system that you establish to operate your classroom on a daily basis,* is different, based on a number of primary beliefs. These foundational beliefs include the following:

1. Classroom management, like assessment and evaluation, *should be seamlessly connected to teaching.* This implies that your approach to dealing with problems and disagreements should reflect the same spirit that you bring to your teaching.

2. *The vast majority of students of all ages sincerely want to learn and can learn* and do not need to be bribed, bullied, or threatened into learning.

3. *Effective teaching will prevent most discipline problems,* and the right approach in the classroom will allow teachers to reach virtually any student.

4. In establishing a management system, teachers should give *students a high degree of genuine responsibility.* This implies that you treat students as responsible young adults who are capable of making important decisions, rather than as children who need to be told what to do and how to act.

Our suggested methods and techniques flow from these beliefs. At this point, we hope that you agree with each of these statements. We hold that these beliefs are profoundly important and should form the central core of beliefs for constructivist teachers. In fact, if you push these statements hard enough, they should influence everything that you do in your classroom and certainly your approach to management. In this section of *Invisible Teaching,* we will present some suggestions that you can revisit on how to establish a system that reflects such core beliefs.

■ GOALS

In presenting a final set of suggestions for establishing a classroom management system, we will address the following questions.

- How can effective teaching prevent most discipline problems?

- How can you involve your students in establishing a management system?

- How can classroom meetings help to address management concerns?

- How can you involve parents as collaborators in the learning process?

In offering the best practical advice that we can regarding these questions, we will rely most heavily on our own classroom experiences; we'll also draw on the advice of a number of educators and theorists.

■ FOCAL POINTS AND DISCUSSIONS

Focal Point 1 **How Can Effective Teaching Help Prevent Discipline Problems?**

In essence, *Invisible Teaching* is about classroom management from the first module onward. Our experiences in dozens of schools over the past twenty years have shown us that most students act up in class because they are bored, frustrated, alienated—in short, *disengaged.* The key to avoiding discipline problems in the classroom, then, is to engage students in truly meaningful learning experiences to the greatest extent possible each and every day.

In making our claim about effective teaching preventing problems, we would make two additional statements. First, there *are* students in every school who, sometimes because of factors outside the control of teachers and schools, are extremely difficult if not impossible to reach. Even the most idealistic of educators would have to admit this reality; and if these students won't meet you halfway, there's not much you can do about it. Second, our intent is not to blame dedicated teachers for discipline problems. As we note throughout this book, a range of factors sometimes forces teachers to take approaches that they wouldn't necessarily take, in essence making the *compromises* that Sizer (1984; 1996) has so eloquently described. A system that emphasizes didactic approaches, coverage of vast amounts of material, and order and enforced silence in classrooms actually makes it more difficult to *manage* things.

With this said, we believe that there is a great deal that you can do, even within fairly traditional school settings, to change this situation. The next section will offer some practical suggestions for doing just this.

Discussion 1   How Can Effective Teaching Help Prevent Discipline Problems?

An interactive, constructivist approach is good preventative medicine against discipline problems because students are likely to be engaged in *relevant, meaningful* experiences on a daily basis. We can make this claim based on a wealth of experience in classrooms from the middle school through the college/university level. Consider once again that our suggested teaching approach places emphasis on meeting the needs of students at Maslow's three highest levels (see Part 1 of Module Two). If you effectively utilize the methods and techniques that we have described, you'll help your students to build personal connections to you and to their peers and to develop their self-esteem and a sense of personal fulfillment. You'll do this by showing them that they can learn something relevant and meaningful that will help them to understand the world around them in new ways.

We've seen this approach serve to encourage and empower the most disheartened individuals and groups of students. In recalling one telling example, one of us remembers working with a particularly discouraged group of high school students in a basic biology class. Initially, these students seemed to have little interest in biology and school in general; they were taking this class simply because they needed to pass one science course to graduate. Some had failed the course once or twice already. We started with a focus on the human body and how it works and what people need to do to stay healthy. We organized the curriculum around guiding questions that the *students* generated as a group and took an inquiry-oriented, hands-on approach. Slowly, student interest grew, to the point where the extra chatter was subsiding, attendance improved dramatically, and several of the students were coming in regularly after school to continue their investigations. In one true breakthrough moment, the class was about to investigate a set of sheep lungs as part of our research on the effects of smoking on the body. One student, a vocal leader within the class who had initially shown little interest in science, was disturbed by some classmates talking as directions for the activity were being explained. He passionately told the class that he and others wanted to focus on the activity, that it was important, and that "anyone who didn't want to be there could get the hell out." At that moment, the extra chatter stopped as the offending students realized that they had stepped outside of the expectations that the students had set for themselves. The entire class then focused on listening to the directions, and the transition from a group of discouraged individuals to a true community was complete. This is the impact that a student-centered approach can have.

We have shared a number of suggestions for implementing each of our methods and techniques. As you consider or expand a constructivist approach in your classroom, here's some overall advice related to effective teaching and the *prevention* of problems.

Never Underestimate the Importance of Planning Thoroughly

Invisible Teaching talks about planning in some depth. Our sincere hope is that you carry this advice into your own classroom. If you don't plan thoroughly and thoughtfully, you're headed for major problems in a student-centered setting. Of course, your plans won't always work, but if you think through potential problems in advance, chances are that you'll have the ability (and the confidence) to make adjustments and to take advantage of the *teachable moments* that will arise.

As you plan, consider and use the teaching methods that we introduce. Plan on utilizing multiple methods within each classroom period. For the most part, don't stick to any one format for more than twenty-five to thirty minutes; this seems to be an upper limit of engagement for most students. This will mean shifting from one method to another at least once in a fifty-minute period. You might, for example, begin a session with a brief Interactive Presentation (Module Twelve), move into a twenty-minute peer-group activity (Module Six, Part 1), then allow students to share ideas generated in a full-class Exploratory Discussion (Module Ten). Using a variety of methods and techniques, even within a single class period, will be a key to your success. This variety addresses different learning styles. *And use all of your time.* Teachers frequently run into trouble when providing free time at the end of any class period.

Whichever method you're using, question your students continuously to help them remain engaged in the learning experience. If you're presenting new ideas, question students to check on their understanding. Even if you have a number of new ideas to convey, don't present information for more than four to five minutes without questioning students; we all know that it's too easy for students to drift off, even if your presentation is interesting.

Find a Way to Relate to Each of Your Students

As a constructivist teacher, you'll have multiple opportunities to interact with your students one-on-one and to really get to know them as individuals. Find out as much as you can about the experiences/interests of each of your students and try to connect to these whenever possible as you plan future lessons. Students who are turned off to school often have special interests and talents that you can tap into (in fact, it's often not the rowdy students that will worry you most, but those who are so discouraged that they don't want to do anything). Providing students with options frequently is a good way to reach them. Let students decide whether they'd rather do a presentation, write a paper, make a film, write a song, or paint a picture to show you and their classmates what they've learned. You ensure rigor by supplying criteria and guidelines.

Reflect Carefully

Don't forget that reflecting realistically on classroom events is an essential dimension to effective, constructivist teaching. You may be trying many of these methods and techniques for the first time when you step into your classroom. As with anything that we try for the first time, there *will be* some bumps, maybe even some outright flops, along the way. Don't be discouraged when something doesn't work as well as you had hoped; this is all part of the learning process. Make adjustments and try again. Don't fall into the student-blaming, complaining-in-the-teachers'-lounge trap when things don't go quite right.

As part of the process of reflecting on your teaching, make it a habit to audio/videotape yourself to monitor your progress. The things that you notice yourself doing (or not doing) on tape are often incredibly revealing. Pay close attention especially to the way that you question your students. Another related suggestion: Find a colleague to serve as a partner and invite that person to watch you teach occasionally. Reciprocating this favor will be doubly instructive, as you can learn from what your partner does as much as from the feedback.

Effective Teaching and Stopping Minor Problems

Thorough planning and engaging methods prevent most problems, but not all of them. A constructivist classroom will often be a loud, active place; students will get excited as they participate in activities/discussions (it's a sad truth that some of the quietest classrooms are actually the *least* productive in terms of meaningful learning). One of the things that you absolutely need to do to be a successful teacher is to be aware of everything that's going on in the room. This sounds like a tall order, but continually scanning the room with your eyes and moving around the room and standing in spots where you can see each student will help you develop this sort of awareness.

Even though you want your classroom to be an active, lively place, it's vital that you react to inappropriate behavior immediately (most often, this behavior will include things like excessive talking). Think of a progression of actions that you can take as the teacher to deal with minor problems, actions that are seamlessly connected to your *teaching.* Consider an example: You're conducting a Directed Discussion (Module Nine), with students seated in a U-shaped arrangement. Three students in the most distant part of the room are talking, and you're relatively sure they've drifted out of the discussion. Try the following progression of actions:

1. Make eye contact/deliver a disapproving look (we can all remember teachers who could deliver a stern message without saying a word).

2. Ask one of the disengaged students a question to pull them into the discussion.

3. Move toward the students as the lesson continues. Stand right next to the student if necessary (your proximity will be enough to stop many problem behaviors). If you can't move toward the student for some reason, say the student's name in a nonthreatening way.

4. If the problem continues or reoccurs, move casually toward the student, bend down, and say something as you stand next to the desk ("Can you please contribute something to the discussion? We'd like to hear your thoughts on this").

5. If the problem continues or reoccurs, ask the student to move to a different part of the room (an unoccupied desk some distance away).

6. If the problem is serious enough, ask the student to talk to you in the hallway. Say that you'd like to have the student's participation and ask if there is a problem (it may have nothing to do with your class). If this is something that has happened before, you can get a bit more assertive in the hall, without starting a confrontation in front of the rest of the class. This is

a real danger if you challenge a student directly in front of peers.

It has been our experience that a progression of responses like this, all of which would seem indistinguishable from the actual teaching of the lesson, will take care of the vast majority of your minor problems, especially social talking at the wrong times.

If the problem that you're facing is more serious (e.g., a heated argument develops between two students), our advice would be to jump to the higher steps in this progression right away (e.g., talk to both of these students in the hall to defuse the situation). In the case of serious problems that continue over time, try as hard as you can to talk to the student involved before or after class, some time when you can communicate one-on-one without interruption. Communicating with colleagues and parents should be an important part of this process as well (more on this later in the module). If you've been teaching awhile, you know that you may rely on administrators for advice and support, but not to solve your problems *for* you.

Focal Point 2 How Can You Involve Students in Establishing a Management System?

If you are beginning the new school year with a shift to constructivist teaching, the first few days that you spend resocializing your class are vitally important. Our advice is to set the stage for the rest of the year by conducting interactive activities. Conduct your initial ILPE lesson (Investigating Learner's Previous Experiences, Module Seven) *on your first day of class* and make this first lesson especially memorable. We have found that doing this will establish some positive expectations among your students.

On the second or third day of class, or if you are switching to a student-centered approach in midyear, *discuss* classroom rules and procedures for a constructivist setting with your students in an open way (we prefer the term *guidelines* over *rules*). There are a variety of approaches that you can take in doing this. We believe that it's useful to think of these approaches as falling on a kind of continuum. At one end of the spectrum is a very direct approach. Tell your students what your expectations are. If you choose this approach, make these expectations high and at least explain your rationale for every guideline that you establish (e.g., "Our number one guideline in this class will be mutual respect for others. This is vital because . . ."). See Part 1 of this module, "Resocializing," for more suggestions.

A Directed Discussion Approach to Establishing Guidelines

The degree to which you allow *student input* in forming class guidelines is up to you. We can tell you from experience that students are much more likely to take ownership of (and then *live by*) rules or guidelines that *they have helped to establish.* Let's return for a moment to our continuum of approaches for establishing class policies and guidelines. In the center of this continuum is what we might consider to be a Directed Discussion approach. We have found that such an approach is far superior to simply *telling* students what the rules will be. You begin the discussion by talking to students about *what you envision the class doing in the coming weeks and months.* You then pose the question, "What guidelines will we need to establish to allow us to do all of these things?" Then, you ask a series of focused questions aimed at helping students to articulate a set of guidelines and procedures for the class ("We're going to have open discussions and activities in this class almost every day. What guidelines regarding *talking* will help us to do this?"). By the end of the discussion, the class will have articulated a set of policies and procedures for the rest of the year.

A Reflective Discussion Approach

The most open, student-centered way to establish class guidelines involves taking a more Reflective Discussion approach (Module Eleven). With this third approach, you begin the discussion by sharing the same kind of vision that you have for what the class will be doing. At this point, you open the discussion for greater class input. What are some of the things that your students would most like to do and to learn about? Then, you let them know that every class does need a set of operating guidelines, and you open the floor for *their suggestions* on what these guidelines should be. As the teacher, you then moderate a discussion in which the students choose, perhaps by consensus or by vote, what the final guidelines will be. As the moderator, you can offer your own input as part of this process.

Why Allow Student Involvement in This Process?

As we've noted, our experience has been that students are far more likely to abide by a set of rules and procedures that they have had some voice in creating. Many teachers might view this process as risky, that it will open a classroom to utter chaos, but this has not been our experience. Students of any age will want to establish consistent procedures so that they know what to expect. We have seen a consistent, if not universal, student desire for the creation of a supportive environment in which everyone feels safe enough to share ideas. In fact, students will often be far tougher on themselves than any teacher might be when it comes to establishing rules.

Our advice is to try either the Directed or Reflective Discussion approach for establishing classroom guidelines. You'll find that students will agree with many/most of your suggestions and that there is a definite empowering feeling for students that comes through these approaches. Starting the school year with such an empowering, democratic approach will send some important messages about what students will experience in your class. If you don't feel secure in allowing this much student input, especially as a new teacher, at least enter the term with a *fair* set of rules/procedures and share these with students in an open way. Let students know what your rules are and *why* you've established them. Remember that rule # 1 for *teachers* should be to treat students like young adults and not like children. Establish an atmosphere of trust and be fair and consistent when it comes to classroom management.

What Classroom Guidelines Might You Consider Adopting?

Make your guidelines and policies simple and straightforward; don't burden students with too many rules, or you'll risk creating an oppressive classroom atmosphere. *Possible* classroom guidelines might include any or all of the following:

- Respect one another's right to speak. Listen carefully to others; one person talks at a time.

- No obscene or abusive language in the classroom.

- All students should be in their seats when the bell rings. Challenge students to consider this possibility because you'll want to use every possible minute of your class time.

- Late assignments will lose 10 percent of their total possible point value for each day they are late. Those turned in over five days late may be turned in for a maximum of 50 percent of their original point value.

- Assignments that include plagiarized material will receive a failing grade.

Our experiences have shown us that these particular guidelines can be very effective in helping you to establish a thinker-friendly community in your classroom. It might help to clarify the last two on the list. We have found that establishing a system for makeup work whereby students are penalized *to a degree* for late assignments works most effectively; this might make more sense when considering the alternatives. One option is to accept assignments anytime, which seemingly penalizes those students who work hard and complete assignments on time. At the other end of the scale is a *turn it in when it's due or not at all* approach. Our problem with this policy is that it could mean that a student who, for example, has serious problems outside of school for a time and misses a series of assignments will not fall so far behind that there is no chance to pass your course. We suggest giving such students some chance to complete assignments and turn them in for at least partial (e.g., 50 percent) credit.

We do highly recommend a very strict plagiarism guideline, especially in an era when abundant references and cut-and-paste options make this kind of cheating relatively easy. We suggest that teachers of all subjects clearly communicate to students *what plagiarism is* (don't assume they know this) and *why it can't be tolerated* in your classroom community.

A list of guidelines similar to these should be all most teachers need when it comes to classroom rules, with a couple of notable exceptions. Science and PE teachers will certainly want to communicate special safety rules from time to time, and PE teachers may want to establish rules related to dressing for activities.

Using the procedures that we have discussed can help you to establish a feeling of community in the classroom. Putting constructivist methods and techniques into practice can enhance and further develop this feeling. We believe that periodic classroom meetings are essential in taking your community to yet higher levels.

Focal Point 3 How Can Classroom Meetings Help Solve Problems That Do Arise?

Within any community, problems are solved (or at least addressed) by committed people who have some stake in the welfare of the community as a whole. This should be the case with your *classroom* community. At both the middle and high school levels, we have found that periodic classroom meetings can provide students with a forum for discussing important issues and further enhance the feeling of empowerment of students within your classroom.

We suggest that you conduct monthly or quarterly meetings in each of your classes, or more frequently if problems arise. In experimenting with this approach in the high school classroom, we have found that the Exploratory Discussion (Module Ten) format worked very effectively. Seat yourself in a circle of chairs with your students. Begin by communicating the purpose for the meeting, which is to assess the recent progress of the class as a community and to address issues of concern. Then ask a broad, inviting question to begin the discussion (e.g., "What have we done as a class recently that helped you to learn something useful?"). Ask other open-ended questions to encourage students to expand on their initial ideas. Then, ask a question aimed at generating suggestions for further improvement (e.g., "What can we do to further improve the learning atmosphere in our classroom?"). If students are reluctant to contribute ideas at first, start with some of your own suggestions to prime the pump (e.g., "One thing that I'd like to see us try would be ____"). As with any effective Exploratory Discussion, try to generate as many ideas as possible; be sure to record these and discuss the class's progress on them periodically.

Meetings are also effective in solving specific problems that arise. Again, set the context for such a meeting, then share your concern (e.g., "I have a problem that I need your help to solve"). In meetings of this type, allow students to share their concerns as well and try to develop a consensus on how to solve the problems discussed ("We agree that all of these concerns need to be addressed. What suggestions do you have for doing that?"). Meetings such as this can be tremendously effective for solving recurring problems in any classroom. We believe that the reason for their effectiveness goes back to issues of *trust* and *responsibility;* if you as the teacher show that you have enough respect for your students to challenge *them* to address problems facing the class, students will generally respond in a positive way.

Focal Point 4 How Can You Engage Parents as Learning Collaborators?

We believe that *parents* are *the* great, untapped resource for middle schools and high schools. Although some schools have developed exemplary programs for promoting parental involvement, we believe that, for the most part, American secondary schools do a woeful job at reaching out to parents (unless, of course, there is a specific problem).

One of your first tasks should be to write the guidelines that you establish as a class into a syllabus. Include within this document some contextual information about the course (e.g., What are your major goals? What kinds of experiences will students share in this course?). Each student should have a copy of your syllabus. You may even consider leaving a copy with the principal. Make sure that parents get a copy of the syllabus as well. One of your primary early-year goals should be to get parents involved as essential collaborators, and the beginning of the year provides you with an opportunity to start this process. If you're shifting to a student-centered approach midyear, it's never too late to involve parents. Write a cover letter introducing yourself, include a copy of your syllabus, and mail this to every parent. Here's the next step in the process of connecting to parents: Call each parent some time during the first month of school or as soon as you "shift gears" as a follow-up to your letter. Introduce yourself, ask them if they'd looked at the syllabus and have any questions, and tell them about what you hope to achieve as a teacher. This sounds like a lot of work, but it pays dividends. You'll establish an early, positive rapport with parents, and if you ever do have concerns about a student, a call home will likely get a positive response. We've found that most parents (over 90 per-

cent) appreciate this initiative. It's especially important these days, when there is a tendency among some to blame *teachers* when problems arise.

Make it a point to contact parents periodically during the school year. Call home with *good news* about a student; this can provide an incredible boost at times for both the parent and the student. Another possibility is to publish a monthly or quarterly class newsletter that can be mailed home. This is relatively easy to do, especially with some of the slick computer programs available today. You can give students the responsibility to write and collect articles for the newsletter and even to produce it on class computers. We have found that this is a great way to keep parents involved and informed and that it can create a wonderful level of excitement and writing motivation for students as well.

■ ROUNDUP ■

In Part 2 of this module, we have addressed just some of the many issues related to classroom management, which we have defined as the daily operation of your classroom. We noted that the best way to approach management is to consider it as an integral part of your *teaching.* We provided numerous, additional examples to support our belief that effective, engaging teaching will prevent most discipline problems in any classroom.

We also presented advice on how to involve your students in establishing a set of guidelines for *their classroom,* and why it is important to do this. We feel that some level of student involvement is essential in creating a thinker-friendly community. In this same section, we suggested possible guidelines that you might consider adopting in some form for your own classroom.

Finally, we discussed the usefulness of classroom meetings as forums for addressing issues of concern to teachers and students and the value of engaging parents as essential collaborators. We have found that both of these initiatives can dramatically enhance the feeling of community in classrooms and create an additional level of commitment and excitement for everyone involved.

REFERENCES

Glasser, W. (1986). *Control theory in the classroom.* New York: Harper and Row.

Kohlberg, L. (1981). *Essays on moral development.* New York: Harper and Row.

Kohn, A. (1996). *Beyond discipline: From compliance to community.* Alexandria, VA: Association for Supervision and Curriculum Development.

Kounin, J. (1970). *Discipline and group management in the classroom.* New York: Holt, Rinehart, and Winston.

Maslow, A. (1968). *Motivation and personality.* New York: D. Van Nostrand.

Sizer, T. (1984). *Horace's compromise: The dilemma of the American high school.* Boston, MA: Houghton Mifflin.

Sizer, T. (1996). *Horace's hope: What works for the American high school.* Boston, MA: Houghton Mifflin.

BrushUp

Overview

In Section B, *BrushUp*, we present a lesson plan structure in Module Three with what we call Core Components. This suggested approach to planning provides a common template in which to embed the constructivist methods for workshop participants, who will inevitably plan lessons in various ways. If you are using this book on your own, we hope that you find the Core Components helpful to refine or experiment with your lesson planning.

Module Four expands on lesson planning with an array of techniques and tools that help to carry out each method. Module Five, "Questioning Skills," and Module Six, "Peer-Group Learning (PGL)," provide expanded focus on those two techniques, which are essential to effective constructivist planning.

B

Planning Professional Lessons

Overview

Goals

Focal Points and Discussions

The Lesson Plan Structure with Core Components

Rationale

Performance Objective

Materials

Hook

Student Aim

Development with Method and Method Markers

The Culmination

Form versus Function

Assessment and Evaluation

Building a Lesson Plan

Roundup

Hands-On Practice

■ OVERVIEW

This module gives you our Core Components for lesson planning. In doing this, we're not suggesting that our format is better than your own. In fact, every so often we change our Core Components, not in concept, but in form, as we work with colleagues and inservice and preservice teachers and explore new ways of planning.

There are two reasons why we're sharing our elements of planning with you. First, you might be curious how other people approach planning and stumble on some new idea that may interest you. The second reason is practical. Because we embed our seven constructivist methods in our lesson plan format, our Core Components create a unifying framework for our methods. This standardization is especially important if you're taking an inservice workshop or other collegial development in which each participant uses a different style of planning lessons.

Because you're most likely a seasoned teacher, we'll just briefly explain each Core Component and the examples so that you'll be able to comfortably follow our method modules.

■ GOALS

We'll describe and demonstrate seven features or Core Components and other aspects of professional planning, whether you're teaching a fifty-minute lesson, a month-long project, or within a block program. In this module, we'll acquaint you with the following.

- Rationale
- Performance Objective
- Materials
- Student Aim
- Hook
- Development
- Culmination
- Form versus Function
- Assessment and Evaluation

■ FOCAL POINTS AND DISCUSSIONS

Core Components of planning as we describe them here are the underpinnings of a constructivist approach to teaching, what we call *invisible teaching*, discussed in Module Two. Briefly, invisible teaching refers to a *facilitative* approach in which you guide or *enable* students to learn. As a facilitator, you must plan thoroughly and reflectively in order to gather together the various instructional materials your students can refer to in addition to a textbook. You also need to plan prompts (questions and directions) and activities that guide students through the learning process via Bloom's Taxonomy (see Module Five, "Questioning Skills"), as well as make yourself available as a live resource in the classroom. In this way, you become invisible as *the teacher* because your students may not be consciously aware of the role you're playing behind the scenes as they learn.

As a constructivist teacher, you learn along with your students, the quintessential mentor. But as your students come closer and closer to this ideal, you will never be idle. In pursuit of independent learning on new levels—for example, with projects—your students will turn to you as their guide, the catalyst who gets them thinking about the next step, about where and how to fill in the gaps, increasingly learning along with your students even as your knowledge helps you point them in the right direction. We have had such experiences with our own secondary students from all types of backgrounds, suburban and urban.

With didacticism, the teacher is the star. With constructivism, your students are the stars. The constructivist teacher shines too, but you can't tell unless you know what to look for. (For more on student and teacher roles, see Module Two, "Resocializing.")

Focal Point 1 **The Lesson Plan Structure with Core Components**

Core Components do not need to be sequenced in a set fashion, though at first we will introduce them in a linear sequence. We encourage you in time to expand and/or combine some of the components to accommodate your teaching style or to accommodate the intentions of a specific lesson or project.

Discussion 1 **The Lesson Plan Structure with Core Components**

We suggest that you start out dividing your lesson plan into two of three lesson segments: *Prelude* and *Enactment*. The Prelude describes the foundation of the lesson, the information for teacher reference. The Enactment describes the process that engages the students in the learning process. In our view, this distinction helps you at the outset to remember what role each Core Component provides. In time you might want to experiment with different structures for your plans according to a given lesson. In this way, you can eventually expand your present repertoire of lesson formats.

Figure 3.1 presents a bird's-eye view of our suggested structure. Figure 3.2 provides a template for the Core Components with the added third segment, *Assessment and Evaluation.*

Focal Point 2 Rationale

The *Rationale* expresses your instructional intention. In this way, the Rationale is the rudder. We recommend focusing on three features to help you plan a strong, meaningful lesson:

1. *What* are you teaching?
2. *Why* are you teaching this?
3. *Justification.*

Discussion 2 Rationale

The *What?* should be from your syllabus, a specific and clear topic—for you as well as your students. Then ask yourself: *Why is this lesson valuable to my students?*

Having fun or even being interesting is an insufficient reason. Yes, the effort should be engaging, stimulating, challenging, and even enjoyable, all qualities integral to instructional soundness. But you are not in the entertainment business. Also, we suggest that, in the *Why?* segment, you include some of Bloom's cognitive skills presented in Module Five (comprehension, application, analysis, synthesis, etc.) that you want your students to cultivate during the lesson. Art, music, and PE teachers should jot down the *perceptual, listening acuity,* and *motor skills,* respectively. As for the *justification,* reflect on the INTASC Standards embodied in your lesson. (See Module One for an overview and the Appendix for a detailed description of these.)

Examples of Rationale

Following are some examples of the Rationale in various subjects. We provide nonexamples contrasted to examples as a way to clarify the importance of a specific focus. Figure 3.3 encapsulates the parts of the Rationale for quick reference. We suggest that you jot down the var-

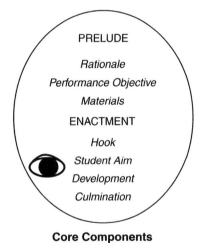

Core Components

Rationale = focused instructional intention that provides cohesion

Performance Objective = activity that generates a physical or digital product in Development (could take twenty-five miutes or two weeks)

Materials = sources of information

Hook = attention grabber; relates to Rationale

Student Aim = captures the Rationale in catchy language

Development = unfolds the method and carries out the Performance Objective (could take thirty minutes or days/weeks for a project)

Culmination = brings together key concepts with new insights (could take several minutes or two days of project presentations)

© 2001 Ina Claire Gabler

FIGURE 3.1 Core Components for Lessons or Projects: Bird's-Eye View of Lesson Planning.

Lesson Segments with Core Components

PRELUDE (for teacher's reference)
1. Rationale
   a. *What* are you teaching?
   b. *Why* are you teaching this?
   c. *Justification* in terms of INTASC Standards (see Appendix)
2. Performance Objective
   a. *Preparation* for creating a product
   b. *Product* that demonstrates learning
   c. *Criteria* that ensure acceptable achievement
3. Materials
   a. *Textbook*
   b. *Primary Sources*
   c. *Audio/Visual*
   d. *Information Technology*
   e. *Etc.*

ENGAGEMENT (student involvement)
4. Student Aim
   Captures the Rationale in colloquial language
5. Hook
   a. Grabs interest
   b. Relates to Rationale
6. Development
   a. Unfolds a given method with the Performance Objective
   b. Contains prompts
7. Culmination
   a. Wrap-Up summarizes the specific key points.
   b. Leap elicits a related new concept or application of the topic.

ASSESSMENT AND EVALUATION PLAN
(what has been learned and how well)
Performance-Based Examination of
- *Student Projects*
- *Presentations*
- *Journals*
- *Portfolios*
- *Group/Lab Activities*
- *Role-Playing*
- *Etc.*

FIGURE 3.2 Template For Lesson Planning with Core Components

ious wordings that introduce the *What?* and *Why?* segments in the examples below. You'll be asked to use these various wordings in the Hands-On Practice at the end of this module.

EXAMPLE #1A/HISTORY (AMERICAN REVOLUTION)

What?: Students will enlarge their understanding of causes of the American Revolution to include economic motives.

Why?: Analyzing and evaluating economic influences provides students a more in-depth understanding of the American Revolution.
Justification: INTASC Standards #2, #5, #6, #8.

Analysis of Example 1A

The *What?* expresses a specific focus, namely, the inclusion of economic conditions as another cause of the revolution. The *Why?* is also specific and indicates the cognitive or thinking skills. The *Justification* cites relevant INTASC Standards.

Nonexample 1B/History

What?: Students will learn more about the American Revolution.

Why?: Better student understanding of the American Revolution.

Justification: Meets four INTASC Standards.

Analysis of Example 1B

The *What?* is too vague. What specifically does "learn more" refer to? Similarly, the *Why?* is nonspecific and does not indicate the nature of the topic's value. The *Justification* must specify which standards.

EXAMPLE #2A/ENGLISH (CHARACTERIZATION)

What?: To explore the behavior of Ichabod Crane and Brom Bones in Washington Irving's *The Legend of Sleepy Hollow.*

Why?: Students will interpret facts about Ichabod Crane in order to analyze Brom Bones's motives. This lesson introduces the concept of characterization.
Justification: INTASC Standards #2, #3, #5, #8.

Analysis of Example #2A

The *What?* is well focused. Similarly, the *Why?* states the specific values of the lesson, both for content and thinking skills. In the *Justification* the focused Rationale makes clear how the INTASC Standards are satisfied.

Nonexample #2B/English

What?: To learn about the characters Ichabod Crane and Brom Bones in *The Legend of Sleepy Hollow* by Washington Irving.

PARTS	PURPOSE
1. *What* are you teaching?	1. Clarifies your instructional intentions
2. *Why* are you teaching this?	2. Establishes worth of the topic
3. *Justification*	3. Confirms instructional value/INTASC Standards

FIGURE 3.3 The Rationale

Why?: Student understanding of Bones and Crane.
Justification: Critical-thinking skills.

Analysis of Nonexample #2B

While the *What?* specifies the characters and the work, the instructional intention is not focused. What will the students "learn about" the two characters? The *Why?* is also vague. What kind of "understanding" does the teacher hope to establish? The *Justification* lacks specific INTASC Standards. In addition, the Rationale is too vague to suggest specific standards.

EXAMPLE #3A/SPANISH (PREPOSITIONS)

What?: Students will learn the pronunciation and meaning of five important Spanish prepositions.
Why?: Prepositions are crucial for conversation and reading. Learners will be encouraged to infer and apply the meanings on their own.
Justification: INTASC Standards #2, #3, #5.

Analysis of Example #3A

The *What?* is well focused. The *Why?* cites the practical use as well as thinking skills and also indicates active student learning. The *Justification* cites specific standards appropriate to the lesson.

Nonexample #3B/Spanish

What? and *Why?:* To teach about prepositions so students can use them effectively.

Analysis of Nonexample #3B

The *What?* and *Why?* are too vague. There is no *Justification*.

Now that you have a taste of the Rationale, take a look at the Performance Objective that follows.

Focal Point 3 **Performance Objective**

As the name suggests, the *Performance Objective* results in a physical, digital, or enacted product that your students create. With this in mind, take a look at our three features for a Performance Objective.

1. *Preparation:* <u>Develops the knowledge and thinking skills</u> necessary to create the product.

2. *Product:* Demonstrates your students' learning with a <u>concrete outcome</u>.

3. *Criteria:* Include a <u>specific, minimum number of items correctly carried out</u> for satisfactory achievement of the product. In PE, art, music, or other subjects, criteria may cite a <u>specific time duration</u> for a given task.

Discussion 3 **Performance Objective**

The Performance Objective directly relates to the Rationale. The Performance Objective is described in the Prelude of the lesson to help you focus as you plan. However, the Performance Objective is carried out in the Development section. Accordingly, the *preparation* helps your students develop the knowledge and skills they need to generate the product. Think of the preparation as the foundation for creating the product. In a fifty-minute lesson, the preparation may take fifteen to twenty minutes. For a project, the preparation may take eight to ten days of research and discussion.

The *product* can be anything concrete: a list, a magazine, a computer graphic, an original concept map, a series of questions, an original Website, a debate, an enactment of a scene from a play, a video minidocumentary, and so on. The product may take twenty-five minutes or three weeks to complete. In the process of creating a product, your students keep learning, hands-on. In addition, you'll also learn as you facilitate and discover new ideas from your students.

Doing versus Talking

The activity product is usually NOT an oral activity such as a student–student discussion or teacher–student dialogue. There are meaningful exceptions to this—oral "products" such as acting scenes from a play or formal debating—so long as every student participates. As you know, in a typical lesson most students will not have the opportunity to orally demonstrate what they've learned because of time constraints—and even shyness. You need evidence that everyone is ready to move on and to spot the students who need extra help. For the most part, oral dialogue is part of the preparation. A concrete *product,* however, demonstrates the quality—and quantity—of learning for an entire class. In addition, the products demonstrate what the students have and have not yet grasped related to the Rationale.

Finally, the *criteria* cite a minimum number of tasks that must be successfully completed. Criteria may also define a length of time for a task, for example, at least twenty minutes of dribbling a basketball across the court. In this way, criteria establish standards.

Performance Objective versus Tests

The Performance Objective is NOT a test, quiz, and so on. These are *assessment instruments that help to judge the quality of learning.* By contrast, a Performance Objective is usually an *integral* part of the *daily* learning experience. We say "usually" because sometimes, for example, a two-day lesson devotes the first day to developing concepts and principles; in this case, the Performance Objective may constitute the entire second day.

A SCENARIO: You're a master pizza chef. Making pizza is the obsession of your life, and you want to pass on your expertise and appreciation of this fantastic food. Disciples surround you in the kitchen. A natural teacher, you use the Socratic method of questioning to open your disciples' eyes to the art of baking incomparable pizza. You direct their attention by questioning their observations as you make the dough and shape it, as you assemble grated cheeses, peppers, mushrooms, sausages, and onions along with anchovies, olives and other assorted toppings. You probe your disciples for the most delicious blends of various combinations; you ask them to justify their conjectures as they strive to orally describe exquisite pizzas for individual tastes. Yes, you have done a beautiful job of facilitating their creative thinking. Your students even make your masterly mouth water at the mere sound of their original concoctions because you have the powers to envision their gustatory glory.

But until each disciple has baked a pizza independently, neither you nor the would-be master can be certain that meaningful learning has taken place. Indeed, the first efforts may show promise but may not yet flood the palate. For this to happen, your disciples must practice, guided by recipes, and be encouraged to explore original versions based on what they've learned. Then and only then will each disciple succeed in creating pizza with pizzaz.

Like baking a pizza, a Performance Objective combines the ingredients of a lesson into a product that affirms learning. In this way, like the pizza, the Performance Objective is greater than the sum of its parts.

Examples of Performance Objectives

Before we give examples in three subjects, take a look at Figure 3.4 for a summary of the Performance Objective that you can match to each example. The following examples are based on actual lessons by teachers trained in constructivist teaching. Consider these examples in terms of Figure 3.4 and Bloom's Taxonomy in Module Five. They include the Rationale so you can see how the Performance Objective relates to the instructional intention.

We suggest that you jot down the introductory phrases to the three parts of the Performance Objectives. You will need this for the Hands-On Practice to come.

EXAMPLE #1/SCIENCE[1] (WATER PURIFICATION)

Rationale

What? and *Why?:* Students will name and comprehend the three steps of water purification and why it is important. Students will analyze facts then apply that knowledge to categorizing bottles of water at different stages of purification.

Justification: INTASC Standards #1, #2, #3, #5, #6, #8, #9.

PARTS	PURPOSE
1. *Preparation* develops the ideas that prepare students for the product or activity.	1. Forces you to plan thoughtfully related to the Rationale; enables your students to generate a physical product that demonstrates learning.
2. *Product* is a physical outcome for a lesson or project. The product must directly relate to the Rationale.	2. Demonstrates to you and the students that they have grasped the concept(s). The constructivist product *demands critical thinking and/or problem solving rather than rote repetition.*
3. *Criteria* include a specific, minimum number of items correctly carried out or a specified time duration, especially in PE and art, for satisfactory performance of the product.	3. Criteria establish standards.

FIGURE 3.4 The Performance Objective

Performance Objective (related to the Rationale)

Preparation: Students will discuss the appearance of different bottles of water. Each student will write a description of a water sample, using pH and visual qualities. A discussion will compare and contrast the various bottles with factual information about water purity and pollution.

Product: In groups of three, learners will be able to compose an overhead transparency that represents the process of water purification either graphically or in writing.

Criteria: Students will be able to establish the three steps of water purification. Students will be able to identify at least two differences and two similarities among all the samples.

EXAMPLE #2/ART[2] (DRAWING)

Rationale

What?: To develop understanding of line, shape, and proportion.

Why?: Learners will heighten their perceptual awareness of the elements of forms and space.

Justification: INTASC Standards #1, #2, #3, #5, #6.

Performance Objective (related to the Rationale)

Preparation: Students will discuss the various types of lines, shapes, and proportions in the upside-down line drawing of Mt. Rushmore projected by the overhead projector. The subject matter is not identifiable upside-down.

Product: Students will be able to draw the upside-down image, imitating the characteristics of line, shape, and proportion.

Criteria: Learners will draw for at least ten minutes or until they complete the task. Then they will turn their work right-side-up and see if they can identify the subject matter without being told. Students will discuss and analyze at least three relationships of lines, shapes, and proportions and their importance in drawing Mt. Rushmore or anything else we see.

EXAMPLE #3/PHYSICAL EDUCATION (THROWING A FOOTBALL)

Rationale

What?: To learn how to successfully throw a football within 25 feet.

Why?: To develop arm–eye coordination, balance, timing. To coordinate movements between arms, feet, and the intended distance.

Justification: INTASC Standards #2, #3, #5, #6.

Performance Objective (related to the Rationale)

Preparation: Demonstration of the proper throwing form. Students asked to identify what they notice first, second, third, and so on. Open discussion analyzing the characteristics of each movement.

Product: Students will be able to successfully throw a football according to the Rationale by the end of class.

Criteria: At least twenty minutes of practice with a partner. Each student will be able to throw a football and succeed with all specified characteristics of a successful throw.

Each student must analyze his throw on a chart for each characteristic.

Focal Point 4 **Materials**

Materials matter. Textbooks may serve as a reference, but for in-depth learning it's a good idea to bring complementary materials into your classroom: primary sources, magazines, newspapers, as well as audio and visual materials, graphics of all kinds, objects, stand-alone software, and so on. Of course, the Internet can also supply valuable information, but your students need to learn to verify the validity and quality of Internet sources. Varied materials not only provide a wider ranger and depth than the textbook alone; they stimulate both the students and you with different perspectives, styles, and visual and aural appeal. Select materials that promote rigor, materials that add color. In short, provide your learners with, and encourage them to contribute to, a cornucopia of resources.

Discussion 4 **Materials**

As your students go beyond the information—when they analyze, synthesize, and evaluate the substance—they can point to the materials to support their assertions. In this constructivist approach, materials provide both the foundation for critical thinking and the validation of those insights.

We recommend that you use Bloom's Taxonomy as your right hand. With questions, directions, and activities, you can guide your students through the abundance of information so that they learn to identify the facts, concepts, principles, and themes that serve as the springboard for their own insights. That way, your students and you explore ideas together.

Selecting appropriate materials is an important skill that takes imagination. Incorporating materials into a constructivist approach that stimulates interest instead of passive ingestion—that's the art and the exciting challenge of being a student-centered teacher.

Examples of Materials

In Figure 3.5 we've organized an overview of materials into categories. The materials described here do not comprise an exhaustive list. But they can help you experiment with a variety of materials. We hope that you embellish the list from your own ideas and experiences.

Focal Point 5 **The Hook**

The *Hook* begins the Student Engagement segment of the lesson for good reason. The Hook is an attention

Textual	Visual	Audio	Objects	Tools	Teacher Designed Tailored to Learning Needs or Topic
books	video and film	songs and music	models (of forms, scenes, relationships, etc.)	chalkboard or white board	scenarios
magazines	cartoons	speeches	physical/visual metaphors	overhead and opaque projectors	fact sheets
lyrics	graphic representations	readings	3-D mockups (e.g., DNA, cubes, sentence structure, etc.)	TV, VCRs, tape and CD players	handouts of various formats (columns, tables, outlines, concept maps, graphs, drawings, activity prompts, etc.)
primary sources	Websites	sound effects		computers (single or networked)	facsimiles for skill building, e.g., simulated reference texts for tailored note-taking and for learning how to organize a bibliography for a research paper
Websites and email; stand-alone software	software simulations for learning in all subject areas; stand-alone software				

© 2001, Ina Claire Gabler.

FIGURE 3.5 Materials

grabber. When you plan a lesson, it's useful to assume that the only person in the classroom interested in the lesson is you. How do you pique the students' interest? For starters, you can use an effective Hook, which has two elements: It is (1) *content based* (relates to the Rationale) and (2) *personalized* (relates to the students in some way).

Discussion 5 The Hook

By *content based* we mean the Hook alludes to facts or concepts in the lesson. But you don't want to be dry. If you tie the Hook to your students' frames of reference, then you'll *personalize* the Hook and capture interest. If planned well with a motivating theme, varied materials, and engaging techniques, the entire lesson should "hook"

the students. But they will often need something catchy to pull them in at the outset.

Sometimes an idea for a Hook will occur to you in a flash of inspiration. Other times, an effective Hook will occur to you as you plan the Performance Objective or the Culmination. There are also times when you will not be able to think of an effective Hook. In that case, the Student Aim, described in Focal Point #6, can double-dip as a Hook. Or a description of the upcoming Performance Objective might engage interest.

A Hook should NOT be merely a gimmick. A meaningful Hook begins the learning process. Every Core Component should contribute to the instructional value.

Examples of Hooks

Here are some sample Hooks. We hope that some are new to you.

- A Hook may be a provocative question. We mean *provocative,* not an academic question that only a teacher could love.
- A Hook may find you in costume, role-playing.
- A Hook may invite students to briefly role-play.
- A Hook may be an engaging videoclip or audio segment.
- A Hook may be a positive, noncompetitive challenge.
- A Hook may be an anecdote that students can relate to, an analogy of the concepts to come.
- A Hook may be a preview of a computer simulation.
- A Hook may be props that represent ideas and concepts in an accessible format.
- A Hook may be anything else you dream up that relates to the lesson and jump-starts your students.

However imaginative the Hook may be, you need to relate it to the heart of the lesson. A question–response dialogue with your students is one way to achieve this. Consider subject-specific examples in terms of Figure 3.6.

EXAMPLE #1/SCIENCE[3] (WATER PURIFICATION)

Hook

Content based: Show class four bottles of water in varying stages of purification.

Personalized: Ask students to describe what they observe and to infer possible significance. Which water would they be willing to drink? not willing to drink? Why? Can they describe various characteristics (odor, color, consistency, etc.) of water they have encountered that has not been safe? of water that has been safe? Are they not sure how to tell if water is safe or not? Have they heard

Content Based	Personalized for Students
Anchored to an integral concept in the lesson	1. Poses an analogy to which students can relate; may employ one or more physical props 2. May challenge students' belief system in a respectful way 3. May involve some or all students in a brief role-play or a demonstration, etc.

FIGURE 3.6 The Hook

of someone drinking impure water? What happened to that person? Would they be willing to swim or wash in impure water? Why?

EXAMPLE #2/ART[4] (DRAWING)

Hook

Content based: Project a black ink drawing of Mount Rushmore on a transparency. The image is upside-down and unrecognizable.

Personalized: What do you have to notice in order to copy this faithfully? Do you think drawing this will be more difficult or easier than drawing it right-side-up? Why? What is the advantage of drawing this upside-down? What do you think I want you to focus on? Why?

Note: In Example #2, the Hook becomes the vehicle of the lesson's substance.

EXAMPLE #3/MATH (DISTANCE PROBLEMS)

Hook

Content based + personalized: How long does it take you to get to the pizza parlor at lunch? Do you need to run there and back to return to school in time? Or can you walk? What determines if you walk or run?

Focal Point 6 **Student Aim**

An effective *Aim* contains the same two elements as the Hook: It is (1) *content based* (points to the heart of the lesson) and (2) *personalized* (relates or speaks to your students in some appealing way). The Student Aim expresses your formal Rationale in colloquial or catchy language. The Aim is a rudder for your students. It should also *whet curiosity.* It sometimes includes the cognitive skill with such words as *list, interpret, analyze,* and so on. The same Aim may be expressed in different language for different classes, tailored to the interests of each student group.

Discussion 6 **The Aim**

Since both the Aim and the Hook are content based and personalized, they can interrelate and build on each other as the heart of the introduction to your lesson. The Aim may be written clearly on the board, an overhead transparency, or other medium. It can be phrased as a statement or a question. The Aim may also serve to steer you back on path, away from digressions, as a look over the shoulder at the Aim on the board or transparency reminds you of your Rationale.

Not every lesson benefits from an Aim at the outset, particularly inductive lessons in which students arrive at the major concepts and principles themselves, with your guidance. For example, the sample lesson plan on metaphor in Focal Point #11 is an inductive lesson: You will see that the students are guided to define a metaphor themselves at the *end* of the lesson.

Sometimes a Hook builds up to the Aim, or you can provide no Aim and at the outset challenge the students to infer the Aim of the lesson later on in the Culmination. In other words, sometimes the Aim is explicit; other times, it's implied. Ideally, you would vary these approaches.

Aim as Hook

Finally, a compelling Aim can substitute for a Hook or serve as an additional Hook. An academic-style Aim, including a question, will *not* likely hook your students even if *you* think the question or statement is brimming with significance. For example, we do not consider the Aim in the sample lesson on metaphors ("What is a metaphor? How do metaphors affect you?") to be intriguing enough to serve as a Hook. A compelling Aim is something surprising, mysterious, inventive. In our sample lesson soon to come, the Hook is a picture of a magician raising a torch at a dragon. An Aim as a Hook could be, "Can you uncover the magician's metaphors in the time limit of this lesson?"

Examples of an Aim

Use Figure 3.7 as a handy reference for each example of an Aim that follows. *Note:* All nonexamples below have one thing in common: They're *dry*.

EXAMPLE #1A/MUSIC (GENRES)

Aim: Rap and Blues: Friends or Foes?

Elements of the Aim	Purpose
1. Content based	1. Captures the heart of the Rationale
2. Personalized	2. Relates or speaks to students in some way

FIGURE 3.7 The Student Aim

NONEXAMPLE #1B/MUSIC

Aim: To learn about the similarities and differences between the Blues and Rap

EXAMPLE #2A/MATH (DISTANCE PROBLEMS)

Aim: How long would it take you to get from your seat to the nearest pizza parlor?

NONEXAMPLE #2B/MATH

Aim: Distance problems

EXAMPLE #3A/SOCIAL STUDIES (POLITICS OF HUNGER)

Aim: There's an overabundance of food in the world, so why are people going hungry?

NONEXAMPLE #3B/SOCIAL STUDIES

Aim: To learn about the politics of world hunger

Focal Point 7 Development with Method and Method Markers

The *Development* contains your chosen method and includes a Performance Objective. Because each method is different, the Development is a variable Core Component, with specific method features that we call *method markers*. For this reason, the Development is only indicated, not demonstrated, in the sample lesson plan in Focal Point #11. In Section C of this book, each method module contains full sample lesson plans with the corresponding Development and method markers. For now, we want you to focus on the Core Components without the method.

Focal Point 8 The Culmination

The *Culmination* contains the following two elements: (1) *Wrap-Up* (*summarizes the key points* of the lesson) and (2) *Leap* (*introduces a related but new concept, principle, or theme,* an implication of one or more of the key points developed in the lesson). The Culmination is otherwise known as a conclusion because it effects closure. Too often, however, the conclusion is considered a throwaway. Teachers often provide a superficial statement such as, "Today we've learned about gases," or, "Tomorrow we'll learn two more drawing techniques." Sometimes teachers ask for or express a summary of the lesson, a meaningful practice. But a lesson's closure can be thought-provoking as well. This is the reason we use the term *Culmination*.

Discussion 8 The Culmination

We recommend that you tie the threads of a lesson together. A strong Culmination, a *terrific* Culmination, is the pinnacle of the lesson. The Culmination should *bring together specific key points*, reaffirming the lesson's Rationale. But the challenge for your students comes when, for example, you prompt them to predict principles or articulate themes beyond those established in the lesson, relating the ideas to today's world. Some examples: What is the significance—beyond the classroom—of Hiroshima, of discovering the atom, of stereotyped characters? How have those events and concepts shaped present-day attitudes? How have they shaped your students' lives? Could McDonald's exist without photosynthesis? Could it exist without geometric proofs? *Why?*

Of course the Culmination supplies cohesion, a practical necessity. For example, referring to the Aim is an effective transition into the Culmination, especially if the Aim asks a question. Or the Culmination can establish the Aim inductively, that is, guide the students to retrospectively determine the Aim themselves. At the same time the Culmination can inspire your students to leave your classroom *still talking about the ideas in the lesson*. So think of the end of a lesson not as a mere summary or disposable formality, but as a *peak*.

Examples of the Culmination

We suggest you compare each of the following subject-specific examples to Figure 3.8.

The Wrap-Up	The Leap
1. Refer to the Aim as a lead-in.	Probe with thought questions:
2. Review key facts and concepts. Be specific.	1. What is the significance of __?
	2. How has __ affected your life, directly or indirectly?
	3. What if __?
	4. Can you compare __ to __?

FIGURE 3.8 The Culmination

EXAMPLE #1/ENGLISH (WRITING WITH MAIN IDEAS AND DETAILS)

Wrap-Up: What is the difference between a main idea and supporting details?

Leap: Think of a profession besides writing that might interest you. How could it be useful to distinguish between main ideas and supporting details in that profession?

EXAMPLE #2/FRENCH (IRREGULAR VERBS)

Wrap-Up: What are the five irregular verbs you've learned today?

Leap: What are some situations in which you would need to use these verbs to make your needs understood?

EXAMPLE #3/SCIENCE (EXPERIMENTAL METHOD)

Wrap-Up: What are the elements of the experimental method?

Leap: What is a real-life situation that we haven't discussed in which the experimental method is useful? If you wanted to find out how much your friends liked you, would the experimental method be effective? Why?

Focal Point 9 Form versus Function

Constructivism highlights the difference between *form* and *function*. Form refers to the *definition* or *content* of the Core Component; for example, the Rationale clarifies the teacher's intention and focus for a given lesson, or the Performance Objective includes an interpretation of the fourth chapter in *Huckleberry Finn* by Mark Twain. Function refers to the *role* of a Core Component. Function separates passive from active student participation and separates memorization from critical thinking. As we've said earlier, memorization is important for important facts, definitions, and so on, but recall should be a stepping-stone to higher-level cognition.

Discussion 9 Form versus Function

Imagine that two Performance Objectives center around the *form* or *content* of an urban design that addresses ecological concerns. The first Performance Objective instructs students to label a diagram, defining and explaining the significance of each feature. This first Performance Objective *functions* on only low cognitive levels; it merely requires the students to paraphrase what you and the textbook have imparted.

The second Performance Objective requires students to plan the urban design from scratch, not only defining and explaining the various features but also analyzing the interrelationships, predicting outcomes with supported judgments. This Performance Objective carries your students across Bloom's Taxonomy, generating a product that embodies original analysis and solutions. It *functions* as an original critical-thinking experience.

Consider another example. In a teacher-centered lesson, the Rationale or *form* is to learn the definition of photosynthesis. For the Performance Objective, students memorize the definition of photosynthesis and explain stages in the process, that is, engage in low-level *functions,* all conveyed with teacher talk or lecture and a textbook. This knowledge may mean nothing to the students beyond the questions on a multiple-choice test.

Or, in a student-focused[5] lesson with the same Rationale, the Performance Objective may *function* as student analysis of photosynthesis as part of the ongoing transformation on earth—energy being converted into matter and matter into energy in countless ways. For the concrete product, your students might generate a concept map with examples from their everyday lives and arrive at the relationship between the process of photosynthesis and this larger perspective. For example, how are a burger and french fries related to photosynthesis? How are the clothes your students wear a product of photosynthesis? What kind of books would we have without photosynthesis? How else are your students' lives affected by photosynthesis?[6]

You can see that the didactic Performance Objectives promote prescribed answers while the constructivist Performance Objectives enable discovery. This is not to imply that all didactic lessons lack value. Minilectures are useful to introduce projects or units, to summarize discussions (Atwell, 1987), and to present information in a content-rich syllabus. In fact, one of our methods, the Interactive Presentation in Module Twelve, incorporates minilectures. However, long lectures or ongoing teacher talk tend to promote a passive student role with little if any critical thinking.

Focal Point 10 Assessment and Evaluation

We'd like to review the difference between *evaluation* and *assessment.* Evaluation is the process of making a judgment about the quality of student learning. Assessment is the means by which you gather information to make these judgments: portfolios, presentations, questionnaires, tests, oral interviews, and so on.

Discussion 10 Assessment and Evaluation

As a constructivist teacher, you need strategies in addition to multiple-choice or fill-in exams for judging what your students have learned. Students in a constructivist environment are active learners. They create original products. They learn to question and think critically. In time, they become independent learners, selecting their own topics for projects and constructing their own insights justified by sources. You can see that as a constructivist teacher you will need strategies for judging your students' performance-based products, instead of checking largely for rote memorization or mere application of facts.

There are three types of assessment:

- *Diagnostic:* Identifies what your students know and need to learn about a given topic.
- *Formative:* Examines your students' progress throughout the learning process.
- *Summative:* Establishes what the students have learned both quantitatively and qualitatively.

To assess and evaluate the quality of learning in a lesson, project, or unit, ask yourself two questions:

- *What products will my students generate?* (research paper, Website, role-play, enactment or debate, video, drawing, portfolio, motor coordination, musical composition, etc.)
- *What are the criteria for acceptable achievement?* (your own rubrics or categories for evaluation of organization, thoroughness, appropriate skills for the task, satisfaction of the Aim, originality, critical thinking, motor ability, growth, test results, etc.)

We define *performance-based assessment techniques* as those that *allow teachers to observe and evaluate what students are able to do as they are engaged in a learning experience that involves thinking at higher cognitive levels.* An important question now becomes: What assessment techniques might be included in the mix of tools that you utilize within your classroom? *Given the right function or role,* a wide range of techniques might be considered performance based. It is our position that tests and quizzes could also be considered performance based, again, *given the right design.*

Examples of Constructivist Assessment and Evaluation

What follows is a list of suggested performance-based student products for constructivist learning that you can include in various lessons, units, and projects.

- *Student presentations* should be frequent events in

all classrooms. Such presentations can promote the confidence of students, help them to develop important communications skills, and significantly enhance their understanding of subject matter. Presentations can range from the brief, informal, and nongraded variety (e.g., pairs of students explaining a process for solving a complex math problem) to extended events that require extensive planning (e.g., groups of students discussing their research findings after a class project).

• *Student journals* can be utilized to challenge students to think about their experiences (and their own thinking processes) in more depth. Math teachers might ask students to write about their thought processes as they complete a difficult proof. Teachers in any subject could invite students to take and defend a final position following a Reflective Discussion. We recommend evaluating student journal responses in terms of how thoroughly they address guiding questions and how effectively they use evidence to support their arguments.

• *Student interviews* can provide exciting learning experiences for students of any age in any subject area. Writing interview questions can immerse students in any topic. Actually conducting interviews can provide students with interesting new insights. We recommend requiring students to write Reaction Papers or to do presentations in response to the interview experience.

• *Themes, papers, and laboratory reports* can take many forms and can be linked directly to authentic, performance-based experiences. Examples could include reports in which students reflect on cultural differences between the United States and another country whose language they are learning, written reflections completed in response to guiding questions related to novels or short stories, or Reaction Papers completed in response to comments made by a guest speaker.

• *Tests and quizzes* can provide interesting insights into students' thinking and understanding and can extend their thinking in new ways. We recommend that you build performance-based elements into your tests (e.g., science students could be challenged to complete brief, hands-on investigations and reflect on the results in a test essay; a math exam could include one complex problem related to their lives that students could work through in pairs, then report on the process and results). Brief quizzes (e.g., four to five short-answer questions) can provide frequent, *formative* insights into the nature of students' understanding.

• *Research projects* should be a major emphasis in all subject areas, at all grade levels. We have found that effec-

tive research projects are driven by intriguing guiding questions (articulated by both teachers and students); allow for a degree of student choice in what is researched, how this is done, and how findings are reported; and feature some kind of sharing event in which students have an opportunity to *teach* their peers what they have learned through the process. Research projects can take a wide range of forms, depending on the subject. They can be conducted by individual students or peer groups and can feature any of the performance-based techniques that we have described.

• *Original Websites, video, audio material, and other media products* can both motivate your students and prove educationally valuable. Your students can create various media products with the content of any of the products described here and produce authentic-learning products for audiences beyond the classroom. In addition to the content, your students would learn the features of the media and how to manipulate them to full educational advantage, following your guidelines and criteria.

We recommend that you utilize a blend of these assessment techniques and that you qualitatively evaluate assessment products with scoring rubrics. Such instruments can provide students with meaningful feedback and make the assessment process manageable. Our final advice is to closely couple the assessment process with your teaching approach, almost to the point where *assessment* and *teaching* are indistinguishable from each other. Figures 3.9 and 3.10 present a template for and examples of assessment products and evaluation criteria.

Focal Point 11 Building a Lesson Plan

Consider the sample lesson that follows. It contains all the Core Components for an eighth-grade lesson on metaphors. We chose this topic because it is accessible to people in all subject areas. Similarly, we chose eighth

Assessment Products	Evaluation Rubric
Diagnostic:	Product:
Formative:	Grading:
Summative:	Relevant Features with Criteria:

FIGURE 3.9 Assessment and Evaluation Plan Template

Sample Products for Assessment	Sample Criteria for Evaluation (create rubrics for the following)
1. Research paper or related products such as magazines 2. Original Website 3. Original video 4. Enactment of a play 5. Role-play or debate based on research 6. Original lab experiment 7. Original drawings or paintings 8. Demonstration of targeted motor skills 9. Role-play conversation in foreign language employing targeted expressions, verbs, etc. 10. Portfolio 11. Presentations 12. Interview skills 13. Student journals 14. Tests	1. Organization and structure 2. Written proficiency (specify skills) 3. Critical thinking: development of concepts, principles, and themes with documentation and clear logic 4. Satisfaction of the goal 5. Satisfaction of the Student Aims 6. Originality 7. Thoroughness (in-depth) 8. Growth from previous performance 9. Diction and enunciation 10. Drawing proficiency for targeted skills 11. Motor coordination 12. Production values 13. Test results in conjunction with other performance-based assessments 14. Completeness (includes all criteria)

FIGURE 3.10 Sample Products and Criteria

grade so that the content would not obstruct the Core Components. An assortment of sample lessons for various levels and subjects awaits you in Modules Seven through Twelve.

In keeping with our discussion on the Development, that Core Component is indicated but not filled in for now because it varies according to the method it unfolds. But even without this crucial Core Component, you can gain a strong sense of the progression or "story" of this lesson from the other Core Components it contains. Note the cognitive skills from Bloom's Taxonomy.

■ EXAMPLE OF BUILDING A LESSON PLAN

Sample Lesson Plan with Core Components
Topic: Metaphors, Eighth Grade

Prelude

A. Rationale

   1. *What?:* To introduce the concept of a metaphor as a concrete image with various interpretations.

   2. *Why?:* Students will comprehend and apply the concept of a metaphor. They will analyze (compare and contrast) symbolic versus literal meanings of various images to develop abstract thinking.

   3. *Justification:* INTASC Standards #2, #3, #4, #5, #6.

B. Performance Objective (carried out in Development)

   1. *Preparation:* Project colorful picture of magician and dragon. Students will write one literal interpretation as a caption. Class discussion will explore different interpretations of the same picture.

   2. *Product:* Students will be able to write a caption that expresses their own symbolic interpretation of the entire picture. Students will compare and contrast the literal and symbolic captions that they wrote for the same picture.

   3. *Criteria*

     a. Students must write one literal and one symbolic caption on their own, without consulting anyone else.

     b. Learners must compare and contrast the literal and symbolic meanings of at least three images they used to write their captions.

     c. Students will work with a partner, comparing and contrasting their captions.

C. Materials

   1. Magician costume

   2. Overhead transparency graphic as the focal point for developing the concept

   3. Chalkboard

Enactment

D. Hook

   1. Dress in a cape and pointed hat as a magician complete with "magic wand." Role-play with "magic" words and "spells." Ask students what

they would wish for. Wave the wand and tell them their wishes are granted.

2. Say, "I am the magician who grants your wishes. Now I'll show you another magician. See if you can figure out what *this* magician is doing."

3. Project a colorful picture of a magician with a burning torch and amulet facing off against a huge dragon.

E. Student Aim (on the board or overhead projector)

What is a metaphor? Can metaphors affect you?

F. Development (Inductive Concept Method in Module Eight with method markers. Carries out Performance Objective)

G. Culmination

1. *Wrap-Up:* Refer to the first question of the Aim, "What is a metaphor?" Elicit a simple definition from students based on the symbolic interpretations, something like: "A metaphor is a concrete image with a symbolic meaning."

2. How many levels of meaning can a metaphor have? Why?

3. *Leap* (second question of Aim): "Can metaphors apply to you?" "How might the different meanings affect the way you understand what you read, see, etc.?"

4. *Leap:* Recount the ending of the film *The Postman* in which the postman asks the poet Neruda, "Is the whole world a metaphor?" Elicit interpretations.

5. "Tomorrow we will expand the definition of a metaphor."

Assessment and Evaluation Plan

For homework: In their own words, students will write the difference between the literal and symbolic meanings of their own and their partner's captions for the same picture. Also in their own words, students will define a metaphor based on the partial definition developed in the lesson. They will also define two ways in which a metaphoric meaning differs in general from the literal meaning. Finally, students will describe an object in their home (e.g., a lamp) from both a literal and metaphoric perspective. To be collected.

■ ROUNDUP ■

Everyone wants to learn. Really learn. There is nothing more stimulating and motivating than a learning challenge that students consider meaningful. The Core Components supply a foundation for just such a learning environment. They are your prompts for direction and focus. Every teaching style can succeed with the Core

Components: the Rationale, Performance Objective, Materials, Hook, Student Aim, Development, and Culmination.

The Development unfolds the method between the Hook and Culmination. As the name implies, the Development builds the substance of the lesson, employing a method (a cohesive template) with method markers (features of a method). Therefore, the format of the Development is different for each method.

The difference between *form* and *function* is crucial. *Form* refers to the definition or procedure of the component; for example, the Rationale clarifies the teacher's intention and focus for a given lesson. But it's *function* that distinguishes between passive and active student participation and that distinguishes between rote learning and the challenge and stimulation of critical thinking. Traditionally, these Core Components have been functional components of lectures and/or teacher-dictated practices that emphasize right answers rather than a *process* of discovery. Both extensive lecture and the right-answer approach assume a passive student role.

Instead, we encourage you to employ the Core Components in a student-as-active-learner approach. Rather than tell your students what they should think, try to foster their critical-thinking skills; emphasize the *process* of learning so that student-generated *products* embody original insights and solutions, products that build their thinking skills. With this approach, student products become milestones in formulating ideas—which goes far beyond filling in blanks on worksheets. We remind you to refer to the template in Figure 3.2.

It's time now to try your hand at writing your own Core Components.

■ HANDS-ON PRACTICE ■

Alone or with a partner, choose a topic from your subject area and develop it sequentially from the Rationale to the Culmination, omitting the Development for now.

Self-Instruct Planner: Core Components

Subject_____ Topic_____
(Work on a separate piece of paper.)

Refer to Bloom's Taxonomy in Module Five as you work with the Self-Instruct Planner.

Prelude: Rationale, Performance Objective, Material

A. Rationale *(refer to Figure 3.3)*

1. *What?* (incorporate italicized words): *To introduce . . . , Students will learn . . . , To increase students' mastery of . . . , To develop . . . , Learners*

will enlarge their understanding of . . . , To develop students' perception of . . . , etc.

2. *Why?* (Be specific. Cite *what* the students will learn, physically coordinate, visually perceive, etc.)

3. *Justification:* Refer to INTASC Standards in the Appendix.

Self-Check

Does your Rationale have a clear and specific focus? Or does it try to do too much? Have the cognitive, perceptual, or motor skills specific application? We encourage you to get feedback from a colleague in a different subject area from your own. Same-subject colleagues may not see conceptual or scope problems as clearly as someone not familiar with your subject—like your students.

B. The Performance Objective (refer to Figure 3.4)

1. *Preparation:*
2. *Product* (*Students will be able to . . .*):
3. *Criteria:*

Self-Check

Does the product relate to the Rationale? Does the product call upon students to bring together and *interpret, analyze,* and/or *synthesize* the significant concepts and principles? Are there clear and specific criteria? Did you fall into the frequent trap of making a discussion the product (except for oral "products" such as debates or enactments)? Get feedback from a colleague.

C. Materials (refer to Figure 3.5)
   Materials (3 or more):

Listing the materials is NOT busywork. Your materials suggest the *variety and scope* of your lessons as a self-check. Most important, thinking through the materials you'll need ensures that you will be fully prepared to facilitate the lesson. In addition, a materials list serves as a check for yourself that you are not falling prey to routinized habits or not using enough substantive sources. The materials you select for a lesson or project should work integrally with and enrich the learning experience.

Enactment: Hook, Student Aim, Development, Culmination

D. Hook (refer to Figure 3.6)

1. *Content Based:*
2. *Personalized:*
3. *Transition from the Hook into the Development of the lesson:*

Self-Check

Does your Hook relate to the lesson's substance? Does your Hook connect to students' frames of reference? Get feedback from a colleague.

E. Student Aim (refer to Figure 3.7)

1. *Heart* of your Rationale:
2. Student Aim/Version #1 (question):
3. Alternate Student Aim/Version #2 (statement):

Self-Check

Does each Aim capture the heart of the Rationale? Or does it indulge in an engaging feature that is not the essential aspect? Is the wording in each version significantly different? Swap with a peer for mutual feedback.

F. Development (Method with method markers)
G. Culmination (refer to Figure 3.8)

1. *Wrap-Up*
   a. Possibly refer to Student Aim (may serve as entree for the Culmination):
   b. Establish key points of the lesson:
2. *Leap*
   a. Two or three possible interpretations related to students' frames of reference:
   b. One or two challenge questions related to students' frames of reference

Self-Check

Does your *Wrap-Up* reestablish key points? Does the *Leap* ask students to arrive at new insights with *justification*? Does at least one challenge question relate to students' frames of reference? Get feedback from a peer.

Assessment and Evaluation

Describe what student materials you will use to assess and evaluate the success of the lesson in terms of the Rationale. What would be the important criteria for each task for acceptable achievement?

ENDNOTES

1. Based on a lesson written by Sarah Holtschlag.
2. Based on a lesson written by Marianne Stanton.
3. Based on a lesson by Sarah Holtschlag.
4. Based on a lesson written by Marianne Stanton.
5. For the difference between student-focused and student-centered lessons, see the Figures 2.1 and 2.3 on Pedagogical Settings in Module Two, "Resocializing."
6. Thanks to Bertram Chip Bruce at the University of Illinois at Urbana-Champaign for this example of meaningful learning.

REFERENCES

Atwell, N. (1987). *In the middle: Writing, reading and learning with adolescents.* Portsmouth, Boynton/Cook Publishers, Inc.

SUGGESTED READING

Arenson, K. W. (2001, October 3). One philosopher's alchemy: Teaching as romance. *The New York Times.*

Bonwell, C. C., & Eison, J. A. (1991). *Active learning: Creating excitement in the classroom.* Washington, DC: Washington University, School of Education and Human Development.

Brooks, G., & Brooks, M. G. (1993). *In search of understanding the case for constructivist classrooms.* Alexandria, VA: Association for Supervision and Curriculum Development.

Perkins, D. (1992). *Smart schools: From training memories to educating minds.* New York: Free Press.

B

Module 4

Techniques and Tools

■ OVERVIEW: A SCENARIO*

You're about to audition at the Village Gate in New York, down in Greenwich Village. It's the first time you'll play the guitar in public, far from the ears of rooting friends and family who think you'll be the blues star of the new millennium. And, man, you sure do play a mean tune. Pickin' up strums here and there, imitating the blues singers you admire, just chompin' at the bit, yeah, to take your place among'em. *Man.* You'll knock those Village Gate gatekeepers off their odd shod feet.

Ahead of you in the auditions is Mame the Dame. Big and brassy. She sings just one number and you deflate down to a punctured balloon. Her guitar astonishes: She runs a real glass bottleneck along the frets (talk about *authentic*), changes keys like a janitor, dazzles with finger picking that leaves you breathless. As for her voice, she sings alto real smooth to a clear falsetto that shakes the glasses on the gatekeepers' table. And being a real pro, Mame the Dame with inimitable style suits her techniques to each song, sometimes uses the same pick but in different rhythm or volume, or uses a technique just once, hitting the mark and knowing when to move on, man, to another effect.

Your turn comes, but man, you're gone, dashing home, determined to learn those techniques yourself.

Hey. You know a mean dose of blues when you see it. Get you some.

A lesson needs effective techniques just like the *real* blues singer in the scenario you just read. After all, the same song has been sung by countless singers. Likewise, the same topic has been taught by many a pedagogical predecessor. It's easy to fool ourselves. A creative idea isn't enough for a lesson or project to have substance. As a budding blues singer in Mame the Dame's wake, you got the idea pretty quick. Whether a beginning or experienced teacher, you also need effective techniques. Lots of them.

■ GOALS

In this section we discuss the following:

- The difference between techniques and tools, with examples
- The interrelationship between techniques and tools
- The difference between techniques and methods

*©2001 Ina Claire Gabler

■ FOCAL POINTS AND DISCUSSIONS

Think of an assortment of techniques and tools as your collection of instruments that work together. Techniques are practices such as brainstorming or using heuristics that can engage your students in critical thinking and active involvement instead of passive repetitions. Techniques also provide procedures for independent learning by both individuals and peer groups. Techniques lend spice and imagination to the learning experience. Tools are materials and devices such as activity sheets and instructional machines. Each tool has its advantages and disadvantages for implementing various techniques.

The Focal Points that follow examine techniques and tools in more depth.

Focal Point 1 **Techniques**

A *technique* is the *use of a task or procedure that helps to carry out a method.* A method, in turn, is a cohesive template or blueprint. For example, a series of techniques like modeling and role-playing can develop the Exploratory Discussion or Interactive Presentation methods (Modules Ten and Twelve, respectively). Expanding a bit, we can say that techniques are practices occurring in a sequence. In this way, techniques develop the Rationale (see Module Three) within a method template.

Discussion 1 **Techniques**

All techniques can be used in all methods. To choose the techniques that will be most effective for a given method with a particular group of students requires experience. Like the Core Components, techniques have been around a long time. It takes clear focus and imagination to design the use of a technique so that it cultivates original thinking instead of lurking too long around those low cognitive levels. The difference between using techniques for passive or active student learning is another example of *form* (a specific technique, like questioning) versus *function* (the role of questions as yes–no vehicles or prompts for critical thinking), as discussed in Module Three.

Consider the following examples of techniques. Two techniques, questioning skills and peer-group learning (PGL) will be expanded on in Modules Five and Six, respectively.

Examples of Techniques

We offer an ample list of examples, but it could never be exhaustive. There are countless techniques or countless adaptations of every technique. You undoubtedly have invented some of your own, tailored to your teaching style(s) and your various students' needs. The only limit is your imagination. So consider this gallery of techniques an overview of the art.

EXAMPLE #1/QUESTIONS

Questions generate teacher–student or student–student dialogue. Questions are the underpinning for many other techniques. The three types of questions that we recommend are *Trigger, Probe,* and *Redirected.*

- *Trigger question:* As the name suggests, a Trigger question opens a discussion. It gets things going. A Trigger generates a broad-based beginning.

- *Probe question:* This type of question asks a respondent to explain her answer further. In other words, a Probe follows a Trigger question and focuses on the same student, probing for more ideas, but in a *nonthreatening* way.

- *Redirected question:* When you pose the same or a related question to various students or the entire class, inviting them to add their ideas to the same issue, you're asking a Redirected question.

Take a brief look at the differences among these question types in Figure 4.1.

EXAMPLE #2/HEURISTICS

A heuristic is a codified procedure. Another way to say it: A heuristic is a formulaic series of steps for carrying out an activity. Perhaps the most famous heuris-

tic is the journalist's *who, what, when, where, why, and how.* You can invent your own heuristics.

English: For peer-group feedback on freshman papers, an English professor[1] invented the following heuristic:

1. *I think your essay (or paper) is about—*

2. *The major points in your essay (or paper) seem to be—*

3. *What I like most about your essay (or paper) is—*

4. *I think your essay (or paper) could be strengthened by—*

Math: Here's a formulaic process for solving word problems:

1. *Work backwards.*

2. *Define the end product.*

3. *List the ingredients of the end product.*

4. *List the sequence for solving the ingredients.*

Heuristics enable students to work independently and/or to interact fruitfully.

EXAMPLE #3/ROLE-PLAYING

Role-playing is the act of adopting another identity. Taking on various identities in role-play enriches discussions, debates, or individual exploration of a concept. Your students play the part of real or imaginary figures. You may supply background information for each role, or students may write their own background information if the role-play serves as a review or the application of research. Students argue according to their roles regardless of their own point of view. Later, students break role and express *their own perspec-*

Trigger Opens discussion with a broad question	Probe Asks respondent to explain further; guides respondent to insight that benefits the student and class	Redirected Poses question on the same issue to other students or the entire class; invites various angles on the same issue
Why did the United States drop an atomic bomb on Japan in World War II?	1. In addition to wanting to win the war, what other reason might have motivated dropping the A-bomb on Japan? 2. That's an interesting idea. Could you explain a bit more how national pride could have been a factor, citing some facts? 3. Can you justify national pride in this situation or not? Why?	1. Could someone put that in your own words? 2. Does anyone agree? disagree? 3. Can anyone think of yet another motive for dropping the A-bomb?

FIGURE 4.1 The Difference Among Trigger, Probe, and Redirected Questions

tives with documented justifications. Or students may argue from their own perspective within the assigned role or the context of a simulation. The continuum of role-play arguments is the following:

- Students argue from their own perspective.
- Students argue from another perspective and break role.
- Students argue completely from another's perspective.

The configurations may vary. For example, students may role-play in groups of three to four members, each group playing out the same roles simultaneously. Or the entire class may sit in a circle in which all students role-play, with several taking on the same role so that all viewpoints are argued by various people. Yet another format: Several students role-play in front of the class while the class in turn poses questions to the role-players. The class itself may role-play a group—for example, Southern plantation owners during the American Civil War.

Here are some other examples. Ask students to briefly role-play a pertinent situation. Here are some ideas.

- Students role-play animals foraging for a limited food supply, "surviving," "breeding," and "perishing" according to their success, prior to a class discussion on ecology.
- Students enact a school board meeting about a controversy.
- Students debate issues related to the Vietnam War, role-playing various figures.

The possibilities are endless. If planned well with *in-depth* materials for background information, role-playing forces students to think critically as they (a) expand on the background information and (b) consider their own viewpoints with justification when they break role. One caveat: Never force a student to take a role that he finds too offensive to represent even in a hypothetical situation.

EXAMPLE #4/PERSONALIZING

Personalizing is the practice of connecting your topic to the students' frames of reference. Personalizing provides a familiar frame of reference, related to the students' own life experience, that connects to a new context. It bridges the familiar to the foreign. When you relate your students' experiences of school, family, friendship, TV shows, popular movies, sports, favorite music, and so on to the knowledge base or concepts in a lesson, you hook student interest and clarify ideas that may be foreign at first. The reason?

Personalizing provides analogies or metaphors in your students' own terms that further understanding. Role-playing is another way to personalize: By pretending to be someone else, a student feels "ownership" of that person and the related situation.

Here are some examples.

- For a social studies miniunit comparing and contrasting the differences and similarities of the American and Russian judicial system, consider this example based on an actual news event: Play a song of a murdered rap singer. Distribute a brief newspaper article or write a brief summary of the news story, with a transparency image if possible, about a record producer accused of murdering the singer. Ask pairs of students to role-play the producer's lawyer and the state prosecutor. Russian and American "lawyers" and "prosecutors" cite their cases and evidence, including the assumption of guilt or innocence. Break roles. The class discusses circumstantial versus documented evidence and possible motives for the murder and motives, if any, to frame the suspect.

- For a unit on characterization in literature: Ask students to write a list of three to five characteristics of the opposite sex. Discuss the responses. Compare and contrast the stereotypes with real boys and girls the students know. Discuss the hallmarks of a stereotype and possible reasons for stereotyping. What role do stereotypes play in society? How might stereotypes weaken or strengthen literature that depicts human life?

- For an art lesson on Cezanne: Ask students to draw three objects in the room as corresponding geometric shapes. Share and compare. Discuss the nature of underlying shapes. Invite your students to discover the underlying geometric shapes in a Cezanne print.

EXAMPLE #5/BRAINSTORMING

Brainstorming is the practice of encouraging students to free associate responses to a question, word, idea, and so on. In a brainstorm session, students call out their ideas, and their responses are written on the board or overhead transparency as an expanding reference. From the potpourri of ideas, students can infer and supply corresponding categories and headings.

You enhance the value of this activity when you pose guiding questions every so often that help your students perceive connections between and among the ideas, thereby generating a network of interrelated concepts, headings, themes, and so on.

Consider Figures 4.2 and 4.3, which build on free association, generating categories and concepts. Students supply the specific items and ideas in Figure 4.2, and the responses are written on the board or transparency for ongoing reference. You facilitate a discussion developing the larger concepts related to the Aim. In the discussion, students would inductively supply the headings or organizers in Figure 4.3 in their own words, similar to our examples: "kinds of transportation," "categories of transportation," as well as "world changes because of transportation." Memory is not always a robust or reliable source for meaningful discussion grounded in facts and a variety of concepts. You and the students therefore benefit when the knowledge base and concepts are visible on the board or overhead transparency for supporting evidence and intellectual rigor.

EXAMPLE #6/CONCEPT MAPPING

Concert mapping is the process of organizing ideas into categories and subcategories represented in a graphic depiction. Often an extension of brainstorming, a concept map is a pictorial representation of the interrelationships of concepts and their facts and examples. Concept maps may employ circles and lines, boxes, a tree effect, and other linking devices. They organize ideas visually into a simple graphic. The process is an effective technique for visual thinkers.

Figure 4.4 employs the brainstorming categorized in Figure 4.3. Notice how the same information is organized differently, delving a bit deeper into categories within categories. Here, too, your students infer and supply the concepts from the variety of examples that they provided in the brainstorm. Your job is to guide their thinking with questions—another technique—without spilling the beans.

Obviously, a lesson on transportation may not reach high cognitive levels if only because of familiarity. But getting learners to identify categories within categories and then to reorganize the examples according to even different categories yet again is the beginning of higher cognitive thinking skills.

Remember that in constructivism, the *thinking process* takes priority over memorizing categories and examples that have been provided. When your students *think their way* to the categories based on their own soup of examples, then reassign the examples according to a different organizing concept—realizing that more than one example can fall under more than one category—*that's* stimulating, especially when the same example, such as "swinging from tree to tree," can fit under opposite categories. From the perspective of how trees grow, "swinging from tree to tree" can be considered a land modality. From the perspective of the nature of travel—through the air—"swinging from tree to tree" can be considered a form of air travel. See if you can find "swinging tree to tree" in other categories as well in Figure 4.4.

Compare the concept map in Figure 4.4 to the original items in the brainstorming activity, represented in Figures 4.2 and 4.3. Note the development of complexity from the brainstorming to the concept map.

EXAMPLE #7/MODELING

Modeling is a demonstration of a task before your students attempt to do the task themselves. Whenever possible, *modeling* includes *teacher direction along with student participation* in a kind of dress rehearsal. Your materials should therefore include a brief sample of the task you want your students to do. Modeling an activity is especially important for projects and peer-group work so that learners will know exactly how they should carry out a given assignment on their own. Think of modeling as a run-through before the cameras roll.

Here are some examples.

- For a lesson on organizing and outlining original notes from source materials (any subject area): Check out Figure 4.5 for modeling the task. Students come up with the categories and reorganize the shopping list under headings (Dairy, Frozen Foods, Fruits and Vegetables, Desserts, Nonedibles, etc.)

EXAMPLE #8/TRANSITIONS

Transitions are statements that logically connect segments in the lesson into a seamless flow. Transi-

---

Aim: How has the evolution of transportation changed the world?

airplanes   horses   walking   cars   boats
rowboats   canoes   rafts   steamboat
horse and buggy   helium balloons
helicopters   walking   running   donkeys
camels   dog teams   trains
chariots   swinging from tree to tree
space missiles   jets

FIGURE 4.2 Brainstorming Examples of Transportation/Free Association

Aim: How has the evolution of transportation changed the world?
Kinds of transportation
airplanes   horses   walking   cars   boats   rowboats   canoes   rafts   steamboat   horse and buggy helium balloons   helicopters   walking   running   donkeys   camels   dog teams   trains chariots   swinging from tree to tree   space missiles   jets
Categories of transportation LAND   AIR   MECHANICAL   ANIMAL   WATER
World changes because of transportation types of war, national power, scope of living, personal power and self-perception, societal changes

FIGURE 4.3 Brainstorming Examples of Transportation: Generating Categories and Concepts

tions bridge what just took place in the lesson with what is about to happen. They are particularly important when moving from the introduction (i.e., after the Aim and Hook or other opening) to the Development (see Module Three). Transitions are also essential within the Development, providing logical connections from one stage of thinking to another, or from one activity, such as discussion, to another activity, such as the Performance Objective.

Examples

- "Now that we have established X, let's see how Y is affected."
- "We've looked at how Huck Finn seems to have matured on the river trip with Jim. Next we're going to see ways in which Huck was not so mature."
- "Let's quickly review the steps of photosynthesis before you represent its various impact on plants—and on human beings."

EXAMPLE #9/ADVANCE ORGANIZERS

Advance Organizers alert students to an upcoming task in order to orient the students' attention. Advance Organizers do as their name suggests: They organize students' focus in advance of a task. They can even activate relevant schemata and can begin to create cognitive dissonance (the clash of new information with one's beliefs) within students—a guaranteed Hook. This forward-looking directive improves your students' attention <u>as</u> they watch, read, or listen and in that way, creates the foundation for a fruitful discussion after the video, reading, or presentations. Otherwise, discussions rely on recall and may not reach the same rigor as discussions founded on notes and focused attention. An Advance Organizer may also be an anticipatory alert for an upcoming task, or it may be a guiding question.

Examples

- "When you read the article, underline at least five causes and effects of obesity."
- "As you listen to your classmates present their conclusions, jot down as many ways as possible in which their views differ from or agree with yours."
- "In the upcoming videoclip from *Frankenstein,* what are at least two reasons to sympathize with the monster?"
- "After designing the concept map, you'll have to write a justification for each of the interrelationships you've depicted."

EXAMPLE #10/PEER-GROUP LEARNING (PGL)

Peer-group learning is a category of various types of peer interaction in dyads or groups. In peer-group learning, your students can be paired in dyads or grouped together, comparing their ideas, problem solving, carrying out an extensive activity, and so on. To be successful, this interactive exchange needs thorough teacher planning of prompts and activities, including activity sheets with defined social roles that enable the students to function independently.

We consider PGL a technique because the practice can be used in every method as appropriate. There is an in-depth description of PGL and activity sheets in Module Six.

Focal Point 2 Tools

As we said earlier, *tools* are materials and various devices, such as activity sheets and instructional machines, respectively. Tools can also generate materials that contain techniques. For example, a computer (tool) may have

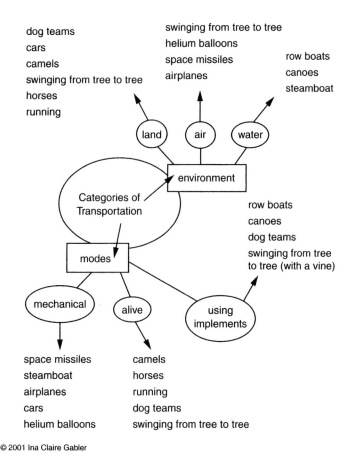

FIGURE 4.4 Concept Map

a program that helps your students categorize (material) and that may contain questions and role-play (techniques). Each device and material has its advantages and disadvantages for implementing various techniques.

Discussion 2 Tools

In this age of dazzling technology, the temptation is to confuse the tool, namely, computers, VCRs and videotapes, closed-circuit TV, and so on, for the substance of a technique or even a method. This confusion is another example of the difference between form and function.

The truth is that tools and their materials are just that—nothing more. How you decide to *implement* the tools as conveyers of techniques—now *that's* the issue. The simplest, conventional-looking overhead transparency (referred to as "transparency" henceforth) can be the vehicle of teacher–student and even student–student dialogue that gets your students thinking. Conversely, a jazzy stand-alone software program or simulation may

look great, but if it's employed for mostly low-level cognitive skills—hey—bring out the transparency.

Examples of Tools

If tools are used flexibly and imaginatively, they can incorporate all the techniques we've described. For example, an activity sheet can include role-playing, questions, modeling, personalizing, concept mapping, and so forth. Similarly, a computer-based project can also utilize those same techniques. So it's important to keep the techniques in mind when you contemplate using instructional tools. Take a look at these examples and imagine how inventive you can be with each one.

EXAMPLE #1/ACTIVITY SHEET

This time-honored material has been largely overused and misused. It has also been an indispensable vehicle for independent student learning. What makes the difference?—form versus function, or the role and content reflecting the teacher's concept of the activity sheet. When thoughtfully prepared, the activity sheet works across a range of contexts: class

---

Shopping List

Directions: Organize this shopping list according to categories. Provide headings for the categories.

milk
bananas
potatoes
cheese
cereal
bread
eggs
grapes
chopped beef
chocolate chip cookies
ice cream
carrots
lettuce
doughnuts
chicken
bagels
soap
frozen juice
shampoo
vitamins

FIGURE 4.5 Organizing a Shopping List

discussion, individual student input, and peer exchange. Let's take a closer look.

For class discussion or individual student input: Effective *activity sheets* help to organize ideas in discussions or for individual reflection. The sheets may be charts, tables, diagrams, or questions that require student response. *The pitfall:* designing short-answer, right-wrong, or fill-in-the-blank worksheets. Try to think of an activity sheet as a compass pointing the way to discovery rather than an exercise that calls for repetition of what you and the textbook have said. Sample activity sheets are in Module Six, Part 2.

EXAMPLE #2/OVERHEAD PROJECTOR AND TRANSPARENCIES

Linguistic prompts and visual grabbers: Even in the computer age with electronic slides, well-planned overhead transparencies remain an effective facilitator for discussions and critical thinking. *Linguistic prompts* may take any written form: for example, questions, quotations, heuristic guides, fill-in or filled-in tables, fill-in or filled-in concept maps. Fill-in materials may be useful in the thinking process as prompts (questions and directions) for discussions or a reference for more in-depth analysis, for example, comparing and con-

trasting differences and similarities. For the most part, however, keep in mind that *fill-in materials should not be used as end products in and of themselves.*

Visual grabbers may be colorful or black-and-white pictures, charts, graphs, and cartoons that hook your learners' attention. Ideally, visual grabbers are accompanied by a thinking task, either oral or written. Both linguistic prompts and visual grabbers help focus your students' thinking, generating ideas for discussion. Transparencies may be used as a Hook to introduce a lesson, as a midpoint or final summary, or as an ongoing reference during activities.

Here are some examples of linguistic prompts followed by examples of visual grabbers.

Linguistic Prompts for Transparencies

- Transparency #1 (Figure 4.6) for class discussion: Science

  Materials: A real, dying plant as a Hook and as a vehicle for introducing elements of a controlled experiment. Students must analyze the symptoms of the plant's distress and infer possible hypotheses for the plant's failure to thrive.[2]

  Transparency: Figure 4.6, which serves as a prompt for focused observations and analysis in class discussion.

- Transparency #2 (Figure 4.7) for class discussion: History

  Materials: History readings about the dire effects on Germany resulting from the Versailles Treaty and about the relationship to Nazi anti-Semitism; excerpts from *Mein Kampf* by Adolf Hitler; photographs of *Kristallnacht*.

  Transparency: Figure 4.7, which serves as a prompt for concept analysis in class discussion.

Examples of Visual Grabbers for Transparencies

- Transparency #3 (Figure 4.8) for Class Discussion: Math

  Materials: Textbook chapter on probability. News article on a topic that includes probability. Probability problem solving in dyads with activity sheet, including a probability problem based on the news article.

  Transparency: Figure 4.8, which serves as a prompt for probability analysis in class activity as a Performance Objective.

  Oral Directions

  - Draw a chart any way you choose that interprets the information in this graph in a different format.

Signs of Pathology	Possible Reasons
A. List 3–6 signs of pathology for the sample plant. 1. 2. 3. 4. 5. 6.	B. List 2 possible reasons for each pathology cited in "A." 1. 2. 3. 4. 5. 6.
Variables to Isolate	**Method of Control**
C. List 3–6 variables that could contribute to the plant's health. 1. 2. 3. 4. 5. 6.	D. List 1 or more methods to control for each variable. 1. 2. 3. 4. 5. 6.

FIGURE 4.6 Designing a Controlled Experiment

- Based on your chart, write an argument that tries to persuade a smoker you know to stop smoking, citing the probability of that person getting lung cancer.
- One rule: use percentages in your argument.

Using overhead transparencies as facilitators for dialogue and critical thinking transforms this simple, traditional material into the vehicle for an interactive technique. The value lies in your implementation as well as the content: the difference between *form* and *function.*

EXAMPLE #3/COMPUTER TECHNOLOGIES

Computers are many tools in one. They utilize many applications in addition to accessing the Internet and the Web.

"If there were no Jews, the anti-Semite would make them."

—*Anti-Semite and Jew* by Jean-Paul Sartre

- Explain Sartre's statement.
- Describe and justify at least 2 reasons why the statement might be true.
- Compare/contrast anti-Semitism with racism.

FIGURE 4.7 Concept Lesson: Bigotry

Computers are one resource among several. In some ways they serve as additional information sources to books and other traditional printed materials. In other ways, the computer is a tool that can facilitate a technique, for example, as a tool for asynchronous discussions with students around the globe or across the country. The computer can also serve, with guiding software, as a vehicle for writing, and so on. Finally, sophisticated stand-alone software in all subject areas embed various methods and techniques for critical thinking in their operations. Our "Methods Finale" in Section C provides a scenario entitled "Fishy Mystery," which depicts the integration of computer use with our constructivist methods. In addition, each method contains a Tip for Integrating Technology section.

Focal Point 3 **Cognitive Frameworks: Deduction and Induction**

Techniques are most effective when intentionally orchestrated deductively or inductively. In deduction, you present the definition of a concept or principle, then your students analyze examples—and, when possible, nonexamples—that characterize the concept or principle. In other words, *deduction moves from the general to the specific.* With induction, students categorize and analyze examples and nonexamples, then generate a definition of the concept or principle. *Induction therefore moves from the specific to the general.* Module Eight describes these

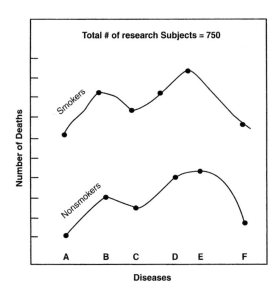

FIGURE 4.8 Concept Lesson: Probability

cognitive frameworks (structures of thinking) in greater detail. See Figure 4.9 for an overview.

■ ROUNDUP ■

The techniques described in this module have been around for a long time. So we want to repeat what we have said here and in Module Three: Try to remember the difference between *form* and *function.*

For example, the form of questioning can function either as a technique of right–wrong answers in a teacher–student exchange OR as a technique that prompts critical thinking. Similarly, activity sheets and overhead transparencies are forms that are being employed nationwide as you read these words. In the hands of some teachers, activity sheets and transparencies function merely as fill-in-the-blank rote repetition exercises; in the hands of other teachers, the same materials serve as prompts for higher-level thinking either in class discussions or among students in peer groups. Even role-playing can end up being nothing more than fun, merely lending some color to a lesson that fosters passive student learning. Conversely, role-playing can be the vehicle for student interaction and interpretation of a unit's facts, principles, and themes.

So you must give a lot of thoughtful planning to the *function* of the techniques you employ. Sometimes you will decide that an entire lesson will be devoted to the establishment of a factual knowledge base, preparing for a second lesson that encourages students to interpret and evaluate the facts, to infer principles and

larger themes based on those facts—or to serve as the foundation for an extensive project. The techniques you use should carry out your instructional intentions in that instance. But even a knowledge-base lesson should engage your students in some interpretation or in organizing the facts according to principles or categories, and so on.

Other times, you will shoot for a lesson with high-level cognition, right up there, your students synthesizing and evaluating, reaching for the moon with feet well grounded in a knowledge base. Most often, you will want to combine establishing a knowledge base of facts with critical thinking, making use of orchestrated deduction and induction. All techniques lend themselves to this variety of instruction.

For the finale we leave you with this thought: You yourself must use critical thinking in order to facilitate your students' critical thinking.

Hey. Now that you've seen a mean dose of techniques, follow Mame the Dame and "get you some"!

■ HANDS-ON PRACTICE ■

Refer to Figure 4.9 as a visual summary, then try hands-on practice with the following techniques.

Self-Instruct Planners: Techniques and Tools

Note: If you like, continue working with the topic you developed in the Core Components Hands-On in Module Three when you plan with the following various techniques and tools.

Subject _____ Topic _____

(Work on a separate piece of paper.)

Directions:

1. Decide on a Core Component you will develop with each technique and tool.

2. Try your hand at some of the techniques and tools that interest you.

3. Whether you work with the topic you developed in the Core Components Hands-On or whether you work with a different topic, write down the complete Rationale as the rudder for selecting techniques and tool materials.

A. Rationale

B. Techniques

  1. Questions (Refer to Bloom's Taxonomy in Module Five)

A Cognitive Framework Directs Thinking

Deduction = development of a concept or principle with facts.
General to specific.

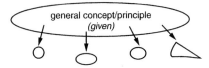

Induction = use of facts to arrive at a concept or principle.
Specific to general.

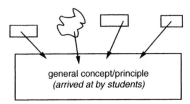

A Technique is a Specific Practice or Procedure

questions   *personalizing*

role-playing

brainstorming   *concept mapping*

peer groups   **modeling**

Techniques Develop Deduction or Induction

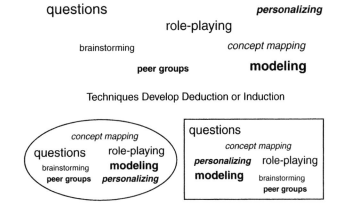

© 2001 Ina Claire Gabler

FIGURE 4.9 Cognitive Framework versus Techniques

Trigger (1):

Probes (3):

Redirected (3):

2. Role-Playing

Describe the context:

Describe three roles and the purpose of each:

3. Heuristic

Invent a pattern or codified steps for carrying out an activity:

4. Brainstorm (work with partner for this and brainstorm together)

Concept to be developed:

Anticipated Responses:

Anticipated Categories of responses:

5. Concept Mapping

Interpret your brainstorming responses and categories from at least two different perspectives and design two concept maps that represent those perspectives.

6. Personalizing

Try inventing a Hook or Aim that includes personalizing.

7. Modeling

Design a brief activity that models the activity in the Performance Objective. Modeling should include student participation via questions, directions, and performing a mini-task.

C. Tools

1. Overhead projector with transparencies

    Design a transparency that will supply prompts to guide student analysis of a concept or principle or theme integral to the Rationale. Describe any visual grabber you may use.

2. Activity sheet (see Module Six, Part 2)

3. Computer technology (see the introduction to Section C and Technology Tips in Modules Seven through Twelve if you're unsure of how to work with this one)

ENDNOTES

1. Written by Allan Brick of Hunter College in New York City.
2. Based on a lesson by Cyndie Morain.

SUGGESTED READING

Ausubel, D. P. (1960). The use of advance organizers in the learning and retention of meaningful verbal material. *Journal of Educational Psychology, 51,* 267–272.

Bruner, J. S. (1960). *The process of education.* Cambridge, MA: Harvard University Press.

Clark, J. H. (1991). *Patterns of teaching.* Boston, MA: Allyn & Bacon.

Dunn, R., & Dunn, K. (1992). *Teaching secondary students through their individual learning styles: Practical approaches for grades 7–12.* Boston, MA: Allyn & Bacon.

Michaels, S. (1987). Text and context: A new approach to the study of classroom writing. *Discourse Processes, 10,* 321–346.

Novak, J. D. (1990). Concept maps and Vee diagrams: Two metacognitive tools to facilitate meaningful learning. *Instructional Science, 19*(1), 29–52.

Richardson, L. (1994, January 31). More schools are trying to write textbooks out of the curriculum. *The New York Times.*

B

Module Five

Questioning Skills

■ OVERVIEW

questions Questions *questions questions*

Ask questions.
Why?
Questions tackle
you
(wrestlin' with askin')
and your students
(wrestlin' with answerin').
Yeah, questions
make you think
about thinking,
make you think, yeah,
about your students'
thinking. About how to make their
brains buzz.
It's tough
stuff. Students,
they ain't
use-ta it.
You ain't
use-ta it. But
once you both get
use-ta it,
the classroom you gave
up for dead
starts a-shakin' with the wind
of wings.
This takes time.
But you've got
that, yeah.
Try again. And again. And—
Hey, you guys. Study
turtles.
You know, you
ain't goin' nowhere with-
out ploddin'
power.
Yeah.

© 2001 Ina Claire Gabler

■ GOALS

So just how do you promote that struggle with new ideas that's so vital in a constructivist classroom? What can you do to challenge your students to immerse themselves in your subject matter? How do you *energize* those passive students and challenge them to truly *think?* That's where *effective questioning* comes in.

Fortunately, there have been a great number of studies completed regarding effective classroom questioning and interaction. This body of research and our own classroom experiences enable us to make a number of suggestions regarding effective teacher questioning techniques in any classroom setting. It is our view that effective questioning is the essence of effective teaching, one of the most useful ways to promote critical thinking. As educator Eleanor Duckworth (1987) has so aptly noted, "The right question at the right time can move (students) to peaks in their thinking that result in significant steps forward and real intellectual excitement" (p. 7). Because of the central importance of questioning in all constructivist teaching methods, we would like to present you with a fairly extensive discussion of effective (and ineffective) questioning techniques and then build on these ideas later in the book.

In Part 1 of this module, we'll focus on several dimensions of effective questioning, including the following:

- The importance of varying the question cognitive level

- The powerful impact of Wait Time I and II

- What you should do *as* your students answer questions

- Effective follow-up questions

- Other things that you should or should not do when interacting with students

As you read and consider our advice on questioning and interaction, try to imagine implementing each of these techniques in your own classroom.

■ FOCAL POINTS AND DISCUSSIONS

Focal Point 1 **The Importance of Varying the Cognitive Level: Bloom's Taxonomy**

In any setting, it will be important for you to use different *kinds* of questions, both to help students make cognitive connections *and* to gain insights into the nature of their thinking. To accomplish this, we will repeatedly suggest that you utilize Bloom's Taxonomy of Educational Objectives (Bloom, 1956). We have found Bloom's Taxonomy to be a useful tool for planning lessons of any kind. It is helpful for making decisions regarding *what* to teach and *how* to go about teaching it. Perhaps the most practical use for the taxonomy is in planning questions that you might ask in the classroom.

We'll call these initial, planned questions *Trigger questions* (see Module Four).

The Importance of Varying the Cognitive Level: Bloom's Taxonomy

What Is *Bloom's Taxonomy*?

As it was developed, Bloom's Taxonomy describes six levels of cognitive activity, with each level presumed to require different kinds of thinking processes. Questions formed at the first two levels of the taxonomy are used to elicit facts or information from students. At these levels, information is recognized and recalled. Students' ability to perform these tasks reflects a *basic* understanding of the ideas involved. The next four levels of the taxonomy represent *higher-cognitive-order* thought processes. Individuals who can function at these levels have a much richer understanding of the facts, concepts, and principles involved. As a result, we can often infer that the relevant learner schemata (conceptual "bundles" or "parcels" of perceptions or beliefs) are well structured and connected to ideas from other domains.

Before discussing the use of Bloom's Taxonomy in more detail, it is important to note the following caveat: We must keep in mind that the contexts in which questions are asked can affect not only students' answers but the way in which we classify or interpret them. For example, the question, "What factors determine an economic recession?" could be used as a knowledge question, a comprehension question, or an analysis question. If students' answers were based on memorized factors listed in a textbook, then the question falls at the knowledge level. However, if the answer was based on speculative trends perceived by a student, the question falls at the analysis level, requiring a much more complex cognitive process. Only by knowing the context for questions can you determine with any certainty if students are working at lower or higher cognitive levels. We have seen teachers fooled into believing that students had developed in-depth understanding of important ideas because they could answer higher-order questions, when in fact they were merely repeating words provided earlier by the teacher.

The First Level In *Bloom's Taxonomy* is Knowledge

At this level, students are asked questions that require recall or recognition of facts, definitions, and observations. In other words, these questions test your students' basic memory. You must use questions at this level to some extent, because facts, definitions, and so on can provide a foundation for higher-level thinking. Keep in mind that the *overuse* of these basic questions can result in students' memorizing information that is largely disconnected from their frames of reference. Such knowledge is not only meaningless to the student but is also quickly lost (or never really connected) to elements of long-term memory.

Examples

The following words are often used when asking knowledge-level questions:

define, recall, recognize, remember, who, what, when, where, repeat, name, list, record, underline

In most contexts, the following examples could be classified as knowledge questions: "In what year did the Civil War begin?" "How is a thesis statement defined?" "What is an independent clause?" "Who developed the first rabies vaccine?" "What is the Spanish word for groundhog?"

The Second Taxonomy Level Is Comprehension

Questions posed at the comprehension level challenge students to phrase information in ways that make sense to them. Students demonstrate that they understand subject matter by being able to rephrase it, to give a description in their own words, and to use information in describing similarities and making comparisons.

Examples

There are four types of comprehension questions: those in which students are asked to *interpret, translate, provide examples, or define in their own words.* Interpretation questions require that students understand the major ideas in a verbal or written statement and how the ideas are related to each other. These relationships are characterized by *how* and *why* questions. Examples would include: "How do the two poems use a bird metaphor?" "How do anthropology and sociology differ in respect to what they study?" "Why would you use this equation to solve this problem?"

In translating ideas for themselves, students change ideas from one form of communication to another while retaining the meaning. Data in a graph may be cast as summarizing statements in a paragraph, for example.

The categories of example and definition consist of asking students to give examples of something and to define concepts or principles *in their own words.* A teacher might ask, for instance, "Who can draw an example of a polygon?" or "Can you tell me in your own words what irony means?" The following words are often used in comprehension questions:

describe, compare, contrast, rephrase, explain, translate, restate, discuss, express, identify, locate, review, tell, summarize

The Third Taxonomy Level Is Application

At this level, students are given a *problem* of some kind and asked to solve it. In doing so, they are able to *use* what they've learned in order to *do* something. They must know when and how to use a particular method of solution. It is important to remember that application is a two-step process. First, students are presented with the problem, requiring that they recognize what kind of problem it is. Second, they must select a solution method and solve the problem. It should be noted that some problems may have only one solution. For other problems, there may be several solutions, and those will depend on students' individual knowledge and perception. In a science class, for example, students could be asked to write an essay in which an environmental problem, such as overuse of pesticides, is described and a solution offered. In a history class, students could be asked to state a problem connected to an event and offer solutions.

Examples

The following verbs are often used in application-level questions:

interpret, apply, employ, use, demonstrate, practice, compute, solve, modify, construct, prove, illustrate

The Fourth Taxonomy Level Is Analysis

Questions at this level require students to look at something as a whole and break it down into component parts. As we'll see later in the text, analysis questions are especially important in helping students to develop critical-thinking skills.

Examples

Analysis questions encourage students to use three kinds of cognitive processes:

1. Identifying motives, reasons, and/or causes for a specific occurrence. Examples of these questions could include: "What factors caused the economic recession of 1893?" "What motivated citizens to riot in Los Angeles after the Rodney King verdict?" "Why haven't the Cubs won a World Series since 1908?"

2. Considering available information to reach a conclusion, an inference, or a generalization based on this information. Examples could include: "What happens at the molecular level if you combine this type of acid with this type of base?" "Why did State Department officials in 2001 believe that the elimination of the Al Qaeda network in Afghanistan would decrease the likelihood of future terrorist attacks in the United States?"

3. Analyzing a conclusion, inference, or generalization to find evidence to support or refute it. In this case, students are asked to present an argument. Examples could include: "How do local recycling programs preserve the quality of the environment?" "What evidence can you give that supports this interpretation of the poem?"

It is important to remember that analysis questions challenge students to learn and understand events and/or concepts and to search for reasons behind those events or concepts.

The following words are often used in analysis questions:

examine, relate, draw a conclusion, provide evidence, support, analyze, why, distinguish, appraise, test, compare/contrast, criticize

The Fifth Taxonomy Level Is Synthesis

Questions at this level promote creativity in students because the teacher is asking them to rely on their individual personalities, experiences, and cultural background to *produce something original.* In constructing knowledge at the synthesis level, students are adding new information and/or developing original products in completing such products as artwork, short stories, orally presented arguments, projects/presentations, research papers, and musical phrasing. The key words related to this cognitive level are *original* and *creativity.*

Examples

Synthesis questions can challenge students to produce original communications, such as poems, plays, and collages; to make predictions (what would happen if . . .); to solve problems; to develop a plan; to compose a piece of music; or to create a set of abstract relations. The following verbs are often used in writing synthesis questions:

predict, produce, write, design, develop, compose, create/construct, organize, prepare, propose

These phrases are often used within synthesis questions:

How can we improve ___?
What would happen if ___?
Can you devise ___?
How can we solve ___?

The Sixth Taxonomy Level Is Evaluation

In asking questions at this level, you'll be challenging your students to combine the cognitive processes used in answering application, analysis, and synthesis questions. In effect, students are being asked to establish a set of appropriate values or standards and then determine how closely the idea or concept meets these standards or values. In other words, students must make value judgments that should be reasonable and rational and then defend those judgments in a logical way. We would emphasize that these judgments should be based primarily on logic rather than emotion and that the processes used include many of those that we have associated with critical thinking. In promoting the development of critical-thinking abilities, evaluation questions allow students to recognize and take a stand on issues, and to reevaluate their own positions as they consider the ideas of others. In providing feedback to evaluation questions, you should remember that there are no *right* and *wrong* answers, *but* that some viewpoints may appear to be more defensible and reasonable than others. We'll investigate these important considerations in more detail in Module Eleven, "The Reflective Discussion Method."

Examples

As you will see, evaluation questions will be especially important in conducting Reflective Discussions, but they can and should be used in many types of lessons. Examples of evaluation questions would include: "Should patients be allowed to choose euthanasia as an option in extreme medical cases?" "Is Communism really 'dead' as a viable form of government?" "What is more important: preserving old-growth forests or providing lumber-related jobs in the Northwest?" "What is the best way to complete this geometric proof?" "Were the actions of Friar Lawrence justified?"

The following verbs are used in writing evaluation questions:

judge, argue, decide, appraise, evaluate, choose,
rate, compare, evaluate, select, assess, select

The following phrases can also be used in writing and asking evaluation questions:

What is your opinion of ___?

Do you agree with this position? Why/why not?

Which is better (more effective, more beautiful, etc.)?

Figure 5.1 summarizes Bloom's Taxonomy.

As we introduce a variety of constructivist methods in Modules Seven through Twelve, you'll see that questions at some cognitive levels are closely associated with certain methods (e.g., Inductive Concept lessons feature an abundance of analysis questions). But remember that almost any kind of lesson should include a mix of questions from these cognitive levels. Varying your Trigger, Probe, and Redirect questions in this way will make your lessons challenging for your students and more intellectually stimulating for you as the teacher. *We would also invite you to teach the taxonomy to your students directly; they can use it to generate their own intriguing questions for you and each other.* Urging students to ask insightful questions should be a major part of the constructivist classroom experience. As you compose questions for future lessons, keep our earlier admonition in mind: The cognitive level and the cognitive processes initiated by any question depends on the context in which the question is asked. Remember that teachers sometimes fool themselves into believing

Questioning Category	Bloom's Category	Student Activity	Questions; Stem Words for Directions
LOWER LEVEL	Knowledge	Memorizing: facts, terms, definitions, concepts, principles	what . . . ?, list . . . , name . . . , define . . . , describe . . .
LOWER LEVEL	Comprehension	Understanding the meaning of material beyond factual recall	explain, interpret, summarize, give examples, predict, translate
LOWER LEVEL	Application	Selecting a concept or skill and using it to solve a problem	compute, solve, apply, modify, construct
HIGHER LEVEL	Analysis	Breaking down material into its parts and explaining the hierarchical relations	How does . . . apply? How does . . . work? How does . . . relate to . . . ? What can we infer from/about . . . ? What distinctions can be made about . . . and . . . ?
HIGHER LEVEL	Synthesis	Creating/producing something original after having broken down the material into its components	How does the data support . . . ? How would you design an experiment which investigates . . . ?
HIGHER LEVEL	Evaluation	Making a judgment based on a preestablished set of criteria	What predictions can you make based on the data? What judgments can you make about . . . ? Compare and contrast . . . criteria for . . .

FIGURE 5.1   Table Of Bloom's Taxonomy

that they are asking higher-order questions when in fact students are relying on lower-order (i.e., memorized) responses. Be careful not to fall into this trap.

Focal Point 2 The Powerful Impact of Wait Time I and II

Imagine that you've stepped into your own classroom with an exciting lesson plan in hand. You've prepared a series of challenging Trigger questions. You begin the lesson and ask the first of these thought-provoking questions. What should you do *immediately after* asking each of these important questions? The answer is simple: *Wait!* Actually give your students enough time to think about the question that you've just posed.

This brief period of silence is known as *wait time*, and it is one of the most important teacher behaviors associated with effective questioning. There are actually two different types of wait time. *Wait Time I* is *the pause between the end of a teacher's question and the teacher saying or doing something else* (calling on another student, rephrasing the question, etc.). *Wait Time II* comes a bit later in the process. It is *the pause between the end of a student's response and the teacher doing something else* (asking another question, giving feedback, etc.).

Discussion 2 The Powerful Impact of Wait Time I and II

Subtle though they may *seem,* a number of studies on classroom interaction have shown that the use of Wait Time I and II are *the most* important variables in effective teacher questioning (Rowe, 1974; Tobin, 1987; Dillon, 1988). In cognitive terms, it is easy to see why wait time is important: Learners of all ages need time to perceive the question, process its meaning, formulate an answer, and begin to respond. It also makes sense that complex, higher-order questions would require extra wait time.

An important question becomes, how long should a teacher wait after asking a question or receiving a student response? Research has shown convincingly that at a *minimum,* teachers should wait three seconds before replying, asking another question, or saying or doing something else (Tobin, 1987). Again, wait time should be considerably longer when associated with more complex questions. These same studies (and our own classroom experiences) have shown us that the benefits of wait time diminish after twenty seconds because students tend to stop thinking about the question at this point and begin to feel uneasy about the silence (though one of your authors once waited about half a minute and was about to move on when a student raised her hand with a response that prompted lively s–s discussion about the issue). Unfortunately, research also shows that average teacher wait time

is *less than* one second (Tobin, 1987), which certainly doesn't leave students much time to come up with thoughtful replies. As a vivid example of a *lack* of wait time, have you ever seen the comedic movie and television teacher who asks students questions, then drones "Anyone, anyone?" before answering the questions *himself?* Apparently, many teachers feel uneasy in allowing even brief periods of silence. One of our most important pieces of advice is to become comfortable with allowing brief periods of silence as vital *thinking time* in your classroom.

Research Findings

Why are these brief periods of silence so important? Researchers have shown that the use of sufficient wait time has a profound effect on the learning of students. For example, the following changes have been noted in classrooms where teachers have been taught to extend wait time:

- Student learning, as reflected in the number of correct oral responses and in scores on written tests, increases significantly.
- The number of students who failed to answer when called upon decreases.
- The number of unsolicited but appropriate responses increased.
- The length of student responses increased.
- The number of student statements where evidence was used to make inferences increased.
- The number of responses from students identified by teachers as less able increased.
- The number of *student–student* interactions increased (i.e., students were more likely to listen and respond to each others' ideas).
- The number of *student* questions increased (Rowe, 1974; Tobin, 1987; Dillon, 1988).

In addition, teachers who extended wait time were perceived by students to be more caring and patient. Students interviewed seemed to feel that these patient teachers were truly interested in their ideas. In extending wait time, it was also found that teachers made fewer errors characterized by responding illogically or inappropriately to student comments; a little silence also provides *teachers* with important thinking time (Tobin, 1987).

The educational benefits of using extended Wait Time I and II are obviously dramatic. This makes sense when you stop to consider that *everyone needs time to think!* This is especially true of students with particular learning-style preferences. Many learners are particularly deliberate and thorough thinkers, and perhaps more cautious when it comes to volunteering ideas. It has been our sad observation that these are the students who don't actively participate in classrooms where teachers fail to extend wait time.

Think of the silence during wait time as a fertilized egg hanging in the air, about to hatch. Figure 5.2 represents this concept.

Specific Recommendations

Based on the extensive research conducted, and on our own classroom experiences, we can make the following recommendations related to wait time:

- Extend Wait Time I to at least three seconds for lower-order, factual questions and to at least five seconds for higher-order questions.

- For particularly complex questions, extend initial wait time and allow students to spend two to three minutes considering the question and noting their initial ideas on paper.

- For complex questions, allow five to ten seconds of thinking time and then ask students what processes they are using to answer the question. This reinforces the critical-thinking notion that the process is as important as the answer and that there may be many ways to solve problems or consider issues.

- After fifteen to twenty seconds of wait time, rephrase or simplify your initial question, *if* you feel that students are unsure of how to begin.

- Extend Wait Time II to promote student–student interaction. As we will have already noted, it is vital for teachers to challenge students to listen to and build on each other's ideas, and extending Wait Time II is a subtle way to do this.

- Explain your reasons for extending wait time to students. Tell the class that you are allowing them a few seconds of thinking time after you ask a question. Some students, like some teachers, are initially uncomfortable with periods of silence.

Focal Point 3 As Your Students Answer Questions

As we have discussed the importance of varying question cognitive level and extending Wait Time I and II, an important question may have occurred to you: What should I do while a student is actually *answering* a question? You can promote a thinker-friendly classroom atmosphere by consciously considering these *attending behaviors.*

Discussion 3 As Your Students Answer Questions

Active Listening

In general, it will be vital for you send the message that you're listening closely to what your students are saying. You'll want to encourage them to continue and to focus the attention of the *entire class* on the student who is responding. You can send these messages by doing the following:

1. Maintain eye contact with the student who is speaking. Glance around the room from time to time to be sure that everyone is listening. If necessary, ask the student to repeat the response, and remind classmates to listen.

2. Use nonverbal gestures to indicate your support and understanding. Our experiences have shown that subtle head nodding, encouraging facial expressions, hand gestures, and assuming an open physical stance that shows that you are thinking about what the student is saying all make a difference.

3. Demonstrate to students that you're listening. *Do not interrupt,* even if you believe the student is headed in the wrong direction; this will discourage students from participating and taking intellectual risks in your classroom. At times, students will realize their mistakes and

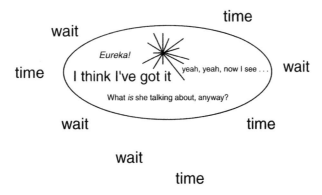

© 2001 Ina Claire Gabler

FIGURE 5.2 Wait Time

correct them. On other occasions, *you* may simply have misunderstood where the student was headed with the response. Even when students do provide partially incorrect or even far-out responses, remember that both you and your students can learn much from mistakes. This is characteristic of thinker-friendly communities. Listening is the best way to encourage further participation and to alert you to the nature of students' understanding.

4. Remember your Wait Time II. Pause for two to three seconds; the student may add to her initial response or a classmate might jump in with an insightful a comment. You might find that using Wait Time II is even more challenging than *Wait Time I,* especially when a student makes a truly insightful statement. *Be patient.*

5. Reply on some occasions with a *reflective* comment. Paraphrase all or part of the student response as a statement or a question ("It sounds like you feel that . . ."). In most cases, we have found that the student will add more detail to his original answer. Again, this technique, when judiciously applied, makes students aware that you are listening and challenges them to expand on their ideas and explain what they've said. Don't overdo it.

We've now taken a close look at that critical few seconds as and after you ask your students a question. Let's now suppose that they've given you a response. What might you do next?

Focal Point 4 Asking Effective Follow-Up Questions

As we'll see when we introduce a series of constructivist methods in later modules, *using* student responses to ask effective follow-up questions will be one of the biggest keys to promoting thought-provoking discourse (i.e., intelligent, purposeful conversation) in your classroom. In this section, we'll discuss two important types of follow-up questions that we'll refer to throughout the text: the *Probe* and the *Redirect.* (See Module Four, Figure 4.1)

Discussion 4 Asking Effective Follow-Up Questions

Probe Questions

It is vitally important to ask *probe questions* during any type of lesson. Probe questions *challenge students to think in more depth and to add detail or otherwise build on what they've said.* More than anything, asking these questions challenges students to think at higher cognitive levels. They are essential if you are to help students move beyond a superficial understanding of ideas.

Examples

Probe questions can take on a variety of forms. When used effectively, they can challenge students to do the following:

1. Clarify and add detail to what they have said

   - What do you mean by _____?
   - Could you say that in another way?
   - Can you give us an example?
   - Would you tell us more about _____?
   - *Why* would you say that?
   - When you say that, do you mean __ or ____?

2. Think about assumptions that they or others might be making

   - What are you assuming in saying this?
   - What assumption is John making here?
   - Why would/could anyone assume that _____?
   - Is this always the case?

3. Provide support for what they are saying

   - Why do you think this is true?
   - How do we know that ____?
   - What evidence do you have for saying that?
   - What other information do we need?
   - Do these reasons provide enough support for your statement?
   - How could we find out whether this is true?

4. Consider the frames of reference of other people

   - How would someone who believes _____ feel about this?
   - What other alternatives are there?
   - What would someone who disagrees say?
   - How would somebody like ____ respond to what you said?

5. Consider implications of a statement

   - What impact would _____ have?
   - Would this always happen in a case like this?
   - Why is this question important/difficult?

As we introduce a series of methods in Modules Seven through Twelve, we'll discuss the use of Probe questions. You'll see that different kinds of Probes are often emphasized when you use certain methods but that asking Probe questions (and encouraging your students to ask them) should be a major part of any constructivist classroom experience.

Redirect Questions

The second type of follow up question is the *Redirect.* In its simplest form, redirecting *refers to repeating the question, not necessarily verbatim, to another student.* This technique is useful for determining the degree of consensus in the group regarding any statement.

Examples

Regardless of which student responded to the question "How would you define surface area?," a math teacher might redirect the question by merely asking, "Does the definition express the concept as you understand it, Vince?" or, "How would you define surface area, Sara?" Another option would be to ask for a quick show of hands to gauge how other students feel about a statement made by a classmate ("How many would agree that ____?"). You can also combine elements of the Probe and Redirect as well by asking something like "How are Sara's and Vince's ideas different?" We have found that using Redirect questions *frequently* will encourage your students to listen to each other and think about what their peers have said, behavior that we certainly want to encourage.

Focal Point 5 **What Else Should Teachers Do (or *Not* Do) to Question Students Effectively*?*

In planning and conducting thought-provoking lessons, there are a number of other important factors for you to consider. In this section, we'll provide you with additional, practical advice for engaging your students in meaningful classroom dialogue.

As we've noted, engaging each of your students through questioning will be a key to your skills as a constructivist teacher. This will be true regardless of the teaching method you utilize. As we introduce a variety of methods, we will place great emphasis on promoting effective classroom interaction. In this way, we hope you can enhance the skills and abilities you've developed over the years.

Discussion 5 **What Else Should Teachers Do (or *Not* Do) to Question Students Effectively*?*

Hints for Involving Students

In continuing our discussion of effective questioning procedures, we have several suggestions for maximizing student participation. When conducting any type of lesson, we recommend that you do the following:

1. *Encourage* students to participate in all of your lessons, especially when using highly student-centered methods. In general, speak in a friendly tone of voice; use positive nonverbal cues (smiling, eye contact, etc.) and provide positive feedback *judiciously* to establish a thinker-friendly environment. When students provide truly insightful comments, be specific with your praise ("Cindy's comment is interesting because ____").

2. Ask questions of the entire class frequently as a way of encouraging all students to participate. One advantage of calling only on volunteers is that this may be less threatening to those who are not used to active participation. One obvious disadvantage is that the same small group of students may answer all of your questions unless you direct some questions to specific students.

3. Call on specific students frequently as a way of gaining insights into the nature of their understanding and to encourage participation. Be sure to ask the question first, pause, then call a student's name. This helps ensure that each student will *listen* to your question. Experience has shown us that calling on a range of students *early* in a lesson can break the ice and encourage even shy students to take part in the lesson. Use a student name first in cases where individual student attention may be lacking. You can deliver an effective wake-up call by doing this.

4. Randomly select students as you ask questions. If you follow a predictable pattern, students may relax if they are sure they will not be called on. Be sure to call on students in the back corners of the room. Researchers have shown that students in the front and center of the room are far more likely to become involved in classroom discussions (Dillon, 1988). In your classroom, you may want to experiment with index cards or popsicle sticks with students' names on them, pulling a stick or card randomly to determine who should answer the question. These methods can be effective if they are not used too often.

5. At all costs, *avoid repeating student responses.* Teacher repetition will result in students listening to *you,* not each other. If necessary, ask students to repeat or rephrase softly stated or vague responses; this will be challenging at first, because many students will not be used to active, thoughtful participation. By *not* repeating responses, you send the message that teachers and textbooks are not the ultimate sources of knowledge in the classroom. In any case, insist that students listen to, and respect, one another's statements.

6. Don't allow certain students to dominate a lesson. Call on other volunteers and nonvolunteers, and remind outspoken students that everyone needs to have a chance to speak as necessary. As we noted in Module One, it is vital to emphasize careful listening in your classroom and model positive listening behaviors yourself.

7. Avoid asking all of your questions at the end of a lesson. When using any teaching method, ask questions throughout your lessons. In this way, you are in a position to challenge your students to process new ideas and to continually assess the nature of student understanding. As a general rule, *never* talk for more than three minutes without asking a question, even when you are presenting new ideas. An exception is the Interactive Presentation method (Module Twelve) in which students carry out prescribed tasks as they listen to minilectures.

8. Encourage students to ask questions of you and each other. As we have noted, meaningful student questions are surprisingly rare in most classrooms. Again, openly praise students who ask thoughtful questions, and tell them WHY the question is worthwhile ("That's a good question because ____"). Make the most of opportunities to explore points that students may find interesting and relevant by redirecting student questions ("Would anyone care to reply to Sue's question?").

9. *Don't* rely on the use of "Any questions?" as a check on student understanding. Some students may be so confused or uninterested that they won't say a word. Never assume that students understand new ideas simply because they don't ask you questions. We have witnessed situations in which students seemed so bored or hopelessly confused that they didn't know *what* to ask.

■ ROUNDUP ■

Effectively questioning students in the classroom is no easy task. But in our view, you *can't become an effective teacher without being an effective questioner.* We hope that the practical advice provided in Part 1 of this module will help you build on your skills as an effective questioner.

In Part 1, we've introduced a number of important ideas that we'll expand on throughout the text. The first of these is the importance of varying cognitive level in the questions that you ask. We have suggested using Bloom's Taxonomy as a tool for planning effective Trigger questions (more on this in Part 2 of this module). You'll find that varying question cognitive level will help your students do more than simply recall information; higher-order questions will challenge them to *think deeply about your subject matter and to use what they've learned.*

We also explained Wait Time I and II and provided a rationale for extending wait time. It has been our experience that providing this thinking time is critical. This can also convey to your students that you really do *care* about what they think, which is an especially important factor in creating a thinker-friendly environment for your students. They'll be much more likely to take desired intellectual risks if they feel that you're a thoughtful and sympathetic listener.

We also introduced Probe and Redirect questions. Asking these follow-up questions will be a major part of every teaching method that we'll introduce in *Invisible Teaching.* Remember that your ultimate goals in asking these questions are to engage more of your students in classroom dialogue and to challenge everyone to think more deeply about the topic at hand. We also invite you to consider the other practical advice regarding questioning as you plan and teach your initial lessons. Always remember that effective teaching can't take place without effective questioning.

REFERENCES

Bloom, B. (1956). *Taxonomy of educational objectives.* New York: David McKay.

Dillon, J. T. (1988). *Questioning and discussion: A multidisciplinary study.* Norwood, NJ: Ablex Publishing.

Duckworth, E. (1987). *The having of wonderful ideas and other essays on teaching and learning.* New York: Teacher's College Press.

Rowe, M. B. (1974). Wait time and rewards as instructional variables, their influence on language, logic, and fate control. *Journal Of Research in Science Teaching, 11,* 81–94.

Tobin, K. (1987, Spring). The role of wait time in higher cognitive learning. *Review of Educational Research, 57,* 69–95.

PART 2

Do's, Don'ts, and Tips

OVERVIEW

Questions. Questions. A mind feels dead without them. The challenge is this: How do you as a teacher pose questions that your students want to answer?

Designing questions is a honed skill before it becomes an art. It all begins with learning how to write a single, well-pitched question. The question itself may actually be very simple—even just a single word, "Why?" or "How?" It's the context and the timing as well as the question itself that combine to make a question sing with just the right pitch. For this reason, writing questions is not as easy as it may seem. Pitfalls await even the experienced teacher: embedded answers, obvious answers, yes-no answers, plain old *boring* answers not worth the effort of your student raising her hand—among other traps that we alert you to here.

GOALS

This section is devoted to *techniques* of writing effective questions. In this roll-up-your-sleeves approach, we will convey the following:

- Do's and Don'ts for all question types
- Effective Trigger, Probe, and Redirect questions described in Part 1 of this module and in Module Four
- Principles of designing question clusters
- Suggestions for question patterns
- A two-part formula for writing any type of individual question

FOCAL POINTS AND DISCUSSIONS

As you've seen in Part 1 of this module, planning is essential for effective question writing. The engaging constructivist teacher poses a thought-provoking individual question as well an effective *question cluster,* a thought-out sequence or "package" of several questions, each one building on the previous one. Imagine a series of question clusters that facilitate higher and higher levels of thinking.

Flexibility

We are *not* advocating prescripting every question. Talented teachers certainly ask pertinent, electric, and challenging questions spontaneously as the discussion or peer exchange requires. We *are* promoting the practice of planning individual questions and question clusters that help move the thought process along, guiding your students to their own interpretations and analysis of the information at hand; planning questions that jump-start the discussion when it stalls; planning questions that motivate your students to research some new angle on a familiar concept.

As an experienced teacher, you know that if you do not thoughtfully plan key questions in advance, then you risk not being able to deviate effectively from your planned lesson, to pluck questions out from under your sleeve and guide the discussion meaningfully if your students take a different route from the one you had anticipated. In fact, we guarantee that your students will explore unexpected terrain—if you engage their interest. So you need preplanned questions to complement spontaneous ones. This way, you'll be prepared to travel the back roads along with your students while you guide them meaningfully.

Focal Point 1 Designing Individual Questions

There is no magic formula to ensure that you compose terrific questions. After all, it's your intelligence and imagination, your grasp of your subject matter, along with context and timing in the moment that combine to generate effective questions—not to mention your experience. With this in mind, we've worked out techniques that give you some tips in designing questions. For starters, we've arranged some Do's and Don'ts.

Examples of Do's and Don'ts

Do's

1. Include **both** a *question word* (who, what, when, where, why, how) along with a *precise term* (a **concrete** concept, detail, or idea).

Examples

    a. *Vague:* "*What* can we say about the main character?"

    b. *Includes precise term:* "*What* was a *strength* of the main character?"

    c. *Vague:* "*How* did we approach this experiment?"

    d. *Includes precise term:* "*Why* was the *first step* important in this experiment?"

    e. *Includes precise terms:* "*What* do you think was *one of the three most important variables* in this experiment?" (Then follow up with "*What* was *another important variable?*," etc.)

Don'ts

1. Don't embed the answer in the question.

Examples:

    a. *Embedded answer:* "So can we say that slavery was a major cause of the Civil War?"

    b. *Nonembedded answer:* "*What* was a *major cause* of the Civil War? Please explain." (Note the question word and the precise term.)

    c. *Nonembedded answer:* "*Why* was *slavery* a *major cause* of the Civil War?"

    d. *Embedded answer:* "Do you see that line and shape affect proportion?" (This question tells the students that line and shape affect proportion.)

    e. *Nonembedded answer:* "*How* do *line and shape* affect proportion?" Or, "*What* are *two elements* that affect proportion?"

2. Don't ask a run-on question (two or three questions in a row). Students don't know which question to answer. In addition, effective questions get lost in the shuffle. Ask one question, then *wait.*

Examples

    a. *Run-on:* "Why did the United States drop the first atomic bomb on Japan? Was it to win the war? Or to demonstrate our military superiority? Do you think the Japanese would have surrendered if we hadn't dropped the bomb?"

    b. *Run-on question organized as a question cluster with individual questions posed between responses:*

    "*Why did the United States drop the first atomic bomb* on Japan?"

    Student response.

    "*Who gained from this?*" (This is a possible question appropriate for the second part of the run-on that asked, "or to demonstrate our military superiority?" The latter contains an embedded answer.)

    Student response.

    "*Do you think the Japanese would have surrendered if we hadn't dropped the bomb? When?*"

    Student response.

    "*Why?*"

Run-ons often result from insufficient planning. The question cluster is far more effective and requires advanced teacher reflection. (There's more on question clusters below.)

3. Don't ask the most challenging questions before a knowledge base has been established. Without lower-level warm-up questions that bring your students into the discussion, guiding their insights, the students won't be prepared to answer the higher-level question(s) and may be intimidated.

Examples

    a. *Higher-level cognitive question at the outset of discussion:* "*What* does the headless horseman *symbolize?*"

    b. *Building knowledge base first according to Bloom's Taxonomy:*

    "*What* is the *conflict* between Brom Bones and Ichabod Crane?"

    "*How* does Brom Bones try *to frighten* Ichabod Crane?"

    "*How* does Brom Bones *succeed or fail* in scaring Ichabod Crane? *What* happens?"

    "*Who* or *what* is the headless horseman?"

    "*What* do you think the headless horseman *symbolizes?*"

4. Avoid yes-no questions without a tag such as "Why?" or "Please explain."

Examples

    a. *Yes-no questions:*

    "Did the United States drop the first atomic bomb on Japan?"

    "Did the bomb demonstrate U.S. military superiority?"

    "Was there a conflict between Brom Bones and Ichabod Crane?"

    "Does the headless horseman symbolize our (ignorance, fear, desire for power, evil, etc.)?"

    b. *With tag:*

    "Did the United States drop the first atomic bomb on Japan? *Why?*"

"Did the bomb demonstrate U.S. military superiority? *Please explain.*"

"Was there a conflict between Brom Bones and Ichabod Crane? *Please describe* it in your own words."

"Does the headless horseman symbolize our (ignorance, fear, desire for power, evil, etc.)? In *what* way?"

5. Don't ask "what about" questions. They always need clarification. Use a precise term.

Examples

a. "What about slavery?"

b. *Instead:* "*Why* did the North *oppose* slavery?"

c. "What about X and Y?"

d. *Instead:* "*How* does X *relate to* Y in this word problem?"

Focal Point 2   Trigger, Probe, and Redirect Questions

An effective question cluster consists of Trigger, Probe, and Redirect questions (see Module Four and Module Five, Part 1). Naturally, specific Probes and Redirects are often improvised, depending on the students' responses. But you can preplan approximations according to your instructional intentions.

Discussion 2   Trigger, Probe, and Redirect Questions

Different types of questions yield different results. As you will soon see, the question *sequence* also matters. It's like building a house from the bottom up. Without a foundation, everything sinks. Trigger, Probe, and Redirect questions work together in a kind of choreography, creating a step-by-step sequence that helps to process information beneath the surface.

A Trigger question opens a topic at any level. You may decide that a principle, for example, may embody three features necessary for your students to grasp in order for them to formulate the principle. You will need at least one Trigger question to introduce each feature. A Trigger question can also spark exploration of a principle (or concept or theme). So think of a Trigger question as a launching pad.

You've launched the idea. What's next? The Probe question does what its name suggests: It digs a bit for substance. Probes elicit examples, further explanations of the response to the Trigger question. "Can you build on that idea?," you say to a student's unfounded assertion, direct-

ing her to the article or video notes or computations in a software application. *Be careful that your Probe questions coax rather than intimidate your students. It helps a lot if you make them aware of what a Probe question is and why you pose them.*

You want to bring everyone into the discussion. That's when you pose a Redirect question. Quite literally, you re-direct the intention of a Trigger or Probe question to another student or to the class at large. Redirects can be broad: "Who has a different point of view about X?" or "Can anyone else think of another example?" or "Who can compare and contrast what Jose and Lucretia have said about Z?"

In this way, you can sequence Trigger, Probe, and Redirect questions to facilitate your students' thinking process.

Insist on Substance

Remember to select pertinent materials. Insist that your students justify their viewpoints by referring to *specific content* in the materials. Assertions made from life experience must also be supported with *specific examples.*

Examples of Trigger, Probe, and Redirect Questions

Take a look at examples of interrelated Trigger, Probe, and Redirect questions in Figure 5.3 for an overview. More examples appear in context in Focal Point 4. "Designing Question Clusters."

Focal Point 3   Question Patterns

Both deductive and inductive frameworks (see Section C, Figure C.1, and Module Eight) are most successful when you interrelate questions progressively. Our examples of question clusters in Focal Point 4 demonstrate this kind of interrelated progression. But first, take a look at some techniques of posing questions, what we call *question patterns,* that can be repeated for a specific outcome. See if you like our examples, and try to come up with your own.

Examples of Question Patterns

Refer to Figure 5.1 for these question patterns.

EXAMPLE #1/QUESTION SEQUENCE TO GUIDE INTERPRETATION

Q1. Ask for a *reaction* to the text, article, visual, etc. "What did you think about . . . ?" or "What was your reaction to . . . ?"

TRIGGER Opens discussion with a broad question	PROBE Asks respondent to explain further; guides respondent to insight that benefits the student and class	REDIRECT Poses question on the same issue to the entire class; invites various angles on the same issue
Why did the United States drop an atomic bomb on Japan in World War II?	1. In addition to wanting to win the war, what other reason might have motivated dropping the A-bomb on Japan? Why? 2. That's an interesting idea. Could you explain a bit more how national pride could have been a factor, citing some facts? 3. Can you justify national pride in this situation or not? Why?	1. Could someone put that in his own words? 2. Does anyone agree? disagree? 3. Can anyone think of yet another motive for dropping the A-bomb?

FIGURE 5.3 Trigger, Probe, and Redirect Questions

Q2. Ask for a textual or visual *example:* "Can you give us an example of X from the text/video/picture?"

Q3. Ask for an *explanation:* "How/why is this description an example of____?" and/or ask any one of the following questions.

EXAMPLE #2/SAMPLE PROBES

1. "Explain the reason for _____."
2. "How does _____ apply?"
3. "Can you predict what would happen if _____?"
4. "Predict the outcome if _____."
5. "Why?"
6. "Compare and contrast _____ and _____? What do you think is significant here?"

EXAMPLE #3/SAMPLE REDIRECTS

1. "Does anyone agree? Why?"
2. "Does someone have a different way of seeing things? Please explain."
3. "What could be another interpretation of _____?"
4. "Could someone find another example that's evidence for _____?"
5. "What do you think the relationship is between _____?"

EXAMPLE #4/SAMPLE MINISUMMARY CLARIFICATIONS DURING DISCUSSIONS

1. "Based on what Ella, David, and Sue have said about _____, we can say that _____."
2. "So are you saying that _____?"
3. "How could you combine these ideas in a single statement?"

EXAMPLE #5/SAMPLE PERSONAL INTERPRETATIONS

1. "How would you feel about _____? Why?"
2. "How might the appearance of things be (misleading/convincing/the opposite of what you would expect, etc.)? Why?"
3. "What do you think is significant about _____ and why?"

Focal Point 4 **Designing Question Clusters**

A *question cluster* is a series of three or more interrelated Trigger questions (along with corresponding Probe and Redirect questions) that are sequenced to guide students' interpretation of a targeted concept, principle, or theme. Effective question clusters take thought: It's a tricky balance of establishing a knowledge base en route to higher-level analysis and synthesis without being too obvious (boring) or intimidating (scaring students away from taking risks).

One approach is to organize your questions into two broad categories that elicit *two strands* of understanding.

Strand One questions elicit the literal information or facts, what we refer to as the *knowledge base. Strand Two* questions elicit analysis, synthesis, and evaluation, the *original insights* founded on the facts. Such insights can be thought of as hidden stories. Each strand of interrelated questions consists of a question cluster.

Both question strands/question clusters are most effective when designed according to Bloom's Taxonomy. Strand One questions correspond to Bloom's lower-level cognitive questions. Strand Two questions correspond to Bloom's higher-level cognitive questions. We recommend that you copy Bloom's table in Figure 5.1 for handy reference.

Discussion 4 **Designing Question Clusters**

To the teacher, Strand Two questions are the most exciting to pose. Typically, new teachers ask these difficult questions first as a way to motivate their students. This often backfires, because you know far more than your students do in your subject area. What is mental fun for you may be beyond the grasp of your students—*at first.*

Sequence Matters

In your effort to stimulate your students with challenging questions early in the lesson, you may only intimidate them. They may not be able to answer an evaluation question posed at the beginning of the lesson, before they are grounded. This inability fosters insecurity and reluctance to answer. But they will be able to answer the very same question toward the middle or end of the lesson after they grow familiar with related facts and concepts.

The Takeoff Factor

Think of an airplane. Before it takes flight, it needs to run along the ground to gain momentum. In the same way, your students need to ground themselves with factual information and basic concepts before they venture into higher thinking. *Your thought-out question sequence facilitates the Takeoff Factor.*

Technique for Designing Question Clusters

Try out these steps for writing question clusters.

1. CONCEPTUALIZE: Reflect on your ideas. *Plan backward* from the insights to the facts. What are the concepts, principles, or themes you want your students to name, interpret, and analyze? What are the facts that build these insights? Reflect on how you can facilitate a thought process to get there. With this approach in mind, consider the following.

   a. *Strand Two/Insights (concepts, principles, themes)*

      • Jot down the concepts, principles, and themes and hidden stories you deem significant for the lesson Rationale.

   b. *Strand One/Salient Facts*

      • Jot down the key facts in the learning materials that are integral to the target concepts, principles, and/or theme.

2. COMPOSE QUESTIONS: Write your questions, referring to your facts and Bloom's Taxonomy (see Module Five, Part 1). Think through the sequence. Order the questions so they facilitate increasing insight for your students.

   a. *Strand One/Fact Questions*

      • Write questions that elicit the important facts you wrote down for Strand One.

      • Start with lower-level questions that interpret and apply the facts.

   b. *Strand Two/Insight Questions (for concepts, principles and themes)*

      • Write Strand Two questions that guide analysis, synthesis, and/or evaluation of the facts from Strand One questions. These questions elicit the concepts, principles, or themes, the hidden stories you identified, or others you may have missed but that the students perceive.

      • Move up the cognitive levels.

   c. *Question Formula*

      • Remember that effective questions contain a *question word* plus a *precise term.* Question words are *who, what, when, where, why* and *how.* A precise, concrete term directs your students' focus.

3. Keep this in mind: *You* must employ imagination and critical thinking as a facilitator of your students' critical thinking.

Example of Question Clusters

Example/Social Studies:

Principle: *The application of justice is inequitable according to economic class and race.*

1. CONCEPTUALIZE

   a. *Strand Two/Insights (concepts, principles, and themes based on sources and life experience)*

- Our society does not value poor racial minorities as much as it does affluent people.

- Despite advances in social practices and professed egalitarian attitudes concerning racial minorities, racism may still pervade on an unspoken level.

- Racism today may have insidious consequences, especially for poor minorities. While racism may not be considered a socially acceptable attitude, it appears to exist, sometimes with pernicious consequences.

  b. *Strand One/List Pertinent Facts*

- Poor minorities are convicted of and executed for committing homicide more frequently than are their white counterparts.

- Poor minority defendants are often assigned a court-appointed lawyer who is significantly underpaid and overworked. Such an attorney will not devote enough time to the client's case.

- Affluent defendants hire clever lawyers equipped with researchers to prepare a strong defense.

- In 2000, Governor George Ryan of Illinois ordered a temporary halt to executions because of the large proportion of prisoners on death row discovered to be innocent based on genetic testing. The majority of those on death row were minorities.

2. COMPOSE QUESTIONS

   a. *Strand One/Fact Questions*

   Cluster 1

- "According to the *New York Times* article, what change did Governor George Ryan order in Illinois prisons in 2000?" (Trigger)

- "Why did Governor Ryan issue this order?" (Probe)

- "Are there any other reasons?" (Redirect)

- "What racial or economic groups of prisoners were affected by this order?" (Trigger)

- "In what way were they affected?" (Probe)

   Cluster 2

- "Based on the videoclip, explain how the racial population on death row compares proportionately with that of the general population." (Trigger; implied question)

- "Based on the article, what is one reason for this disparity?" (Probe=inferior legal defense versus strong legal defense of the more affluent)

- "What is another reason?" (Redirect=possible racism)

- "Support your answer." (Probe)

   b. *Strand Two/Insight Questions (for concepts, principles, themes)*

   Cluster 1

- "In what ways can racism be obvious?" (Trigger)

- "Can you think of another way? Explain." (Probe)

- "Can anyone think of yet another?" (Redirect)

- "Give us an example." (Probe)

   Cluster 2

- "What distinction can be made about open racism and concealed racism?" (Trigger)

- "Can you give an example?" (Probe)

- "What could be another example?" (Redirect)

- "What other differences could there be between open and concealed racism?" (Redirect)

- "What are some examples of this second distinction?" (Probe)

   Cluster 3

- "In the *Newsweek* article, how does the data support the relationship between poverty and race? Explain." (Trigger)

- "How does the data support the relationship between poverty and crime?" (Probe)

- "Support your answer. Be specific." (Implied Probe)

- "How might all this apply to prisoners on death row?" (Trigger)

- "Explain." (Probe)

   Cluster 4

- "How could concealed racism affect our society in general?" (Trigger)

- "Please give an example." (Probe)

- "Any other examples?" (Redirect)

- "What is a possible definition of justice?" (Trigger)

- "What is another possible definition of justice?" (Redirect)

- "What supports this definition?" (Probe)

Cluster 5

- "According to your definition and based on the topic of our discussion, what limited judgments can you make about the application of justice in our society and why?" (Trigger)

- "How could the application of justice be more equitable?" (Probe)

- "Who can add to that?" (Redirect)

Remember: *You* must employ creative critical thinking as a facilitator of your students' critical thinking. The importance of wait time also bears repeating. Wait time is difficult for teachers because we have a particular answer in mind and expect the students to arrive at the same answer immediately: It seems so obvious to us! The silence after a question also makes us nervous that our students aren't "getting it," and many teachers are accustomed to doing most of the talking in class (Johnson, D., & Johnson, R., 1989; Putnam, J., 1997; Slavin, R., 1995). But without Wait Time I and II, the best-planned question clusters may not achieve what you had hoped for.

■ ROUNDUP ■

Who gains from questions?

What are the gains?

Where are the gains found?

When?

Why?

How do you keep the gains coming?

Effective questioning is essential for the constructivist teacher; it is the technique that wears the crown of all methods. A lesson or project planned without effective questions, whether written on an activity sheet or posed orally, is like a house built without a strong framework. It all tumbles down, despite the best of ideas.

Relying predominantly on questions-in-action (the inspiration of the moment) to articulate questions is risky. The result may likely be run-on questions as you think aloud, or vague questions, or questions with embedded answers—or all of the above.

We urge you to preplan, that is, preTHINK your Trigger, Probe, and Redirect questions and question clusters, those inquiries that keep the lesson on target, even as your students take you down unexpected roads. The masterful teacher can improvise effective questions amidst the unexpected because she has preplanned and thought out the essential questions, thereby keeping a mental compass. Be that master teacher.

■ HANDS-ON PRACTICE ■

We invite you to try your hand at composing two question clusters for the following song, then posing those questions to your colleagues in peer groups. If you prefer, use different lyrics of your choice. Check that the literal story contains elements of a larger theme. You might also want to use lyrics in addition to those here so that members in each peer group work with different texts. The advantage of practicing with your colleagues is that you can give and receive helpful feedback about what questions worked and how to improve others. A Self-Instruct Planner follows the lyrics.

Sample Text: *John Henry,* Traditional American Folk Song

John Henry is a song about a nineteenth-century African American folk hero. He was known for hammering many of the first railroad tracks in the country at astonishing speed. Many people had claimed to know him. He has become a legend, both for his tremendous strength and for what he represented.

John Henry

When John Henry was a little baby,
Sitting on his mama's knee.
Well, he picked up a hammer and a little piece of steel.
He said, "This hammer's gonna be the death of me,
   Lord, Lord."
He said, "This hammer's gonna be the death of me."

Well, the Captain said to John Henry,
"I believe this mountain's cavin' in."
John Henry said to the Captain,
"'T'ain't nothin' but my hammer suckin' wind, Lord,
   Lord.
'T'ain't nothin' but my hammer suckin' wind."

Then the captain said to John Henry,
"I'm gonna bring that steam drill around.
I'm gonna bring that steam drill out on the job,
I'm gonna whack that steel on down, Lord, Lord.
I'm gonna whack that steel on down."

And John Henry said to the Captain,
"Lord, a man ain't nothin' but a man.

And before I let that steam drill beat me down,
I'm gonna die with a hammer in my hand, Lord, Lord.
I'm gonna die with a hammer in my hand."

Now John Henry said to the Shaker,
"Shaker, why don't you sing?
You know I'm throwing thirty pounds from my hips on
    down,
Just listen to that cold steel ring, Lord, Lord.
Just listen to that cold steel ring."
The man that invented the steam drill,
You know, he thought that he was mighty fine;
But John Henry hammered his seventeen feet,
The steam drill only made nine, Lord, Lord.
You know, the steam drill only made nine.

When John Henry went down to the railroad
With a twelve-pound hammer at his side,
He walked down the track but he ain't come back,
'Cause he laid down his hammer and he died, Lord,
    Lord.
'Cause he laid down his hammer and he died.

Oh, they took John Henry to the graveyard,
And they buried him in the sand.
And every locomotive that came a-ridin' by
Said, "There lies a steel-drivin' man Lord, Lord."
Said, "There lies a steel-drivin' man."

Now John Henry had himself a woman,
And her name was Polly Ann.
On the day John Henry died a-hammerin' the track,
Polly Ann hammered steel like a man Lord, Lord.
Polly Ann hammered steel like a man.

There's a widow that comes to the graveyard.
And her name is Polly Ann.
Now every time that church bell tolls,
She says, "There lies my steel-drivin' man, Lord, Lord."
She says, "There lies my steel-drivin' man."

Designing Questions: Activity Sheet for *John Henry*

Overarching Question

Write two question clusters, one that elicits the literal story and one that elicits one hidden story or theme in *John Henry.*

Reminder

Effective questions contain a question word plus a precise term. All Trigger questions need Probe and Redirect questions for development of an idea.

Your Job

1. Read the lyrics twice. Once to establish the literal story in your mind. Then once again to infer at least one other story or theme between the lines.
2. CONCEPTUALIZE your ideas. Work backward from Strand Two, the large picture.
   - Briefly jot down the literal story.
   - Jot down one possible hidden story or one theme. Justify your own interpretation to yourself with facts from the literal story. Jot down your own justification based on details in the lyrics. Your written ideas serve as a reference for designing questions.
3. COMPOSE your questions.
   - Write a question cluster of at least three Strand One Trigger questions that elicit the complete *literal* story first. This establishes the knowledge base. Be creative.
   - Write a second question cluster of at least three Strand Two Trigger questions that attempt to elicit the hidden story or theme that you have perceived.
4. POSE your story questions to your colleagues and see what happens. As you probe, ask people to justify their own interpretations and analyses by citing specific details in the song. Insist on this justification whether or not a respondent's story or theme agrees with your own. It's the *thought process that matters—the logic and critical thinking*—more than a particular answer.

Self-Instruct Planner: *John Henry*

(Work on a separate piece of paper.)
Refer to the complete Bloom's Taxonomy in Module Five, Part 1, and to Figure 5.1.

A. Question Cluster for the Literal Story
   1. CONCEPTUALIZE: What are the distinctive details that comprise the literal story?
   2. COMPOSE: Refer to the details in #1 just above. Sequence a question cluster of at least three Strand One Trigger questions along with corresponding Probe and Redirect questions designed to elicit the literal story. Avoid chronology questions, that is, asking what happened first, second, and so on. Instead, use the question formula (question word + a precise term) to briefly elicit the setting and events in an interesting way.
B. Question Cluster for the Hidden Story or Larger Theme
   1. CONCEPTUALIZE: What is the hidden story or theme that you perceive? What details or facts in the lyrics lead you to this perception?

2. COMPOSE: Refer to the details or facts in #1 just above. Sequence a question cluster of at least three Strand Two Trigger questions along with corresponding Probe and Redirect questions designed to facilitate a discussion of the hidden story or theme.

Focus on posing questions that guide people to support their assertions. Encourage logic by your questioning. Try to facilitate higher cognitive skills of analysis (comparing and contrasting the elements), synthesis, and evaluation once the knowledge base has been established. If you achieve all this, even if your colleagues arrive at different hidden stories and themes than you had intended, you will have been successful.

Remember that you are not aiming for agreement with your own perceptions. A constructivist approach fosters the *process* of critical thinking. This means that insights *must be justified* by a knowledge base and concepts. Critical thinking matters more than a desired answer without sound logic.

REFERENCES

Johnson, D., & Johnson, R. (1989). *Cooperation and competition: Theory and research.* Edina, MN: Interaction Books.

Putnam, J. (1997). *Cooperative learning in diverse classrooms.* Upper Saddle River, NJ: Merrill.

Slavin, R. (1995). *Cooperative learning: Theory, research, and practice.* Boston: Allyn & Bacon.

SUGGESTED READING

Armstrong, T. (1994). *Multiple intelligences in the classroom.* Alexandria, VA: Association for Supervision and Curriculum Development.

Bloom, B. (Ed.). (1956). *A taxonomy of educational objectives: Handbook I. Cognitive domain.* New York: McKay.

Gardner, H. (1983). *Frames of mind.* New York: Basic Books.

Nickerson, R., Perkins, D., & Smith, E. (1985). *The teaching of thinking.* Hillsdale, NJ: Lawrence Erlbaum.

Rowe, M. (1974). Wait time and reward as instructional variables, their influence on language, logic and fate control. Part 1: Wait time. *Journal of Research on Science Teaching, 11,* 81–94.

Module Six

Peer-Group Learning (PGL)

■ OVERVIEW

groups *peer groups* peer groups
peer groups peer groups

Peer groups?
Plain and simple
I'll tell you how
it's gonna go.
They won't have a clue,
that's what.
Go tell your theory types—
Peer groups are a hype.
I've been in the real world and I
know that
kids in groups don't hack
it. Why, I tell 'em
what to do and they
don't do it. I give 'em
worksheets, fill up
the blanks, I say,
copy
from the board or the textbook,
tank up
real
easy.
I tried it once, all
day. But
their lives are so messy.
They can't get it
on their own,
you see.
I've got to be the one that
tells 'em. Then they
know the scoop.
That's the way to get 'em to write
the right words in groups.
Now, that's the way it
really
is.
And I still have to
tell 'em what
to write on
my test.
I've got to be the whiz.
I fill up their tanks.
They don't even say
thanks.
Go and tell the professors
that.

© 2001 Ina Claire Gabler

■ GOALS

We talked about it Module Three: As our opening verse hints, there's a long tradition of whole-group, teacher-led instruction in our schools, and change is difficult when it comes to breaking the traditional way of doing things in classrooms. Some teachers resist it; many still see the instructor's role as one of *filling students' tanks* with information. At times, even students resist being shaken out of their comfort zones when it comes to new or different classroom approaches. But over the last ten to fifteen years, we have witnessed an increasing acceptance of what we would call *peer-group learning* (PGL) *techniques,* approaches that *allow students to work together in at least semiautonomous groups of two to eight to accomplish an academic task.* We consider *cooperative-learning techniques* to be a special subset of peer-group techniques; they *feature heterogeneous groups of students working together for common academic and social purposes, with an emphasis on group and individual accountability* (based on Johnson & Johnson, 1989).

Remember that a constructivist classroom is an *ACTIVE* classroom and, as we'll see in this module, peer-group techniques are an essential ingredient in the mix of techniques and methods in a constructivist learning experience. Not only do they allow learners enhanced opportunities for collaboration, student–student interaction, and direct involvement with materials but they create a feeling of *positive interdependence* that affects the entire group.

In the sections that follow, we'll address the following series of important guiding questions:

- Why should teachers use peer-group learning techniques?
- What should teachers do to make peer-group learning experiences worthwhile?
- What peer-group and cooperative-learning techniques have been shown to be effective in the classroom?

■ FOCAL POINTS AND DISCUSSIONS

Focal Point 1 **Why Should Teachers Use Peer-Group Learning Techniques?**

Peer-group techniques, especially cooperative-learning techniques, are among the most widely researched instructional approaches. Well over 300 studies focused on the effectiveness of group work have been conducted over the past twenty-five years (Johnson & Johnson, 1993). This body of research represents a compelling case for making PGL techniques a major focus in your classroom. The following discussion of these studies is by no means comprehensive, but it will provide you with some food for thought when it comes to using peer-group techniques.

Discussion 1 Why Should Teachers Use Peer-Group Learning Techniques

Just what does this research show? That peer-group, and especially cooperative-learning, techniques, when properly implemented, offer a number of advantages as compared to approaches that emphasize individualized, competitive learning situations. Cooperative-learning techniques have been shown to have the following impacts when properly implemented.

* They enhance how much and how deeply students learn material, how long they remember it, and how effectively they can use higher-cognitive-level reasoning strategies. In reviewing and analyzing data from hundreds of studies (using a process known as meta-analysis), Johnson and Johnson (1993) and Slavin (1995) found that from 50–72 percent of the studies completed showed enhanced student learning when teachers emphasized cooperative-learning techniques in the classroom. Only 10–12 percent of such studies found learning advantages in classrooms featuring individualized, competitive, whole-group instruction. Moreover, those studies that did find an advantage to a more competitive approach tended to emphasize rote learning skills (i.e., memorizing information at the knowledge level) as compared to *higher-order* understanding of material (Putnam, 1997). Most encouragingly, researchers have shown these PGL advantages hold for students who were considered low achieving as well as for those who were considered gifted.

* A number of researchers have shown that the use of peer-group and cooperative-learning techniques also have wide-ranging *affective* benefits. A number of these studies show that the use of peer-group techniques enhances student self-esteem (Johnson & Johnson, 1989; Slavin, 1995). Happily, we have experienced this positive trend directly while teaching in middle school, high school, and college classrooms. Students working in peer-group settings very often *come to feel that they have something meaningful to contribute to the group,* and this seems to have a powerful impact on their feeling of self-worth (see Module Two, "Resocializing").

* In addition, the use of peer-group techniques seems to have a highly positive impact on the degree of acceptance and understanding between students of different racial and ethnic groups (Sharan, 1990; Slavin, 1990, 1995) and between students with and without disabilities (Johnson & Johnson, 1989). As David Johnson (1989) summarized, the use of peer groups promoted positive interactions between individual students and allowed them "to perceive one another in multi-dimensional rather than stereotypic ways."

* Many students seem to make impressive gains in developing their own written and especially verbal communications skills as a result of peer-group experiences (Putnam, 1997). Again, we have noted this trend in a wide range of classrooms, and the reason seems clear to us: Students who are regularly challenged to express opinions and listen to and respond to others, rather than sit passively listening to a teacher, will become better communicators.

* Finally, students working in classrooms in which cooperative-learning techniques are a central feature tend to show more positive attitudes toward school in general, less disruptive behavior, a greater feeling of autonomy in the classroom, and enhanced conflict-resolution skills (Johnson, Johnson, & Holubec, 1990).

We see these findings as significant for two main reasons. First, they should dispel the fear that many teachers have that giving up a degree of control will result in increased discipline problems; in fact, *just the opposite effect has been shown.* This leads to a second point that we expand on in Module Two, Part 2 ("Constructivist Classroom Management"): *The best way to prevent discipline problems in the classroom is to keep students engaged in meaningful learning experiences.*

Again, space allows but a brief review of the many interesting studies done regarding the impacts of peer-group learning experiences on students. The reference list for this module lists a number of terrific resource materials focused on these studies if you're interested. Certainly, this body of research, and our own classroom experiences, have clearly demonstrated to us that peer-group techniques are incredibly beneficial to students. The question now becomes: How *do* you properly implement such techniques? This will be our focus in the sections that follow.

Focal Point 2 What Should You Do to Make Peer-Group Learning Experiences Worthwhile?

The next two sections will clarify the somewhat mysterious caveat that we frequently used earlier in this module: *when properly implemented.* Let's start first with some practical advice that cuts across each technique before getting specific about different techniques that you might use in conjunction with constructivist methods.

Discussion 2 What Should You Do to Make Peer-Group Learning Experiences Worthwhile?

Keep in mind that when we say *peer-group technique,* we're referring to any technique that would feature your inviting students to work together autonomously in small groups. This would include such informal arrangements as asking randomly chosen partners to work together for a few minutes on a single task. It would also include co-operative-learning arrangements that might feature groups of students working together in specialized ways for several days or longer. The *general* advice that we'll provide in this section applies to this whole range of peer-group possibilities.

In making these suggestions we felt that it might be most effective to address questions and concerns that many beginning (and even veteran) teachers have regarding group work. Research and our own classroom experiences have shown us that there are specific things that you can do to make group work *work.*

How Often Should You Challenge Your Students to Work Together in Peer Groups?

We recommend that you try to spend from one quarter to one third of your total classroom time with students working in peer groups. This doesn't mean that you should earmark fifteen to twenty minutes per day for peer-group work; we're referring to more of a long-term guideline in this case. Some class periods will include no peer-group work at all; others will feature students working in groups for almost entire periods. It all depends on what your objectives (instructional intentions) are for that session and what methods you'll use to carry out these objectives.

Remember that before they reach your classroom, students have probably had a huge range of experiences working in groups. They've been in classrooms where they never worked in groups. They may have worked in groups in which either they had to do most of the work *or* they could get away with doing almost nothing. Some will have had some very enjoyable and academically worthwhile experiences in group settings. Our advice is to tell your students early on that working in peer groups will be an important part of their experience in your classroom. Then tell them *why.* Invite your students to share any positive or negative experiences they've experienced working in groups, and describe how you will attempt to address

any of their concerns. We have found that taking this approach helps students to understand what you're doing and will result in them taking peer-group learning opportunities more seriously. See other ideas for peer-group implementation in Module Two, Part 1.

Should You Assign Students to Groups in Advance? Allow Them to Choose Groups? or Arrange Them Randomly?

You've made the commitment to make peer-group work an integral part of your students' experience. How should you start this process?

One of your first considerations is how to arrange the groups. We suggest that, for the most part, you assign students to heterogeneous groups based on academic (and other) talents, gender, ethnicity, and personality. Make your groups *diverse.* Research on cooperative learning has shown that heterogeneous groups have academic and social benefits. Invite students who would not normally socialize to work together; this will allow you to break down some of the cliques that you'll find in middle and high schools. We have seen this approach produce dramatic effects in the classroom. Students who would normally never associate with one another will come to know and better understand each other. On most occasions, especially if you're forming groups that are going to work together for days or weeks, we suggest assigning groups intentionally. Here's a suggestion: When you have extended peer-group work planned for a class period, arrange your desks in pods (i.e., groups of three to four) in advance, and place index cards with group members' names on the cards on their table/pod before the class enters the room. It's a real time-saver.

Randomly chosen groups can accomplish many of these same objectives. If you're transitioning from a full-class setting to peer groups (often the case as part of constructivist experiences) and your students are seated in a large circle, ask them to count off in 2's, 3's, 4's, and so on or to pick numbers written on slips of paper out of a hat and then meet with their group in some predetermined part of the room. This is usually quick and efficient, and chances are you'll end up with diversity built into your groups.

For the most part, we don't recommend letting students choose their own groups. What happens when you do this? The same circles of friends tend to sit together, and students who are typically left out will be left out of the peer groups. You might make occasional exceptions to this in the case of projects or presentations. If you're going to ask students to spend time working together outside of class, let them pick partners that might make this more convenient, but make sure that everybody *gets* a partner.

What Group Size Is Optimal?

It takes time for students to develop small-group communications skills, so we recommend starting with smaller peer groups and shorter, more structured tasks or assignments. Early in the school year, experiment with groups of two, three, or four, and ask students to work together for a few (five to ten) minutes. It has been our experience that asking students to work in groups larger than four, especially early in the school year, will lessen the positive impact of the peer-group experience. With larger groups, some students will likely feel left out of the conversation. Easing into peer-group experiences like this will tend to smooth over any *transitions* that your students will need to make. Over time, you'll find that they'll be able to work productively together for extended periods.

What Should You Do to Make Your Expectations Clear?

Experience has shown us the importance of explaining specifically what you'd like students to accomplish when they work together in peer groups. Of course, in a constructivist classroom, you'll be allowing students greater freedom and responsibility than they've likely experienced before. When it comes to peer-group work, you still need to talk to your students specifically about what can and should happen in their groups. What are they going to *produce* as a result of their work together? If you're going to allow them options in this regard, what will they be? How much time will they have? Significantly, how will you build group and individual accountability into the activity? This last point is important; you've got to convey to your students that there's a good reason for them to work together and that each person in the group will be responsible in some way for learning something as a result of the experience. Ask each group to produce something that shows critical thought, creativity, and a degree of teamwork. Let each student know that she will need to understand the important ideas that were a part of the group experience when you ask the class to write a reflective essay, take a quiz or test, or complete some other kind of assignment. You can assign two grades: individual grades for individual tasks and a group grade. That way, each student can weigh his impact on the overall performance, and assiduous students won't be penalized for the lesser effort of others if there's only a collective grade.

How Can You Help Groups Develop Communication Skills?

Whether you're teaching art, PE, math, or any other subject, this is an important question. It's vital to help your students develop their abilities to work together in peer groups. We have found that it helps to develop guidelines with input from your students, that will help them become better communicators. Early in the school year, ask your students what might help them to work together productively in groups; give them your suggestions on this. When you do this, consider some of the suggestions that we've made regarding critical thinking. For example, adopting guidelines like these will help students work together effectively:

- Criticize ideas, not people.
- Listen to other ideas, even if you don't agree.
- Ask each other clarifying questions when you don't understand something.
- Change your mind when evidence suggests you should do so.
- Encourage everyone in your group to participate.

There's an important, implicit message that you send students when you help them to develop guidelines like this: Peer-group work is important; it's an opportunity for you to think about something important and share your thoughts and opinions (See Module Two, Part 1, for more ideas on modeling peer-group interaction.)

Is It Helpful to Have Students Play Certain Roles within Their Groups?

Has a teacher ever asked you to play a *social role* within a group? We have found that this will help your peer groups to be more productive, and that it can help students to develop those communication skills that we just mentioned. What are some possible roles? Consider just a few of these options as responsibilities for group members:

- Leader/moderator
- Recorder
- Presenter
- Spokesperson
- Prompter (who specializes in asking probing questions of other group members)
- Timekeeper
- Reference person (who has sole responsibility for finding necessary information in available material or on the Internet)
- Gatekeeper (who ensures respectful exchange; who prevents domination by a few)

Most often, we suggest allowing students to choose roles. Occasionally, assign roles and ask students to rotate periodically ("Sue, I'd like you to act as group leader today"). This last option is especially effective when students are working in peer groups for extended periods. See Part 2 of this module, "Activity Sheets," for a discussion of the difference between social and task roles.

As the Teacher, What Should You Do As Students Are Working in Groups?

This is a major consideration. There are some important (and often very subtle) things that you can do to help make peer-group work effective. Our suggestion is to become an active *facilitator* whenever your students are working in peer groups. Move around the room. When you approach a group, sit down with the students; towering over the students usually disrupts the interaction. Listen for at least thirty seconds before saying anything; this will allow you to pick up the gist of the conversation without disrupting. At that point, you might interject with appropriate Trigger or Probe questions, modeling effective questioning for the students. If a student raises an important point, let the group know—it's a great way to encourage them to think in more depth. Finally, you might make suggestions on points the group could consider next. If the group interaction is productive and on target, you might even move on to the next group without saying anything.

A very practical suggestion: When you sit with individual groups, try to put yourself in a place where you can see the entire room. Over time, you'll find that you'll be able to listen and watch multiple groups at the same time and to pick up a lot about the progress of other groups just by noticing subtle visual clues.

Any Other Suggestions?

When reconvening the full class after a peer-group activity, allow students to share ideas generated in the groups. This is crucial and again reinforces the notion that what happens in the peer groups is important. For extended peer-group experiences, we also suggest allowing group members to monitor the progress of the group in writing. Ask each student to respond to a questionnaire that challenges him to reflect on what he's learned and to describe which students contributed what to the group's progress (an effective final question on such a questionnaire: "Our group could have accomplished more if _____ ").

So much for the general advice on making peer-group work productive. At this point, let's take a look at some specific peer-group/cooperative-learning techniques that have been shown to be effective across subjects and grade levels.

Focal Point 3 What Peer-Group and Cooperative-Learning Techniques Have Been Shown to Be Effective in the Classroom?

Jigsaw I and II

One of the most frequently used cooperative-learning techniques is called *Jigsaw*. Developed by Aronson (1978), Jigsaw has proven to be highly successful subject areas and grade levels. We highly recommend the technique to both middle- and high-school teachers. Jigsaw is based on the belief that you can learn a lot about important facts, concepts, and principles by trying to teach them to another person. Jigsaw events usually focus on a unit of study that can be broken up into four to six component pieces, or sections.

Discussion 3 What Peer-Group and Cooperative-Learning Techniques Have Been Shown to Be Effective in the Classroom?

Let's say that Mr. Nathan, an eighth-grade geography teacher, is preparing to teach a unit on India, and he wishes to make the Jigsaw technique a major focus. He could break the material into five essential geographical themes: location, place, human–environment interactions, movement, and regions. He would then arrange his students in heterogeneous groups of five, and each student would then choose (or be assigned) to become an expert with regard to one of the chosen themes as it relates to India. The Jigsaw groups are then broken up; all of the students who have chosen to investigate the same theme then meet together in what are known as *expert groups* (e.g., all students investigating location as it relates to India meet in one group). Students in each expert group then research their part of the unit, learning as much as they can about it, and make decisions about how they might *teach* their theme effectively to the members of their Jigsaw group. The teacher facilitates this researching process (note the terrific opportunities here for using the Internet and investigating relevant Websites as part of this research). After some period of time, the Jigsaw groups then reconvene, and each *expert* has a chance to teach her subject to the rest of the group. To ensure some level of group and individual accountability, all students are tested or complete some other assignment on the entire unit and also receive a group grade based on the cumulative grades received by all other members. We have found that the Jigsaw approach allows for other forms of assessment as well; there are wonderful opportunities for students to complete individual or group projects as part of this process.

Again, research has shown the Jigsaw method to be highly effective in a wide range of settings. As for using the technique in a constructivist classroom setting, we encourage you to connect projects with the process and to allow groups of students options in choosing how they show what they have learned.

The Structured Controversy Approach

One of our favorite techniques, known as the *Structured Controversy Approach* (Johnson & Johnson, 1988), features structured debate and an emphasis on development of critical-thinking abilities within a peer-group setting. The process starts with students working together in heterogeneous groups of four. At that point, the entire class is introduced to a controversial issue; within each group of four, pairs of students are asked to argue for one side of the issue. Students in each group are given time to research their side of the issue and to prepare arguments (again, note the opportunities here for emphasizing in-depth student research and the use of outside resources). The groups then meet for a discussion, with each group presenting its arguments on both sides of the issue. As an interesting twist, toward the end of the session, challenge the pairs to switch sides and argue for the *other* position. We suggest asking each group to try to reach consensus on a solution (although this isn't always possible, or desirable, it is a worthwhile goal for the groups to often strive for).

You can tie a range of assessment approaches to this technique. The students can write group or individual reports, prepare presentations, or develop HyperStudio or PowerPoint presentations that convey their position on the issues. As a variation, you can ask different groups in your class to research and debate related but *different* issues, then report their findings to the rest of the class through presentations.

We have had a great deal of success with this technique in a wide range of classroom settings and in different subjects, and we highly recommend the approach. All subjects *do* lend themselves to this technique. For example, one recent student teacher working with one of the authors included a structured controversy debate on the possible repeal of legalized gambling in the state of Illinois as part of a high school probability and statistics course. The students found the experience tremendously effective because it challenged them to apply statistical concepts at the highest levels as they researched an issue that was real and highly relevant.

Teams-Games-Tournaments

This approach (Slavin, 1990) combines elements of cooperative learning and individual and team competition. We would advise you not to overuse the technique in a constructivist classroom setting, but we have found that it can provide an interesting change of pace if used infrequently.

To start, arrange your students in heterogeneous peer groups of four to six. The members of each group are asked to study (and possibly research) assigned material together and to help one another understand the main ideas as deeply as possible; this interaction is one of the best features of this approach. After this researching/studying period, assign your students to sit in groups of three with members from other groups. This provides the tournament setting. As the tournament leader, you now direct questions to the entire class, with each student an-

swering the questions on paper; 1, 2, or 3 points are awarded to the original teams based on how well team members do in comparison with students from other teams seated at the same table. Individual scores on the tournament test are also recorded, again emphasizing group and individual accountability. The process is later repeated with different material and new tournament groups. Keep track of the points earned by the teams over time, and make these team points a part of each student's overall course grade.

Because of the highly competitive nature of this technique, we'd suggest being careful not to overuse it. It can be an effective change of pace if utilized once in a while.

Group Retellings

This relatively simple peer-group technique can be used in the context of many of the methods that we'll introduce later in this guide book. You divide your class into heterogeneous groups of two to four. Ask each person in each group to read different material on the same subject. For example, a biology teacher conducting a unit on immunology might ask students to read different articles focused on the AIDS epidemic. One student in each group might read an article on the latest research findings on treatment of the disease; another might read about the scope of the epidemic in Africa; a third might read a position paper calling for increased funding for research. After the students read the articles (possibly as homework), convene the groups and ask students to take turns *telling* others in the group about their article in detail (again, we find the knowing-through-teaching approach). Listeners *retell* the ideas in their peers' articles, then add to the retelling with a related point from their own articles or from their own experiences (here's where facilitating/asking of follow-up questions by the teacher can help). After the completion of the small-group discussions, you can challenge the groups to *process* the discussions by summarizing the main points emphasized for the rest of the class or through some kind of group or individual writing assignment.

Again, this is a very versatile technique suited to any subject or grade level. We have found it to be particularly useful when the discussion focuses on recent articles that reflect differing viewpoints on important issues.

Response Groups

In groups of three or four, each member reads or presents a piece of original work she has done for the course; for example, an essay, a brief experiment, an original drawing. The other group members respond to the presenter according to a heuristic (a coded pattern of response; see Module Four) that ensures they are both supportive as well as critically helpful. Response groups can be motivating when the presentations consist of products that will be evaluated by the teacher, peers, or professionals as part of authentic learning.

Cybernetic Sessions

This final peer-group technique is a great way to review ideas in any subject area and at any grade level. The basic idea is to help students through a process of analysis, synthesis, and problem solving by discussion of thought-provoking questions. Prepare for a Cybernetic Session by writing six to ten challenging new questions regarding important concepts or principles introduced earlier. For example, an English teacher conducting a unit on Shakespearean tragedy might prepare questions based on the way that different players are characterized during the first act of *Hamlet*. A science teacher might write the kinds of questions that would be included in a lab practicum and assemble materials that might allow students to determine or discover the answers.

The next step is to prepare your classroom for the session. We suggest writing your questions on poster boards and fastening them to the walls in different parts of your room, placing any accompanying materials nearby. Arrange your class in groups of three to five for the start of the session and begin with each group placed at a different station. Start the session by asking the groups to consider and discuss the question at their station, with a recorder in each group jotting down a group response. After a set time period, ask the group to rotate to the next station and continue until each group has completed the entire circuit. After the session, you might include any number of assessment approaches. We also suggest asking the groups to process the experience by sharing ideas in a *wrap-up* discussion.

■ ROUNDUP ■

In Part 1 of this module, we've addressed some of the initial questions regarding peer-group work in the classroom. We noted that the impact of group work, and especially cooperative-learning techniques, has been studied in some depth over the past twenty years. These findings, and our own classroom experiences, have provided us with convincing evidence that peer-group techniques can have a dramatic, positive impact on the learning of students across subjects and grade levels. Not only do these techniques enhance students' understanding of new ideas, and their abilities to utilize higher-cognitive-level reasoning strategies but they also provide

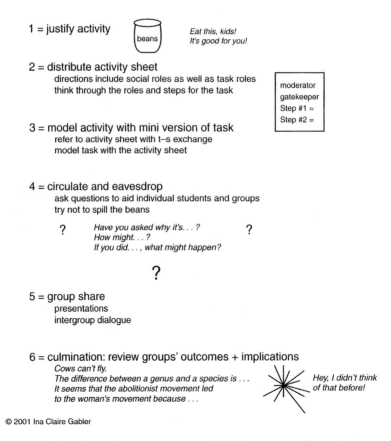

1 = justify activity   *Eat this, kids!*
    beans   *It's good for you!*

2 = distribute activity sheet
    directions include social roles as well as task roles
    think through the roles and steps for the task

    moderator
    gatekeeper
    Step #1 =
    Step #2 =

3 = model activity with mini version of task
    refer to activity sheet with t–s exchange
    model task with the activity sheet

4 = circulate and eavesdrop
    ask questions to aid individual students and groups
    try not to spill the beans

    ?   *Have you asked why it's. . . ?*   ?
        How might. . . ?
        If you did. . . , what might happen?

    ?

5 = group share
    presentations
    intergroup dialogue

6 = culmination: review groups' outcomes + implications
    Cows can't fly.
    The difference between a genus and a species is . . .
    It seems that the abolitionist movement led   *Hey, I didn't think*
    to the woman's movement because . . .   *of that before!*

© 2001 Ina Claire Gabler

FIGURE 6.1 Peer-Group Learning (PGL) Technique Flowchart

a wide range of positive *affective* benefits. We have seen firsthand the impact that well-planned peer-group experiences can have on students who are discouraged, alienated, and/or struggling to understand material.

In addressing our second guiding question, we provided you some important practical advice for implementing peer-group events in your classroom. Remember that peer-group events take a lot of thought and careful planning. We've also seen firsthand the impact that *negative* group experiences can have on young people, so remember to be thoughtful and intentional when implementing group events.

Finally, we took a look at some of the many possible techniques available to you. In later modules, we'll provide additional examples and discuss in more detail what it takes to embed peer-group techniques into larger teaching *methods.* As we move on, remember that PGL events are *quintessential* components of the constructivist classroom; they provide students with thought-provoking and truly empowering learning experiences.

Our flowchart in Figure 6.1 gives you a look at the generic features of a PGL.

■ HANDS-ON PRACTICE ■

1. Start by writing a Rationale (see Module Three) for your PGL event: What will you challenge students to do? How will you accomplish this?

2. Will you utilize a specific peer-group or cooperative-learning technique? If so, which one?

3. How will you arrange students for the peer-group event (e.g., randomly, in assigned groups)? What is the optimum group size?

4. What will you ask students to *do* in their groups? Try phrasing your instructions as you you would provide them for your students. Consider roles for group members.

5. How much time will you allow for this event?

6. What questions *might* you ask group members as they work?

7. How will you *process* the group learning event (e.g., through a summarizing discussion)?

REFERENCES

Aronson, E. (1978). *The jigsaw classroom.* Beverly Hills, CA: Sage Publications.

Johnson, R., & Johnson, D. (1988, May). Critical thinking through structured controversy. *Educational Leadership, 58–64.*

Johnson, R., & Johnson, D. (1989). *Cooperation and competition: Theory and research.* Edina, MN: Interaction Books.

Johnson, D., & Johnson, R. (1993). *Cooperation in the classroom.* Edina, MN: Interaction Books.

Johnson, D., Johnson, R., & Holubec, E. (1990). *Circles of learning: Cooperation in the classroom.* Edina, MN: Interaction Books.

Putnam, J. (1997). *Cooperative learning in diverse classrooms.* Upper Saddle River, NJ: Merrill.

Sharan, S. (1990). *Handbook of cooperative learning methods.* Westport, CT: Greenwood Press.

Slavin, R. (1990). *Cooperative learning: Theory, research, and practice.* Englewood Cliffs, NJ: Prentice-Hall.

Slavin, R. (1995). *Cooperative learning.* Boston, MA: Allyn & Bacon.

PART 2
Activity Sheets

Overview

Goals

Focal Point and Discussion

Varied Quality of Handouts

Putting It All Together

Roundup

Hands-On practice

■ OVERVIEW

Your students, heads bowed close to the desk, scratching their answers on paper, are industriously at work. The principal glimpses your class through the door window, and she nods approval.

But the story isn't over. Not until we look at those papers and the nature of your students' responses.

Aye, here's the rub: What <u>kinds of questions</u> are your students answering? Neat blanks that fit into statements like pieces in a jigsaw puzzle? a collection of "right" answers? multiple choices? responses that repeat what you and the textbook said?

Reflect on what your students have *learned*. What will they retain in a week? a month? a year? Will they remember just a handful of facts—or will they be contemplating interrelated concepts that give meaning to facts?

■ GOALS

Our intention is to convey the difference between effective activity sheets and busywork sheets. We'll discuss the following topics:

- Activity sheets versus worksheets
- Activity sheets and techniques
- Activity sheets as versatile learning guides
- Effective and ineffective handouts
- Activity sheets for peer-group learning

■ FOCAL POINTS AND DISCUSSIONS

Broadly speaking, we categorize handouts under two categories, *worksheets* and *activity sheets*. Worksheets, which we call busywork sheets, are about inserting and circling discrete answers or completing limited statements. They tend to operate at lower cognitive levels, rarely challenging students to think critically; they imply low expectations. In addition, for the most part, they're boring. Why should your students care? If they don't care, they won't retain much. That's when you and they think that they're not "good learners." Or, just as undesirable, because your students may be able to temporarily rattle off a string of dates, events, and details or briefly complete a sentence, they think they're learning a lot.

Activity sheets, by contrast, serve as *prompts* (questions, directions, and tasks that generate original interpretation) for critical thinking and problem solving—not for squeezing a word or two into a blank or completing a statement as the terminal point. No. Instead, your students are writing original, justified interpretations; drawing original diagrams or graphics like concept maps; exploring both sides of an event, issue, or hypothesis; then producing the answers to conceptual and thematic questions.

If this is the case when the principal looks in, then your students are gainfully employed with an *activity sheet,* a tool of *invisible teaching.*

The more students are challenged with high expectations, the higher their performance level. This applies *especially* to students whose abilities are often underestimated because conventional teaching methods fail to relate to their frames of reference and, as a result, fail to motivate. This phenomenon is no great surprise. Boredom deadens the mind and will.

Activity sheets need a careful balance of the familiar with the new, a balance of Bloom's lower-cognitive prompts and higher-cognitive prompts, so that learners gain firm footing before they take leaps with critical thinking. We'll discuss other significant details about the design of activity sheets later on. For now, we want to emphasize the importance of careful planning and reflection each time you write an activity sheet. Writing an effective activity sheet should be a creative process for you. If writing it feels mechanical or formulaic, then working on it will merely be busywork for your students, so start over!

Focal Point 1 **Varied Quality of Handouts**

Form versus Function

Handouts vary greatly in their role, that is, their function, while the form (e.g., questions and fill-in tables) may be identical (see Module Three). Even when two handouts both contain open-ended questions that invite students to respond in their own words, there may be tremendous difference between those handouts regarding cohesion and cognitive demands. Our aim here is to distinguish mediocre handouts like busywork sheets or worksheets from activity sheets. We suspect that when you were a student, you worked mostly on worksheets, especially fill-in-the-blanks along with open-ended statements that required repetition of what the teacher or textbook said. This *apprenticeship by observation* (Lortie, 1975) can foil you as a constructivist teacher.

Discussion 1 Varied Quality of Handouts Examples of Handouts

Let's start by comparing and contrasting Figures 6.3 and 6.4. They both attempt to promote original thinking for the same lesson on solving a riddle, but they function differently. For each example, jot down what you think are the strengths and weaknesses. Then compare your analysis to ours after each figure. We provide the riddle in Figure 6.2 and the lesson Rationale to orient you. (Refer to Module Three for Core Components if necessary.)

Social Roles and Task Roles

Notice that there are two sets of roles. *Social roles* help your students to interact productively and to carry out the task well. *Task roles* describe the steps that carry out the learning activity.

EXAMPLE #1/ENGLISH LESSON FOR SEVENTH GRADE (CLASS ARRANGED IN GROUPS OF FOUR)

Rationale

> *What?:* To solve the riddle, *What's This?,* by Ina Claire Gabler.
>
> *Why?:* To build further understanding of how metaphors work. To develop higher-level cognitive skills, especially analysis and synthesis applied to the clues and solution of this riddle.
>
> *Justification:* To be determined by you after you analyze the handouts in Figures 6.3a, 6.3b, 6.4a, and 6.4b.

Now consider Figures 6.4a, 6.4b as handouts for the same lesson. Be ready to compare and contrast the handouts in Figures 6.3a/b and 6.4a/b.

What's This?

Within a moon that has no face,
A curtain shields a silent place
In which a sea both still and clear
Contains a sun that doesn't sear.

The moon is cracked; the sun goes free—
Until it's part of you or me.

Answer (backwards): gge na.

FIGURE 6.2 A Riddle
© 2001 Ina Claire Gabler

Can you solve the riddle "What's This?" by Ina Claire Gabler

1. Social Roles
   a. Moderator—makes sure that everyone participates at least twice. Moderator starts off the activity by responding first.
   b. Prompter—probes and encourages others when responses need more explanation.
   c. Gatekeeper—makes sure everyone is respectful of others' ideas.
   d. Timekeeper—watches the time indicated and announces when there are two minutes left.
2. Task Roles: Follow directions on the handout.

FIGURE 6.3A Active or Passive Thinking?

Compare and contrast the strengths and weaknesses in Figures 6.3a, 6.3b, 6.4a, and 6.4b from a student's point of view. Consider these features:

- Sequence of questions and tasks
- Clarity
- Cohesion
- Cognitive levels

Also consider possible strengths in terms of how the peer-group learning technique has been organized. From the student perspective, what do you experience as weaknesses or omissions? What other features might help learners succeed with the task of deciphering clues that are charged with cognitive dissonance (contradictions with commonly held associations)? After you analyze Figures 6.3a/b and 6.4a/b, see if you agree with our analysis, which follows.

Our Analysis of Figures 6.3a and b

STRENGTHS

- Clear social roles for productive student exchange
- Question at the top of the handout for direction
- Attempts to challenge students to think on higher cognitive levels
- Clear criteria for the product (combining at least three clues to write a possible solution)

WEAKNESSES AND OMISSIONS

- Allotted time for the task not specified, thereby making the role of timekeeper superfluous. Also, students need to learn to gauge their time.
- Similarly, there are not enough prompts (guiding questions and tasks) in Part 1 for each member in the group of four to participate at least twice, as specified in the moderator's role.

Your Goal: Solving the Riddle!!!

Part One

Directions: Define a metaphor. Then choose the best answer for each clue.

A. A metaphor is a(n)_____ that has a_____ meaning.

B. Tell how each clue is a metaphor. Choose the best answer for each clue.

  1. " . . . moon without a face . . . "

  (a) a monster (b) dark moon (c) something smooth and white

  2. "A curtain shields a silent place"

  (a) something protective (b) a cover (c) a kind of flimsy wall

  3. " . . . a sea both still and clear"

  (a) a large crossing (b) calmness (c) a pool of liquid

  4. " . . . a sun that doesn't sear"

  (a) a picture of a sun (b) something round and yellow (c) a happy event

C. What is the answer to the riddle? Put your heads together to figure it out!

Part Two

Directions: Complete each statement as a group. Be thoughtful.

1. What are at least three clues in the riddle that you think are most important. Why?
2. Try to integrate these clues to guess the riddle's answer. Defend your answer.
3. Why are metaphors important to solving the riddle?

FIGURE 6.3B Active or Passive Thinking?

Reading between the lines of "What's This?" by Ina Claire Gabler

1. Assign Social Roles
  a. Moderator—makes sure that everyone participates at least twice. Moderator starts off the activity by responding first.
  b. Prompter—probes and encourages others when responses need more explanation.
  c. Gatekeeper—makes sure everyone is respectful of others' ideas.
  d. Timekeeper—watches the time indicated and announces when there are two minutes left.
2. Task Roles
  a. (*20 minutes*) Write down each clue in the riddle on the accompanying chart and describe your associations with that clue.
  b. When you finish with task "a," discuss possible metaphoric meanings with each clue and jot them down alongside the literal associations.
  c. Decide if the answer is animal, mineral, or vegetable. Explain why.
  d. (*10 minutes*) Try to guess the answer to the riddle.
3. Can you explain how *every clue* fits the answer?

FIGURE 6.4A Active or Passive Thinking?

- Neither the title question in Figure 6.3A nor the goal in Figure 6.3B gives insight into the value of the task beyond "getting the answer" to the riddle. An improved goal as a question might be, "What metaphors in the clues help you solve this riddle?" This is another example of the difference between the *form* (the definition or intention of a goal) and its *function* (the role or instructional value).

- No model item. Even open-ended questions like the ones in Part Two of Figure 6.3b can be modeled to demonstrate how the answer must be thorough. Modeling can also address the criteria in the questions; for example, whether the answers must be written in complete sentences, whether phrases will do, and so on.

- In Part One, metaphoric meaning is not effectively integrated into the task despite an effort to do so. The clues provided along with multiple-choice answers reduce this task to a mechanical exercise. Teacher expectations are low because there is too much spoonfeeding. Compare this approach with that in the table in Figure 6.4b, where prompts encourage student interpretation.

- In Part Two, metaphoric meaning is brought in only as a sudden and separate concept in question 3 in Figure 6.3b. Compare this approach with that in the

Big Question: What metaphors in the clues help solve the riddle?

Clues	Associations for Each Clue = (literal and metaphoric)	How Each Clue Fits the Same Possible Solution
1. "A moon without a face. . . ." (Model this example with student input.)	1. (student responses to the model =) literal = unlit moon, a moon of another planet; metaphoric = something not fully formed, something sad, something resembling a moon without markings.	1. An egg resembles a moon and has no markings.
2.	2.	2.
3.	3.	3.
4.	4.	4.
5.	5.	5.
6.	6.	6.
7.	7.	7.
8.	8.	8.

Is the answer, mineral, or vegetable, and why?

What do you think the answer is?
Prove it in the last column!

FIGURE 6.4B   Big Question: What metaphors in the clues help solve the riddle?

table in Figure 6.4b. Thinking metaphorically is the only way to solve the riddle.

- Because thinking metaphorically all along is essential to succeeding in the task, the prompts in Part Two as questions 1 and 2 might frustrate rather than assist the students in thinking through a solution.
- Compromised rigor. In Part 2, the critera call for only three clues. Not only is this too easy but also, ironically, makes the task more difficult. The demands are insufficient for students to succeed with the task.
- The Rationale may fail because of the flaws in the handout.

Our Analysis of Figure 6.4a and b

STRENGTHS

- Clear social roles that facilitate productive student exchange.
- Clear and well-sequenced task guidelines.
- The overarching question refers to the content, that is, applying metaphors, not just to the task itself of solving the riddle.
- Rigor: every clue must be matched to a possible solution.
- The table includes a model example for which students must provide responses as a rehearsal

for the task, perhaps in a teacher-led minidiscussion.

- The *animal, mineral, vegetable* question helps to synthesize students' thinking about the metaphoric value of the clues.
- Cohesion carries out the Rationale by guiding the thinking process from literal to metaphoric meanings of the riddle's clues according to Bloom's Taxonomy. Metaphoric thinking is *integrated into the task* that's structured by the table, yet open-ended for original input.
- Prompts and criteria are clear and provide appropriate focus.

"And the Winner Is . . ."

Figure 6.4a and b contains an activity sheet rather than a busywork sheet because it encourages students to work independently and think creatively. Remember that the social roles are clear. The task is also clear and well sequenced, integrating metaphoric thinking, crucial for success in solving the riddle. The prompts (items in the table) guide students to focus their thinking process and keep their eye on the metaphoric values. The *animal, mineral, or vegetable* question helps students to zero in on the answer. Overall, this activity sheet unfolds a cohesive process and is designed for peer groups to utilize social

---

The dare: Prepare a case that argues (for/against) flying the Confederate flag in public today

Your Job
1. Dig up as much information about the Confederate flag as you can from various sources (books, journals, newspapers, the Internet, documentaries, etc.).
2. Employ this information to write a persuasive argument that either (a) supports the right to fly the Confederate flag in public or (b) denies the right to fly the Confederate flag anywhere in the United States.

The Challenge
1. You will be assigned to a group that argues for a given position (for or against flying the Confederate flag in public) regardless of your personal view on the matter. Your group will establish its own social roles and delegate appropriate tasks.
2. You will assume the identity of an historical figure of your choice who would support your assigned viewpoint. This may be a famous person of your choice (American President, military general, writer, abolitionist, etc.) or a typical private citizen of your choice (Northern industrialist, plantation owner, freed slave, religious person, racial or religious minority child, etc.). EACH PERSON IN THE GROUP MUST ASSUME A DIFFERENT IDENTITY.
3. You must argue from the historical perspective to people in the 21st century. This means that your research must focus on the individual perspective you select.

Prompts
1. Is flying the Confederate flag today in the 21st century an act of treason or an expression of First Amendment rights of free speech?
2. Is the Civil War really over? Explain fully.
3. What does the Confederate flag symbolize? To whom?

Criteria
1. Refer to a minimum of six *substantive* sources. This includes the following.
   a. at least two books (no textbooks)
   b. at least one Website with *documented* sources
   c. at least one reputable journal or newspaper with *documented* sources (may include historical publications from past centuries on microfiche)
2. The written argument must adhere to the form of a persuasive essay learned in English class, complete with bibliography.
   a. Include at least six paragraphs: Introduction, Conclusion, and at least four paragraphs in the body. Each body paragraph should have at least three details to support its main idea.
   b. Cite and counter at least one opposing argument to your position.
   c. Include historical background as well as cultural factors. Include at least one authentic anecdote to support your position or to undermine your opposition.
3. The oral debate must employ your research findings from the individual perspective you assume. Be prepared to debate one other group for fifteen minutes. There will be three rounds with different groups.

FIGURE 6.5 Social Studies/Twelfth Grade: Role-Play

roles to full advantage. That means that the activity has a high chance of satisfying the Rationale: Even if the students don't solve the riddle, this activity sheet promotes a successful lesson because the prompts and criteria keep learners thinking—and guided so that their frustration level is minimized.

Contrast Figure 6.3a and b. The latter is too teacher controlled. The handout employs too few clues. This approach may appear to be less overwhelming to the students, but it also utilizes insufficient information. In Figure 6.3b, the teacher's attempt to be helpful results in spoon-feeding in the multiple-choice questions and shuts the door to critical thinking before it opens. For these reasons, Figure 6.3a and b contains a *busywork* sheet.

EXAMPLE #2/SOCIAL STUDIES LESSON F R TWELFTH GRADE

Now that you have an idea of the difference be-tween a busywork sheet and an activity sheet, see what you think of the example in Figure 6.5. W not asking you to compare and contrast different sions for the same lesson this time. Instead, try to spot the strengths and weaknesses in each example, applying what you've learned from the handouts in Example #1. For starters, we think you'll have fun with Figure 6.5. Jot down your own analysis before you look at ours.

Our Analysis

This activity sheet is designed for students socialized for cooperative learning in which each member contributes individually. Did you catch that students are even instructed to define and assign their own social roles within the group? The role-play technique is applied to a research assignment, thereby personalizing the application of the research findings. The debate as a Performance Objective demands the higher-level cognitive skills of analyzing, synthesizing, and evaluation. The activity sheet governs this self-directed project so that the teacher becomes a facilitator or mentor. Finally, this project is an example of what constructivist teaching aspires to. If you resocialize even middle school students from all backgrounds to shift from passive to active learners, they will be able to carry out this project with just such an activity sheet and amaze themselves. (See Module Two, "Resocializing.")

EXAMPLE #3/SCIENCE LESSON FOR TENTH GRADE

You might want to steal the idea in Figure 6.6a–c even if you're not a science teacher. The idea in Figure 6.6b is to model two different ways of organizing the same data. In Figure 6.6c, the same principle is applied to designing two different concept maps for fruits and vegetables. Pause to consider what you think the strengths and weaknesses are of Figure 6.6c. Then compare your analysis with ours.

Our Analysis

This lesson is another example of what constructivist teaching aims for. The task of reorganizing the same data under different characteristics or criteria requires students to move through Bloom's Taxonomy from definition, comprehension, and application to the higher cognitive levels of analysis and synthesis, all as independent learners, guided by the activity sheet. It also demonstrates the enormous flexibility and potential of the activity sheet as a tool that uses a wide variety of techniques. *Figures 6.6b and 6.6c could also be used for individuals without peer exchange.*

Putting It All Together

We've designed this part of Module Six as an inductive learning experience for you. In other words, we've displayed and analyzed several examples of the concept of an activity sheet, invited you to analyze along the way, and now invite you to identify or define the salient elements of an effective activity sheet. You may want to review the examples to refresh your memory and even to catch new details you may have missed.

Big Question: Can you design two concept maps that depict two valid taxonomies for fruits and vegetables?

Social Roles
1. Approach this brainstorm as a fully cooperative team.
2. Take turns being prompters who ask something like "What are the distinguishing characteristics in this (tomato, avocado, potato, etc.)?" "How does this (tomato, avocado, potato) compare to the (banana, coconut, etc.)?" The person with the earliest birthday begins.
3. Select a scribe who draws the concept maps.
4. Select a presenter who will share your concept maps with the class.
5. Assign a timekeeper who alerts the group when only five minutes is left.

Your Job
1. Problem solve in groups of four. You have forty minutes.
2. Cut open and examine the fruits and vegetables given you. (Each group has different specimens.) Observe textures, inner contents, shape, manner of growth, and so on.
3. Infer what characteristics fruits have in common and what characteristics vegetables have in common.
4. Design concept map #1 that demonstrates the interrelationship between larger categories and subcategories.
   a. Decide on at least three broad categories for the taxonomy.
   b. Identify at least two characteristics for each category.
   c. Compare and contrast your specimens to sharpen your observations.
5. Then reconsider the categories represented by concept map #1 and use different characteristics to establish different categories. Represent this second taxonomy in concept map #2. Repeat the criteria in instruction #4 above.

FIGURE 6.6A Science: Designing Concept Maps

Big Question: Can you organize data for a concept map that depicts a valid taxonomy for animals?	**Big Question: Can you organize data for a concept map that depicts a valid but different taxonomy for animals?**
Sample Concept Map #1/Data:	Sample Concept Map #2/Data:
[Filled in with student responses for modeling purposes. *Italics represents student input.*]	[Filled in with student responses for modeling purposes. *Italics represents student input.*]
Broad category: Animals Characteristics: 1. self-reproduce (given) 2. *respire* 3. *eliminate bodily wastes, etc.*	Broad category: Animals Characteristics: 1. self-reproduce (given) 2. *respire* 3. *eliminate bodily wastes, etc.*

Subcategories and characteristics #1:
1. fish (given)
   a. *have gills*
   b. *live in water*
   c. *carnivorous and herbivorous*
2. *mammals*
   a. *warm-blooded*
   b. *live births (etc.)*
3. *reptiles*
   a. *cold-blooded*
   b. *external birth (eggs), etc.*
	Subcategories and characteristics #2:
	1. land animals (given)
	   a. *human beings walk on 2 legs, warm-blooded, mammals, have live births, different racial groups*
	   b. *lizards, reptiles, cold-blooded, lay eggs*
	2. *sea animals*
	   a. *fish have gills, swim, lay eggs*
	   b. *whales, mammals, live births*
	3. *amphibians*
	   a. *frogs develop as tadpoles in water, adults live on land and in water, lay eggs*
	   b. *turtles, etc.*

FIGURE 6.6B Science: Designing Concept Maps (continued)

Stop here to do this task, then read on and compare your key elements to ours. If you caught some addition to our list, please let us know via the editor for Curriculum and Instruction.

Elements of an Activity Sheet

1. Provides an *overarching question* that relates to the *Rationale,* not to the task itself

2. Unfolds the *Performance Objective*

3. Embeds the parts of the Performance Objective into the *directions* of the activity sheet

4. Incorporates various *techniques,* including, but not limited to, the traditional use of questions and fill-ins that carry out the Performance Objective

5. Contains clear prompts for the Performance Objective

6. Provides fill-ins that serve as stepping-stones to critical thinking and that are *not the terminal task*

7. Applies to peer-group or solo activity with directions written accordingly and specifies *social roles* for a peer-group activity (see Module Six, Part 1, "Peer-Group Learning")

8. Includes or describes any necessary *materials*

■ ROUNDUP ■

An activity sheet can function as a compass for your students, guiding them independently through a lesson or project that involves traditional sources and/or technology. Substance is revealed and critical thinking is achieved through effective instructional methods, such as those in this guide book. Techniques, as you recall, are practices and procedures that carry out a method or a combination of methods, so your students need techniques that enable them to meaningfully learn with and without a computer. One effective material that maximizes learning with any resource and numerous techniques is the activity sheet.

We recommend that you don't limit your handouts to fill-in questions, even those that facilitate critical thinking. Use your imagination to incorporate other techniques into the activity sheet, similar to those in this module and in Module Four. For example, you can include Hooks that personalize a frame of reference; write prompts for role-playing animate or inanimate figures; require original concept maps; employ heuristics, brainstorming, or guidelines for question writing for peers, and so on. The list is as endless as your imagination.

For practice writing activity sheets, use the following Hands-On Practice.

■ HANDS-ON PRACTICE ■

Writing a constructivist activity sheet combines intellectual rigor with creativity and clear focus with an understanding of how your students learn at a given point in time. We'll supply some prompts here to get you going and to remind you to draw on a full repertoire of techniques. In addition, you may want to use your own techniques that have not been included here.

Self-Instruct Planners: Designing Activity Sheets

(Work on a separate piece of paper.)

Note: If you want, keep building on the same topic you used in other self-instruct planners. Or choose another topic. Remember to refer to Bloom's Taxonomy as you plan.

Subject_____

Topic_____

Prompts to Help You Focus

1. Formulate your *Rationale.*

2. Decide on an *overarching question* that relates to the Rationale, not to the task itself.

3. Decide on an appropriate *Performance Objective.*

4. Embed the Performance Objective in the *directions* of the activity sheet.

5. Review the various *techniques* you have learned, including those you used in the Hands-On Practice in Module Four.

6. Decide which technique(s) will carry out the Performance Objective.

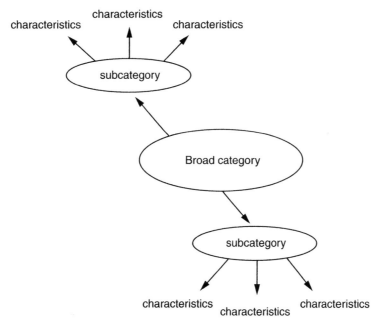

Big Question: Can you design two concept maps that depict different taxonomies for fruits and vegetables?

Directions: Fill in and enlarge this concept map for fruits and vegetables similar to how you organized the data in the "animal" sample.

FIGURE 6.6c Science: Designing Concept Maps

7. Write several clear step-by-step prompts, like the ones here.

8. Decide if you want this to be a peer-group activity or a solo activity. Write directions accordingly. For a peer-group activity, remember to specify *social roles.*

9. Include or describe any necessary *materials.*

SUGGESTED READING

Bonwell, C. C., & Eison, J. A. (1991). *Active learning: Creating excitement in the classroom.* Washington, DC: Washington University, School of Education and Human Development.

Dale, H. (1994). Collaborative writing interactions in one ninth-grade classroom. *Journal of Educational Research, 87*(6), 334–344.

Fenton, C. (1992). Cooperative learning: A view from the inside. *Contemporary Education, 63*(3), 207–209.

Hill, M. (1992). Strategies for encouraging collaborative learning with a traditional classroom. *Contemporary Education, 63*(3), 213–215.

Jacobs, G. (1988). Co-operative goal structure: A way to improve group activities. *ELT Journal, 42*(2), 97–101.

Johnson, D. W., & Johnson, R. (1990). *Learning together and alone.* Englewood Cliffs, NJ: Prentice-Hall.

Kahn, E. A., Walter, C. C., & Johannessen, L. R. (1984, February). Making small groups work: Controversy is the key. *English Journal,* 63–65.

Lortie, D. C. (1975). *Schoolteacher: A sociological study.* Chicago: University of Chicago Press.

Putnam, J. (1997). *Cooperative learning in diverse classrooms.* Columbus, OH: Prentice-Hall.

Sharan, S. (1980). Cooperative learning in small groups: Recent methods and effects on achievement, attitudes and ethnic relations. *Review of Educational Research* (2), 241–271.

Wood, K. D. (1987, October). Fostering cooperative learning in middle and secondary level classrooms. *Journal of Reading,* 10–19.

CONSTRUCTIVIST METHODS

Our methods section contains seven constructivist methods, each with a discrete instructional strategy. Our method templates are intended to provide cohesive direction as you plan individual lessons and units. We believe that the variety of templates will help you expand your repertoire as a creative as well as intellectually rigorous teacher. Please keep in mind that the variety of individual templates is enhanced by possible *combo* lessons, in which you combine two or more methods in minisegments in a single lesson plan according to your instructional intentions.

Deductive and inductive frameworks and techniques (see Module Four) support the different methods in a similar way in which generic floor plan supports variations of buildings: a private dwelling, a house of worship, a factory. You'll find a graphic representation of this relationship in Figure C.1.

Summary of Methods

Here's a brief description of each method in Section C to give you a bird's-eye view, an advance organizer, of what's ahead.

1. ILPE Method (Investigating Learner's Previous Experiences). This method has two goals: (1) to introduce the teacher and to begin to know the students and (2) to discover what the students know about a given topic. Mostly, the teacher employs selective techniques that elicit students' ideas. This information will be used to plan future lessons, adjusted to student needs.

2. Deductive Concept Method. In this approach, the teacher defines the concept first and provides specific examples and nonexamples of the concept. Your students arrive at classifications, using feature analysis and comparison/contrast of examples and nonexamples (general to specific).

3. Inductive Concept Method. One or more concepts are taught inductively. The format is the reverse of the deductive format. You provide examples and nonexamples of a concept. With questions (NOT teacher talk), you lead students to a conceptual understanding, which includes student generation of the concept (specific to general).

4. Directed Discussion Method. Teacher-to-student interaction is emphasized here. Your series of questions related to materials facilitate students' grasp of one or more principles. The teacher's role is more dominant in this type of discussion than in the two subsequent discussion methods.

5. Exploratory Discussion Method. Through promotion of student-to-student interaction, this discussion allows the class to examine different perspectives of one concept or controversial issue. Students DO NOT arrive at a value judgment. Rather, they explore different points of view based on documentation. This is a student-centered method that may include role-play. The teacher's role is to ask

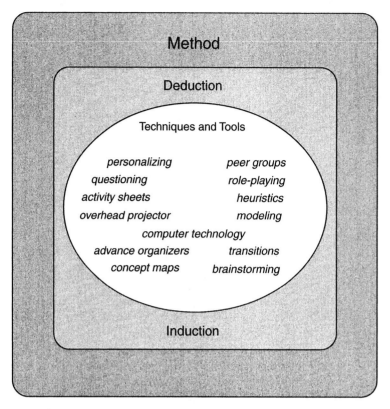

© 2001 Ina Claire Gabler

FIGURE C.1 Methods with Cognitive Frameworks, Techniques, and Tools

broad questions to steer the discussion if necessary—a prime example of *invisible teaching.*

6. Reflective Discussion Method. This is similar to the Exploratory Discussion method. The significant difference is that this method both explores different viewpoints and also requires students to arrive at their individual value judgments with logic based on documented *justification.* It may include role-play and is another prime example of *invisible teaching.*

7. Interactive Presentation Method. This template combines discrete parcels consisting of teacher mini-talks and student mini-tasks. The object is to engage students in active rather than passive listening and in independent thinking in a presentational format.

Each method also includes at least one Tip for Technology Integration.

Our methods are more than templates. They hold the potential to create a learning environment, a *context,* an approach to learning that expands the classroom. The student's role in learning becomes that of critical thinker, initiator of ideas and learning procedures. Your role becomes that of informed catalyst and even co-learner as your students mature as learners (see Module Two, "Resocializing").

As you read this section and possibly feel some resistance to implementing a given method, keep in mind that, yes, this method applies to *your* subject. In fact, you may be surprised by the sense of freedom and endless possibilities that these methods and your own future adaptations can realize.

Investigating Learners' Previous Experiences (ILPE) Method

Overview: Scenario Depicting an ILPE Lesson

Focal Points and Discussions

What Makes the ILPE Method Distinctive?

ILPE Lesson Planning Template

ILPE Method Markers

Up Close: Planning and Conducting an ILPE Lesson

When Should You Use the ILPE Method in Your Classroom?

Tips for Technology Integration

Roundup

ILPE Flowchart

ILPE Sample Lesson Plan

Hands-On Practice

■ OVERVIEW: SCENARIO DEPICTING AN ILPE LESSON

It's Monday morning, just before the start of Mr. Newman's third period physical science class. The students had taken a test the previous Friday, and they are about to embark on a new unit. There's an air of anticipation among the ninth- and tenth-grade students in the room. They know that their teacher likes to introduce new topics with open-ended, interactive activities.

The students settle into their seats, which are arranged in a circle today. The bell rings, and Mr. Newman steps out of the stockroom door. The students laugh as they see their teacher. He's wearing a string of blinking Christmas lights!

"Isn't it a little late for the lights, Mr. N.? It's March!" laughs Andy.

"Ha—it's never too late for this kind of excitement," replies Mr. Newman in mock surprise. "We're going to talk about a subject today that's a little shocking. I hope nobody minds." Nobody seems to mind; the students watch Newman as he trails his string of lights into the circle of seats, dropping carefully into an empty chair. "What do you think of when you hear the word *electricity*?" Hands fly into the air, and the teacher begins calling on students. The responses vary widely. Students mention things like microwaves, computers, cords, power plants, energy, batteries, and more. After most of the responses, Mr. Newman asks a follow-up question: "Why did you say energy, Nicole?" "How are power plants connected to electricity, Casey?" At one point, Nick volunteers "lightning."

"That's an interesting answer! Can anyone tell us how lightning is connected to electricity?" says Newman enthusiastically.

"I remember hearing that people a long time ago weren't sure what lightning was," responds Ami. "Didn't Ben Franklin fly a kite during a storm to learn more about lightning? I saw something about that at the museum." Other students add to Ami's answer; Mr. N. encourages this sharing of ideas with further questions. After a brief exchange, he tells the students that the class can investigate what Franklin did if they are interested.

Over the next five minutes, Newman asks more open-ended questions and receives a range of ideas. "How have you used electricity in the last twenty-four hours?" provokes the most responses. The students seem to recognize that this mysterious *thing* called electricity plays a big part in everyone's life, although they express a lot of wonder about what electricity is really like.

Ten minutes into the class period, Mr. Newman thanks the students for their input and tells them that they'll have a chance to learn more about many of the ideas that they have listed. "Now, I'm going to invite you to investigate electricity. A few minutes ago, Nick told us that batteries can supply electricity to toys and radios and other things. We're going to learn what we can about electricity by trying to get batteries to do some work." Newman, now without the blinking lights, moves to the projector screen, which had been covering part of the board and rolls it up with a dramatic flourish, revealing directions for a class activity. He provides pairs of students with a D battery, two wires, and a small lightbulb; their challenge is to find as many ways as they can to light the bulb, using these materials.

For the next twenty-five minutes, Newman moves around the room, watching each pair of students work to light the bulbs, asking occasional questions. There is a buzz of excitement in the room as successive pairs of students discover ways to meet this challenge. Some groups make their discoveries quickly, while others struggle; Mr. N. encourages these groups but never directs them toward a solution. He invites those groups that find more than one way to light the bulb to try other configurations and to vary the number of batteries, wires, and bulbs in what they would later call the *circuits*. The teacher also asks each group to diagram any configuration of materials that lights the bulb. He is especially careful to ask probe questions regarding their use of terms ("What do you mean by voltage, Keelan?") and to make careful observations. With a few minutes left in the period, Newman asks the students to turn in their materials and to share what they had learned, comparing and contrasting their diagrams (again, lots of teacher- and student-generated questions). The period ends with students writing a one-minute essay in response to the question, "What is one important question that you now have regarding electricity?"

■ FOCAL POINTS AND DISCUSSIONS

Focal Point 1 **What Makes the ILPE Method Distinctive?**

Welcome back from your short classroom visit. You have just taken part in what we call an ILPE lesson. ILPE is an acronym for "Investigating Learners' Previous Experiences." The main goals of a lesson like this are the following:

- To gain insights into your students' initial understanding of and interest in a topic
- To introduce a new topic in an engaging way

We like to think of ILPE lessons as opportunities for you to open windows into your students' minds. Although there are countless ways to do an ILPE lesson, these lessons generally include our main Core Components and some distinctive method markers, as we'll see in the sections that follow. You'll also discover that these lessons may last from a few minutes to an entire class period, depending on a number of factors.

Discussion 1 What Makes the ILPE Method Distinctive?

From a constructivist perspective, it makes sense to purposefully investigate the nature of student understanding frequently, because much of what they will learn depends on their prior experiences and associated frames of reference. In any case, students' varying frames of reference regarding any topic will have a major impact on their understanding of subject matter. It follows that one of the most important tasks for teachers is to investigate the nature of knowledge that students have regarding important concepts and principles, how this knowledge is organized, and how learners use the knowledge. Student attitudes regarding topics (and entire subjects), or perhaps how these topics were *taught,* also have an impact on their subsequent learning, so it makes sense to learn as much as we can about these attitudes as well.

In addition, two of the biggest decisions that we face as teachers are where to begin and how to proceed when embarking on a new instructional unit. These important decisions will depend in part on your curriculum, but also on your students and their initial understanding of important ideas related to your topic. It is obvious that a lesson focused on limits in a calculus class will fail if students have little grasp of important algebraic concepts. Similarly, if each student had played competitive volleyball for years, a lesson on the general rules of the game would be a waste of their time. You've probably discovered yourself that most individual differences in understanding are much more subtle. As a constructivist teacher, one of your most important goals will be to get into your students' heads to the greatest extent possible when deciding not only *what* to teach but *how* to teach it.

Gaining insights such as these are really what ILPE lessons are all about. Whether these lessons last from a few minutes to an entire class period, they can provide you with some important perspectives regarding the existing conceptions that your students hold and also offer glimpses into their attitudes, values, *and* preferred learning styles and modalities. In addition, these lessons provide students with opportunities to *generate questions that might serve to structure future lessons,* all in a highly interactive, motivational setting.

In Modules Seven through Twelve, we introduce a series of constructivist methods. Early in each of these modules, we'll share what we call a *lesson planning template,* which is a *suggested* outline for a lesson or a portion of a

lesson featuring that method. Before we describe the features of an ILPE lesson in more detail, take a look at Figure 7.1. This template should help you to gain some initial insights into what it takes to plan and conduct a lesson like this.

Focal Point 2 ILPE Method Markers

The following method markers make the ILPE method unique among the constructivist methods that we'll introduce in the next several modules. This list will help you to get acquainted with the method before we discuss planning such lessons in more detail and can in fact serve as a sort of an *ILPE schema* (global concept; a bundle of information with characteristics).

- The Hook and/or Student Aim will include some kind of *introduction to the topic,* and may also include teacher and student *personal introductions* if the lesson is planned for early in the school year.
- The Development of an ILPE lesson will include a sequence of broad Trigger questions that will serve as an initial *inquiry* into student experiences related to the topic.
- The Development will also include an *open-ended activity* that will provide you with further insights regarding students' understanding of important facts, concepts, and principles related to your topic.
- The Culmination will usually include a *look ahead* in addition to the *Wrap-Up* and *Leap.* You'll let your students know what's in store for them in future lessons and why the topic is important.

Again, we invite you to keep these distinctive features in mind as we now investigate the ILPE method in depth.

Focal Point 3 Up Close: Planning and Conducting an ILPE Lesson

As we begin our discussion of planning ILPE lessons, think back to the general planning suggestions that we presented in Modules Three and Four. After you've outlined the complete lesson, your actual planning with ANY of our methods might begin at various points. You might find yourself beginning a planning process for a unit by considering a set of district unit objectives and then searching for appropriate materials as you make decisions on possible methods. On occasion, you might read about or participate in an interesting activity during an inservice experience and think about how you might incorporate the activity in your classroom. Or you may become familiar with a new piece of technology (e.g., a Palm Pilot) and instantly brainstorm ways to incorporate the new gizmo into future lessons.

Prelude

- Rationale (with connection to national standards)
- Performance Objective
- Materials and Lesson Aids

Enactment

- Hook (an attention-grabbing question, demonstration, problem, skit/performance)
  1. Teacher/student introduction (in a start-of-the-year ILPE)
  2. Brief introduction/discussion of the topic, using the Hook as a springboard
- Student Aim: Your statement of purpose for the lesson; remember that it can be effective *not* to be too specific about what the students will be doing! You can *keep them wondering. . . .*
- Development
  1. Inquiry
     a. Assess students' initial understanding regarding topic through questions (open-ended Trigger questions are especially useful at this point).
     b. Probe and redirect, based on students' responses.
     c. As an option, list student-generated questions, or construct a concept map.
  2. Open-Ended Activity
     a. Conduct a related activity that will allow you to assess students' understanding of important facts, concepts, principles, and attitudes.
     b. Observe students' actions and listen to the interaction. Ask Trigger, Probe, and Redirect questions when appropriate. Encourage them to expand on ideas presented by others.
- Culmination
  1. Wrap-Up: Ask students to summarize the information gathered. As the teacher, what did you learn about their understanding, interest, etc.?
  2. Leap: Project what's in store as the unit progresses. Then ask students to explore the value of the topic in a brief discussion.

Assessment and Evaluation Plan

- Assessment products (What will students produce in this/a later lesson?)
- Evaluation (How will you evaluate this product, e.g., with a scoring rubric?)

FIGURE 7.1 ILPE Lesson Planning Template

As we introduce each of a series of constructivist teaching methods, we'll walk you through this planning process, in a start-to-finish way, in the belief that this will allow you to feel confident in planning lessons in which you'll utilize each method.

Now to the specific processes involved in planning and teaching an ILPE lesson. Our detailed discussion of the integration of Core Components with ILPE method markers (i.e., specific features) includes suggestions related to both the planning and conducting of lessons utilizing this method.

 **Up Close: Planning and Conducting an ILPE Lesson**

Rationale

In Module Three, a lesson Rationale includes some mention of the content involved, the cognitive skills that students might develop through the experience, and some

justification for conducting the lesson as intended (addressing what we call the "So what?" question—why would you ask students to do this?).

We find ourselves in a standards-driven era. Learned societies, such as the National Council of Teachers of Mathematics (NCTM) and the National Council of Teachers of English (NCTE), have established curriculum standards that have heavily influenced state and local standards. In considering your justification for any lesson, we suggest that you consider curriculum standards established for your subject area. To help illustrate this process, we will refer to the national standards for training teachers in all disciplines developed by the Interstate New Teacher Assessment and Support Consortium (IN-TASC; see Module One and Appendix) as we walk you through the planning process for each method.

Let's consider the electricity lesson conducted by Mr. Newman as we think about writing a Rationale for an ILPE lesson. In this lesson, Mr. N. is most interested in gaining insights into his students' thinking regarding the nature of electricity. In starting the planning process for this lesson, he might have combined the three elements of a Rationale (What? Why? Justification) like this: "Students will first reveal some of their conceptions regarding electricity by responding to open-ended questions. They will then be challenged to apply their understanding of this topic by attempting to create (*synthesize*) as many electrical circuits as possible in a group setting. The experience will enhance individual and group communication and abstract thinking abilities and connects to INTASC Standards 1, 3, 4, 5, 6, 7, and 8." In many cases, your planning for any lesson, including one in which you use the ILPE method, should start with writing such a Rationale. In these three sentences, Mr. Newman has clearly conveyed some powerful reasons for conducting the lesson in this way and has begun to specify what his students *might* be able to do as a result of this experience. That's where the next Core Component, the Performance Objective, comes into play.

Performance Objective

Keep in mind that when you provide what we would call constructivist learning experiences for your students, they will often surprise you by doing the wonderfully unexpected (e.g., by asking important new questions or expressing new insights that you hadn't considered). This is the real beauty of a student-centered classroom. By setting the stage with intellectually challenging lessons, you can provide opportunities for students to make exciting leaps in their thinking. In addition to the wonderfully unexpected, we as teachers also need to get specific as we plan what our students should be able to *do* as the result of the experiences that we provide and how they will be able to *demonstrate* to us and themselves what they've learned. This is where Performance Objectives fall in the planning process.

Module Three states that a Performance Objective includes statements indicating how you'll help students *prepare* for the learning experience, what they'll *produce,* and something about the *criteria* for or quality of the product. In planning any lesson, including an ILPE, think specifically about what you'll expect (or at least *hope*) that your students will be able to do and what they can say, do, or create to show you that they've learned something. For example, our science teacher may have written a Performance Objective like this as he planned his shocking ILPE lesson: "Students will share their conceptions related to electricity during the early phases of the lesson (preparation). Then, using a set of batteries, bulbs, and wires and working with a partner, they will light the bulb in as many ways as possible, diagramming each successful method (product). In a full class setting, each group will then share its diagrams and discover at least three similarities in each *circuit* (criteria)." Note that Mr. N. is definitely encouraging his students to take risks and experiment. We

have conducted similar lessons in our respective subjects in seventh grade, high school, and college classrooms and have found the experience to be extremely challenging (and often motivationally frustrating at first) for students at each grade level.

In his Performance Objective, Newman has specified preparation (setting the stage), what the students will produce, as well as the relevant *criteria* (how many, for how long, etc.). Writing Performance Objectives for ILPE lessons can be tricky because *you can never be sure, in advance, about students' experiences related to the new topic.* As you plan your first ILPE lessons, try to predict what your students might be able to do, and specify how they can show you what they know. This is the heart of a Performance Objective, which can then serve as a road map for planning the Enactment section of your lesson.

Materials

We strongly urge you to list necessary materials directly on your lesson plan. This is especially important in ILPE lessons because they almost always include an activity. In considering materials, one of your biggest concerns will be the *setting* for your activity. Will students do their *creating* alone? In pairs? In groups of three to six? In general, we suggest a small-group setting for ILPE activities; this setting provides more students with an opportunity to get directly involved and a greater chance for the teacher to observe, listen to the interaction, and ask the right question at the right time. Mr. Newman conducted his activity in pairs. For his class of twenty-four, he would need at least twelve bulbs and batteries and twenty-four pieces of wire—and certainly plenty of extras, in case things get misplaced or students wish to use extra materials to construct more complex circuits. Whatever you choose to do during your ILPE lessons, list your materials. It will help you to clearly envision the activity.

We hope that this behind-the-scenes discussion of the lesson Prelude section provides you with a feel for the initial planning that you'll need to do for ILPE lessons. Let's now move onstage for the Enactment section of an ILPE.

The Hook

In planning an ILPE Hook, you'll be seeking to establish the mood for the lesson, to share general information about your purposes, to convey something about the nature of the lesson, and to model the kind of interaction desired from your students. When entering any new situation, people tend to form impressions quickly of the norms and expectations involved. For us as teachers, either meeting a new group of students or reconvening a familiar class at the start of a period, the first five to ten minutes of class time provide an opportunity to orient the group to a set of positive expectations that can help to establish an open, thinker-friendly environment.

We suggest that you set high expectations in your ILPE lessons, especially those conducted early in the school year. To help do this, *hook* the group with an attention-grabbing question, picture, statement, cartoon, poem, problem, demonstration, song, skit, film clip, and so on that will serve to preview the lesson. A chemistry teacher could dress as a wizard and demonstrate a chemical reaction; an English teacher might do a dramatic or comical reading; a history teacher might dress as an historical figure; a math teacher might begin with a puzzling, real-world problem. The possibilities are endless, and a start like this to any lesson can create some excitement and make your students feel more comfortable with you and one another. Our science teacher certainly grabbed the attention of his students with his string of blinking lights. It's a little gimmicky, perhaps, but certainly something that would cause students to wonder what's in store.

An effective introductory technique for an early-year ILPE is for you as the teacher to introduce yourself in the manner that you would like the students to introduce *themselves.* Simply let your students know what you'd like to know about them, and then model that introduction by revealing something about yourself. It is often effective to work an activity, such as a simple game, into your Hook (this is a good option later in the lesson, too). These activities can often serve as effective icebreakers, encouraging your students to be more open with their thoughts than they would be given a more straightforward introduction. Activity options include asking students to interview each other and then introduce their partner to the class; inviting everyone to grab a handful of candy and, for each piece taken, to reveal something about themselves; having the group fill out a brief questionnaire and then find others with common answers; or playing a bingo game in which players answer questions about themselves and try to match answers with classmates, winning the game when they complete a row. Again, a key to the success of any such activity is for you to model desired behaviors for the students. They will tend to follow your lead.

Frequently, this introductory process can lead to a general discussion of student experiences and attitudes related to your topic and subject matter area, especially if there is some topic connection to your initial questions. You can enhance chances for a natural transition into the rest of the lesson by planning appropriate elements to include in the Hook and asking the right questions. For example, foreign language teachers might describe their own experiences in traveling abroad in their self-introduction and ask students to discuss places that they'd like to visit. Physical education, dance, and music teachers might choose to discuss preferred leisure-time activities. English teachers might poll students' reading habits or talk about favorite films, plays, novels, or authors ("If you had a free afternoon and could read anything, what would you choose?").

Student Aim

After a brief, general discussion, you can begin to focus the interaction on your specific topic(s). Planning an introductory statement of purpose as a Student Aim can facilitate this transition. Your purpose statement could include: (1) a tentative overview of the content to be explored in this lesson and throughout your unit ("For the next two weeks, our lessons are going to focus on cross-cultural interpretations of Romeo and Juliet"; "Now I'm going to invite you to investigate electricity"); and (2) the Rationale for later discussion and activity. A brief (one or two sentences) statement regarding your topic will help orient your students as the unit begins. Remember that a structured, specific Student Aim (i.e., previewing statement) is optional. Another possibility is to keep your students in suspense, initially, about your topic, revealing it late in the lesson. We have found that an approach like this can lead to curiosity within any class ("I wonder why she's asking us these questions").

Lessons of all kinds should usually include a statement *at some point* as to why the lesson is important and what purpose it serves (exceptions would include lessons in which the teacher wishes students to make these connections on their own). These statements help overcome the recurring (but often appropriate) question from students: "Why are we doing this?" A statement such as "Today, we're going to be talking about the 1980s. I hope to find out how much you know about this period in history in order to help me plan future lessons," accomplishes this purpose. Again, you can save a statement like this for later in the lesson if you think it's a good idea; this approach is characteristic of more inductive teaching approaches, as we'll see. But do address what we call the "So what?" question in some way during each lesson that you plan.

Development: Using Questions and an Activity to Open Windows into Your Students' Minds

Properly planned, your Hook and Student Aim will lead smoothly into the Development phase of the ILPE. Early in the Development, we recommend asking open-ended, brainstorming-type Trigger questions that invite multiple student responses. Without a doubt, one of the very best ways to assess the nature of students' understanding is to ask them questions. As part of ILPE lessons, questions can be addressed to students in a full-class setting, in small groups, or as part of a written assignment. In our introductory scenario, for example, Mr. Newman asked his class, "How have you used electricity in the last twenty-four hours?" A question like this could offer you a wide range of insights into your students' understanding of what electricity is, how it is generated, and how natural resources must be utilized to produce and distribute it. The question also connects directly to the personal experiences of students (i.e., they have to think about and share something that they have done). In our experience, word-association Trigger questions are especially effective during this phase of the lesson (e.g., "What do you think of when I say the word ____?"). You may ask questions that relate more directly to the past experiences of students at this point (e.g., "How many of you have ever visited ____? How would you describe it to your classmates?"). We suggest writing important Trigger questions like this directly into your lesson plan. This can help you to avoid fumbling for words, asking run-on questions (i.e., asking-rephrasing-rephrasing, see Module Five, Part 2), or doing too much talking yourself.

The questions planned for ILPE lessons should be designed to touch on as many aspects of the topic involved as possible. For example, suppose a geometry teacher wanted to investigate her students' initial understanding of the concept of volume. The teacher could begin with a structuring statement before asking her students a series of questions:

Teacher: I am going to ask some questions related to the term *volume* because I want to know what that word means to you before we begin the unit. What do you think about when you hear the term *volume*, Jake?

Jake: . . .

Teacher: Good! You mentioned that containers have volumes. What do you mean by that?

Jake: . . .

Teacher: Can you add anything to Jake's definition of volume, Candy?

Candy: . . .

Again, in planning the Development of your ILPE lessons, it is important to plan a brief sequence of such open-ended Trigger questions. You're not necessarily seeking right answers, but inquiring into the current thinking of your students.

As we discuss in Module Five, there are two general types of teacher follow-up questions asked after a student responds: the Probe and the Redirect. Although Probe and Redirect questions aren't planned in advance, because they depend on initial student responses—although you can anticipate some as a mental rudder—the use of these follow-up questions is especially important in ILPE lessons. Probe questions acknowledge student responses and encourage them to expand on their ideas, as in the teacher's reply to Jake. In asking students to expand on a response, the teacher may request clarification of something that the student said, justification of an idea expressed, or the adding of information to a previous response. The type of Probe question used depends on the nature of the initial answer; asking the right Probe question at the right time can allow you to take advantage of the teachable moments that students provide with their initial responses. Remember that in an ILPE lesson your main goal is to gain insights into your students' understanding of and attitude toward your topic, so asking clarifying Probes will be vital. We will see that when using other methods, asking other types of Probe questions will become equally important (see Module Five, Parts 1 and 2 for a description and examples of Probe and other types of questions).

The second type of follow-up question is the Redirect. Recall that in its simplest form, redirecting refers to repeating the question, not necessarily verbatim, to another student. This technique is useful for determining the degree of consensus in the group regarding an expressed idea. Regardless of which student responded to the query, "How would you define the term *volume*?," the teacher can redirect the question by merely asking, "Does Jake's definition express the concept as you understand it, Candy?" or, "How would you define volume, Candy?" You can combine elements of the Probe and Redirect as well or ask something like, "How are Pam and Marty's ideas different?" Another useful redirecting technique is to ask for a show of hands to see who agrees/disagrees with a certain statement. Using Redirect questions is crucial: Far too often, teachers who receive a detailed, accurate response from one student will assume that everyone else holds a similar level of understanding. This is almost always far from the case.

In the sample questions discussed so far, note that you can invite specific students or anyone in the class to respond. Directing questions to particular students will allow you to sample the understanding that particular individuals hold. In general, we recommend that about half of the questions designed to elicit learners' previous experiences should be addressed to specific students. Remember to state the question followed by the name of the student, as in the questions addressed by the teacher in the example to Jake and Candy. In this way, the teacher improves the chance that each student will begin to respond cognitively to the question.

As you conduct ILPE lessons, remember that your main purpose will be to determine what your students know or don't know about the topic, and not for the students to be impressed by *your* knowledge, so these questions should be answered by students, not by you. As they discuss your topic, students will certainly learn something more about it, and it will be worthwhile to expand on ideas that students introduce. Be careful not to turn any ILPE lesson into a lecture on your topic. As in any teaching situation, if students can't answer a question, then you have several options. You may wish to rephrase or simplify the question, breaking a complex concept down into its component parts. If necessary, you could also direct the question to another student or to the entire group in a way that minimizes potential embarrassment to the student who couldn't answer the question. Remember that one absolute key to successfully eliciting student responses is to extend wait time before rephrasing or redirecting questions (Module Five). In our view, it is always more useful for you to identify the reason that students cannot answer questions rather than to answer the question for them. Don't feel that you're not accomplishing anything simply because the students fail to give the correct responses to the questions posed. In ILPE lessons, you can learn a lot by finding out what students *don't* understand.

You have a wide range of other options available during the development of an ILPE lesson. You can do a demonstration, read a piece of text (e.g., a poem or quote), or show a videoclip, photo, or piece of artwork and ask students for a personal response. It is often useful for a teacher to list student-generated ideas on the board or overhead sheet or to arrange these ideas within a concept map so that you and your students have a developing reference point. Whatever you choose to do, try to involve each of your students during this portion of the lesson through directed Trigger, Probe, and Redirect questions.

An Open-Ended Activity

We also recommend planning an activity of some kind during the Development Section of ILPE lessons. Engaging your classes in activities, especially those that are open-ended and that provide students with an array of options or choices, can provide you with some terrific insights into their established ideas (and possibly their misconceptions) regarding your topic. They also provide you with further opportunities to investigate students' personalities, learning styles, and attitudes toward this and other topics.

Why are more open-ended activities, like Mr. Newman's batteries and bulbs investigation, especially well suited to ILPE lessons? In activities like these, students are challenged to rely on their current frames of reference to make sense of the situation and consider their past experiences as well as elements of the current situation to decide where to start and how to proceed. Challenging your students to participate in such activities in groups of two to four is a terrific option; this allows you to make observations, listen to student–student interaction, and to ask the right question at the right time to push their thinking deeper or in new directions.

In deciding what kind of activity to plan for your ILPE lessons, ask yourself the following questions.

1. What could I ask my students to do that would provide me with insights into their current ways of thinking about this topic?

The good news is that your options are almost unlimited in this regard. A science teacher might challenge students to do a hands-on activity in which they investigate a mysterious substance, process, collection of objects, and so on, as Mr. Newman did. A math teacher could ask students to work through a puzzling, mathematics-rich problem or situation, as recommended in current NCTM standards. A speech or theater teacher might have her students write and perform a brief skit or presentation on a topic chosen at random. A history teacher could challenge his students to analyze a set of drawings or photographs and sequence them chronologically, defending their choices on the basis of what they see in the pictures. Again, the actions of your students in any of these activities could provide you with invaluable insights.

2. Is the activity best suited for a large- or small-group setting? What size group might be advisable?

This is a crucial question. Smaller groups allow for greater observable interaction among students, so consider groups as small as two to four. You'll have to consider the materials and space that you'll need when making this decision; lack of necessary materials and space might dictate larger groups. Management considerations might play a part in this decision as well. It might be difficult for fifteen pairs of students in some classes to maintain their focus and to later share their ideas. As in any activity, you'll also need to decide whether to arrange the groups heterogeneously, in advance, or perhaps randomly.

3. How should I explain/provide directions for the activity?

As we noted in discussing peer-group learning techniques (Module Six), this is a big question whenever activities are involved. In general, you want your directions to be thorough without being overly restrictive (see sample lesson plans throughout *Invisible Teaching* for examples of directions). In suggesting that ILPE activities be more open-ended or exploratory in nature, we recommend giving students options to the greatest extent possible. *What* they decide to do and *how* they decide to do it will reveal a great deal. But even in an open-ended activity, you'll want to explain carefully that the students *have* options; you may want to suggest possible ways to do the activity. As in planning for any direction-giving situation, we would suggest being ready to show directions on the board, overhead transparency, computer-generated slide, or on a handout and to explain them verbally (you'll tend to catch students with strong visual and auditory modal ity preferences this way). Question students during and after giving directions to check on their understanding ("To review, what will each group want to do FIRST? Jamal?"). Remember to model any tricky or potentially unsafe procedures for students, and perhaps allow them to practice before going any further.

Note that in an ILPE lesson, the activity usually provides the setting for students to carry out the Performance Objective. Whenever possible, challenge students to produce some physical product that will show you something about the nature of their understanding. In his science lesson, Mr. N. asked his students to diagram every arrangement of batteries, bulbs, and wires that produced a lighted bulb. There are several advantages to doing something like this in an ILPE. Students can share and discuss their products later in the lesson or even the next day, a process that can push their thinking in new directions. You could collect, examine, and use in later classes physical products like this; an interesting product might even serve as a useful Hook for a future lesson. So think carefully about what you might ask your students to create (i.e., synthesize) in your ILPE activities.

As in the Hook and inquiry, teacher questioning during your activity will play a big part in the success of the lesson. Watch and listen carefully as students do the activity; look for clues about their attitudes toward the topic. Are they thoroughly engaged in what they are doing, asking each other questions? (Carry a notepad with you as you move among groups, and record meaningful questions or comments to share later with the whole class.) Or is their interest level less intense? Remember that the ways in which students interact in any group setting can reveal a great deal about not only their previous experiences but about their learning style preferences as well. These are insights that you can use to your advantage in planning future lessons. As always, put yourself in a position to ask Trigger, Probe, and Redirect questions to push their thinking in new directions. In completing your ILPE activity, be sure to first plan a sequence of questions that will challenge students to share and think deeply about what they experienced during the activity (again, see sample lesson plans for examples). Whenever possible, use these questions as a springboard to your Culmination.

Culmination: Concluding Your ILPE Lesson

As an ILPE Wrap-Up, we suggest providing your students with a summary of some of the things that *you* learned, as a teacher, during the lesson. This summary could include mention of the knowledge that some students have demonstrated and may mention areas on which you will focus during future lessons ("Today, I've learned that we'll need to review mean, median, and mode before we conduct our first class poll"). This can be a very effective way of addressing the "So what?" question. Let the students know what you've learned from them and how the class will be using the information.

In many instances, planning a *closing statement* is helpful in wrapping up an ILPE lesson. A closing statement, as used here, simply refers to a final sentence indicating that the lesson, or this part of the lesson, is over. In the *Leap,* encourage your students to apply the concepts in new ways. Finally, it's often a good idea to use the closing statement as a transition into the next lesson, what we call the *Look Ahead* (e.g., "From today's lesson it is apparent that many of you are very familiar with the Great Depression. So tomorrow, we'll begin to look at . . .").

As a constructivist teacher, one of your main goals will be to challenge your students to generate questions that they have regarding a topic. We recommend that you make these student-generated questions a central, curriculum-driving focus as you proceed into each instructional unit. The concluding portion of an ILPE lesson presents a golden opportunity to allow students to voice burning questions that they may have regarding the topic at hand. You can challenge your students to do this orally and cover the chalkboard with relevant student questions, or you can ask students to write questions on index cards and turn these in ("One thing I'm wondering about _____ is _____"). Yet another option is to give students some kind of written questionnaire that they can complete in class or at home.

Assessment and Evaluation

Remember that ILPE lessons won't usually include a *formal* assessment and evaluation event. As is the case with many ILPE lessons, Mr. N.'s electricity lesson included many opportunities for the teacher to *informally* assess and evaluate the nature of his students' learning by observing their actions and listening to their comments. As you plan your own ILPE lessons, we invite you to consider possible assessment *products* (i.e., something that the students would produce during or immediately after the lesson) that you might evaluate. Examples could include reflective papers, drawings, journal entries, or presentations.

Focal Point 4 **When Should You Use the ILPE Method in Your Classroom?**

Obviously, the ILPE method is very well suited for the opening day of the school year or whenever you meet with a group for the first time. Plan a brief ILPE lesson every time you introduce major topics or units of instruction. During the school year, a brief ILPE lesson may consist of just a few relevant questions. ILPE lessons and ILPE minisegments in other types of lessons can be highly motivating and fun for students and teachers, because they are fast paced and center on students' ideas. In addition, you will send the positive message that you truly care about what students think, an important step in creating that thinker-friendly community in your classroom.

Asking your students to answer written questions or to complete other assignments will help in discovering clues as to the nature of your students' understanding. Supplement your classroom ILPE lessons with creative writing assignments, or design questionnaires to gauge students' knowledge and interest. Remember that assigning what we call a *one-minute essay* (e.g., "On your index card, complete the following sentence: When it comes to American culture in the 1960s, I'm most curious about _____") can provide you with a range of valuable insights. Remember that this does *not* imply that the only time that you would assess student interest and knowledge level is at the outset or conclusion of a lesson or unit. This kind of assessment must be an *ongoing* process. A conscious, concerted effort at such an assessment *is* vital when meeting a class for the first time or when introducing a new topic to a familiar group of students.

Keep in mind that challenging students to articulate questions that can be investigated within a unit should be a major emphasis in a constructivist classroom. Concluding lessons with one-minute essays, as mentioned, can provide students with opportunities to generate questions. What *do* they wonder most about when they consider your topic? Starting future lessons by returning to these student-generated questions is not only highly motivating but also truly *empowering.*

In any case, conduct frequent ILPE lessons in your classroom. All that you learn about your students will prove invaluable as you plan future lessons.

■ TIPS FOR TECHNOLOGY INTEGRATION

- A middle- or high-school teacher in any subject could develop a biographical computer program entitled "About Me" and share this with the class as part of an early-year ILPE lesson. Later in this lesson, students might work in small groups to plan and share ideas for personal "About Me" programs as a way to introduce themselves to classmates and later develop their own program as an introduction to programming.[2]

- In pairs, students can explore relevant Websites as part of ILPE lessons, completing and later sharing responses to questions on a teacher-provided Treasure Hunt activity sheet. This is another example of a multifaceted experience—students are provided with an introduction to a new topic and further develop their ability to use the Internet, all in a highly interactive setting.

■ ROUNDUP ■

ILPE lessons are planned with a number of important goals in mind. First and foremost, they are designed to allow you to gain insights into the *thinking* of your students. What is the nature of their understanding regarding important facts, concepts, and principles related to some new topic? What are their beliefs and attitudes regarding these ideas? How have their previous experiences impacted their thinking? Addressing these questions is

---

Ms. Klein is beginning a theater unit that will focus primarily on playwriting. After learning about her students' theatergoing and acting experiences during the inquiry phase of her ILPE, she asks the class, "Has anyone ever heard of *improv* before?" Many of the students were able to explain something about improv to the rest of the class. "At this point, I'd like to challenge each of you to take part in your first improv-type experience!" says Ms. K. enthusiastically. She explains the situation. Each person in the class will choose a partner; each pair of students will have five minutes to write (and later act) a scene involving a waiter and a customer ordering dinner. "To add another twist, I'm going to ask each of you to choose a persona for the character that you'll portray," Ms. Klein continues. "Write and act the scene as you think a person like this would react." There is a buzz of excitement as each student reaches into a bag to choose a slip of paper describing their persona. The students excitedly begin to write scenes involving conflicts between such characters as a knight of the round table, a lady of the Old South, a 1940s New York detective, a modern-day talk show host, and a range of other characters. The teacher learns a great deal about the initial playwriting and acting abilities of her students, their understanding of history and culture, as well as their personalities as the class watches and discusses each performance.[1]

FIGURE 7.2 A Glimpse into a Constructivist Classroom

vital for any teacher working from a constructivist learning perspective, and conducting ILPE lessons will allow you to do this directly.

These lessons also allow you to introduce a new topic in an engaging, motivating way. ILPE lessons tend to be highly interactive and fast-paced. They also send the message that you truly care about what your students think. Another unmistakable message is that student questions will influence what subsequently happens in future classes. Make sure that you later address questions raised in the course of ILPEs.

Remember that ILPE lessons can vary in length from a few minutes to an entire class period, depending on a number of factors. In seeking to establish a thinker-friendly, constructivist setting, we recommend conducting such lessons whenever you embark on a new topic. You'll not only gain invaluable insights, but you'll send some powerful messages about the nature of learning within your classroom.

We now invite you to consider Figure 7.3, which will help you to review the main components of an ILPE lesson. Then read the sample lesson plan that follows to enhance your understanding of this method.

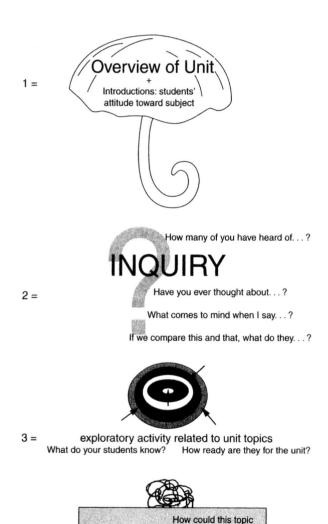

1 =

Overview of Unit
+
Introductions: students'
attitude toward subject

2 =

How many of you have heard of. . . ?

INQUIRY

Have you ever thought about. . . ?

What comes to mind when I say. . . ?

If we compare this and that, what do they. . . ?

3 =   exploratory activity related to unit topics
What do your students know?   How ready are they for the unit?

4 =   culmination: How could this topic relate to your life? Any idea of where it could lead?

© 2001 Ina Claire Gabler

FIGURE 7.3 ILPE Flowchart

■ ILPE SAMPLE LESSON PLAN ■

Unit Title: Developing Effective Communications Skills (Intended for: high school speech class)[3]

Prelude

Rationale

(Combines What? Why? Justification): By conducting a lesson that includes both performance components and an exploratory-type discussion, I will have an opportunity to assess students' speaking skills and confidence level with regard to public speaking as well as to begin to establish an open, relaxed classroom atmosphere conducive to the development of effective communications skills. The experience will enhance verbal communication skills and connects to INTASC Standards 1, 3, 4, 5, 6, 7, and 8.

Performance Objective

(Combines Preparation, Product, and Criteria): After drawing a personal question at random, students will display and then reflect on their speaking skills by providing a one-minute response to the question chosen. In the final phase of the lesson, students will reveal a possible professional/career aspiration and state in writing at least three ways in which effective communications skills could be a part of the chosen profession.

Materials and Lesson Aids

1. A set of questions designed to encourage student response, written on individual slips of paper

2. Poster board with "What makes me most nervous?" poll results

Enactment

Time Estimate	Core Components and Method Markers
7–8 minutes	*Hook:* We're going to start today with an important question.

- What does it mean to be "nervous" (Trigger)?
- The first thing that I'd like to do today is to talk about things that make you nervous!
- What are some things that make you nervous (survey class; list ideas provided; Probe/Redirect)?
- How many of you like to speak in front of people? To perform/act? To appear on camera (Probe/Redirect)?

20 minutes

Student Aim
- Our goal in this lesson will be to begin to ease some of those nervous feelings! The first thing that we're going to do is play a game.

Development: Open-Ended Activity
- What I'd like to do is ask for a volunteer to pull a slip of paper from the hat. Tell us what your question is, and then take 30 seconds to a minute to answer your question in front of the class. Answering some of the questions might require that you do some acting—don't be afraid to do this, everyone is going to have a chance to try it. I'll go first! (Teacher models procedure; volunteers answer questions; Probe/Redirect based on responses.)

Opening questions addressed include:
- If you had one day to do whatever you like, what would you do and why would you do it?
- In your mind, what is a perfect world?
- If you could be any animal, what animal would you choose to be and why?
- How would you describe your worst date?
- Describe your most embarrassing moment in a classroom.
- If you could choose to give a speech on any topic in front of a group of strangers, what would you talk about and why?
- What is your favorite school subject and why is it your favorite?

5–6 minutes

Transition: In the first part of the lesson, a number of you said that speaking in front of people makes you nervous.

Inquiry: Open-Ended Questions
- Why do you think public speaking frightens people so much (Probe/Redirect; possible responses: fear of criticism, self-disclosure, others not paying attention)?
- If we were to do a poll to see what situations make people nervous, what do you think we'd find (Probe/Redirect based on responses)?

(Reveal poll results on poster board, showing public speaking, attending a party with strangers, meeting a date's parents, and going to a job interview as top four "nervous situations")
- Is anyone surprised at these results?
- What do all of these situations have in common (meeting people for the first time, trying to communicate with strangers in new settings)?

Our first unit is going to focus on effective public speaking. One of my major goals will be to help you feel more comfortable doing this! (provide brief overview of the unit)

Culmination
Wrap-Up

6–8 minutes

- I have another important question for you. What do you hope to become once you finish high school and college (survey class; Probe/Redirect, based on responses)?
- Think about the answers that you and your classmates gave us. Choose one of these professions, and describe at least three ways in which effective communications would be a part of that profession.

Leap/Share Responses:
- What role would effective communication play in any of these professions (direct questions based on professions chosen)?
- How might any of these professions involve giving speeches or speaking in front of other people?
- What *kinds* of *speeches* might be involved?

Notice that in one way or another, every profession that you might choose involves effective communication skills.

Provide summary of student comments.

3–4 minutes   Thanks for participating in the lesson today! I learned a lot about you, including some of your fears and your aspirations (review student comments).

Look Ahead
- Over the next few weeks, we're going to focus on effective communications skills. We're going to learn about: relaxation techniques, speech genres, and how effective communications skills apply to you in general.
- For next time, think about at least one topic that you would feel comfortable talking about in front of a group of classmates. See you then!

Note: This individual lesson would not include a *formal* assessment and evaluation event. As is the case with many ILPE lessons, assessment and evaluation would be of an informal and formative nature and would come mainly through teacher observations of student performance, resulting in notes for future planning.

■ HANDS-ON PRACTICE ■

Try planning an ILPE lesson by using the following lesson template. Refer to Module Three, "Planning Professional Lessons," and to Module Six for suggestions.

Prelude

1. Start your planning process by writing a Rationale for the ILPE.

   Briefly describe the *content* that will serve as the focus of the lesson (consider your unit topic.)

   What will you be teaching?

   Why will you be teaching this? (What *cognitive, motor, perceptual,* or *auditory skills* might be emphasized in this experience?)

   What overall *justification* (e.g., standards) could you provide for doing the lesson this way?

2. Now connect your Performance Objective to your Rationale. In writing your Performance Objective, first articulate your *preparation.* What will you do to prepare your students to complete the task that you have in mind?

   Next, describe the *product*—what will you ask students to do during the lesson?

What *criteria* will you use to evaluate the quality of this product (e.g., how many, for how long)?

3. What *materials and lesson aids* will you need for the lesson?

Enactment

4. Next, think about what you'll actually say, do, and ask during the lesson. First, the *Hook.* What will you do to grab the attention of your students?

5. Consider the *Student Aim.* What might you say to let the students know where the lesson is going? (Remember: You can be direct with the Aim or a bit more open and mysterious.)

6. Now plan the *Development,* the true heart of a lesson. We suggest asking *open-ended questions* to gain initial insights into you students' thinking. What might you ask?

7. Include an *open-ended activity.* This approach can be extremely effective in telling you something about your students' prior experiences and their initial understanding of your topic. Describe an activity that you might do as part of your ILPE lesson.

8. Finally, the lesson *Culmination.* What might you do/say/ask to provide a lesson *Wrap-Up?* Now consider the *Leap.* What might you say/do/ask to elicit new insights related to the lesson or new application of the ideas in the lesson?

9. For the *Look Ahead,* can you preview the rest of the unit to let them know how you might use the insights you've gained? (*Hint:* Remember that planning a specific closing statement is an option. Leaving them with a question to consider for next time is often very effective.)

10. What could you do to *evaluate* student products from this lesson? We invite you to develop an evaluation instrument (i.e., rubric) for this assessment product by (1) specifying the key product features, and (2) a point scale.

Congratulations—by addressing these questions, you've planned your first ILPE lesson. Now add some detail and a timeline, and you'll have a lesson plan that's ready to use.

ENDNOTES

1. Thanks to Sara Marquis, Augustana College Class of 2001, for her contributions to this scenario.
2. Thanks to Dr. Randy Hengst, Augustana College Education Department, for contributing this suggestion.
3. Thanks to Megan Peterson, Augustana College Class of 1998, for her contributions to this lesson plan.

Module 8

Teaching Concepts

■ OVERVIEW: SCENARIO DEPICTING A DEDUCTIVE CONCEPT LESSON

Students enter Ms. Vargas's Spanish I class one Monday morning to the lively sound of traditional Spanish music. It's early in the school year, but the class has already become accustomed to the sound of music from Spain and Central and South America. The rhythm seems to energize the students just a bit as they take their seats, which are arranged in a horseshoe today.

As the bell rings, Ms. Vargas says, "Welcome back! Hope everyone had a terrific weekend. Today, we're going to think about a term that we often hear in our day-to-day lives. What do you think of when you hear the word *culture?*"

Hands shoot up as the students recognize this invitation to brainstorm. Their contributions vary widely. They quickly mention various kinds of food (Mexican food seems to be popular), including some made by their relatives and music ("People from different parts of the world like really different kinds of music"), and Maria mentions the Cinco de Mayo parade that she attended last year.

"That's interesting!" says the teacher enthusiastically. She asks Maria what she saw in the parade and what this tells her about Mexican culture, as the other students listen. After this exchange, Ms. Vargas tells the class, "We're off to a great start. In this class, we're going to define *culture* as *the way of life of a group of people who share similar customs, beliefs, and values.* We're also going to investigate *cultural artifacts,* which are *objects that reflect something about the people who made them.*" Students busily write both definitions, which Ms. Vargas has revealed on the overhead. "Let's talk about what this means and why it's important in Spanish and how it will help us to learn the language."

Vargas first invites the class to expand on the list that they've begun to brainstorm by asking, "What might we mean by 'way of life'?" and then, "What could be a part of the way of life of a group of people?" She lists *food, music/art, holidays,* on the board and the students provide a range of new ideas. In the next few minutes, *language, books/literature, clothes, family structure and values, religion,* and *living space* are all added to the list during the conversation. The teacher asks Trigger questions that push the students' thinking further. They add *recreation, forms of government,* and *technology* to the list as the teacher subtly introduces some Spanish vocabulary ("*Repitan clase, por favor—familia*"; ". . . . *fiesta*", ". . . . . *tecnica*").

"Outstanding list! Now we're going to expand on some of these dimensions of culture—investigating Spanish culture is going to be a big part of what we do in this class," emphasizes Ms. Vargas. "Let's take a look at some cultural artifacts produced in Spain over the last fifty years. As we look at these items, tell me what they tell you about Spanish culture." Over the next ten minutes, Vargas pulls a succession of artifacts, or pictures of artifacts, from a large bag. There's a noticeable sense of anticipation as students examine articles of clothing, a movie poster, an intricately carved wooden box, a collection of money, menus, CD covers, pictures of homes and family holiday gatherings (including a recent picture of the royal family), and other items, many of which were collected by the teacher on her recent trip to Spain. For each item, Ms. V. first holds up the object, lets the students know how to say the relevant term in Spanish, and then passes it around the circle of seats as students share observations and impressions of what each artifact might reveal about Spanish culture. Vargas asks frequent Probe and Redirect questions as students excitedly share ideas. After the class examines all of the Spanish artifacts, she asks, "So based on everything that we've seen so far, what words would you use to describe Spanish culture today?" She lists over twenty words that the students agree on, challenging them to provide support for each contribution.

"We'll expand on many of these ideas over the next few months. We'll talk a lot about culture as we learn the language," concludes the teacher. During the last fifteen minutes of class, Ms. Vargas reminds the students that cultures can be broadly or narrowly defined, and that "we actually have a culture here at Carver High School." She quickly arranges the class into groups of four and challenges each group to brainstorm and later share a list of cultural artifacts that they would include in a Carver High School time capsule. The resulting lists reveal a lot about the students' understanding of the main concepts and about their initial feelings regarding their new high school.[1]

■ FOCAL POINTS AND DISCUSSIONS

Focal Point 1 What Makes the Deductive Concept Method Distinctive?

You have just participated in what we (and other educators) call a *Deductive Concept lesson.* Based on what we've already said in the Overview to Section C about deductive thinking, ask yourself, "What made this lesson deductive and what concepts were involved?"

Discussion 1 What Makes the Deductive Concept Method Distinctive?

Deductive teaching is defined as *a style of teaching in which the instructor presents the class with one or con-*

cepts or principles, challenges students to investigate a set of examples that are related to these main ideas, and then asks the students to test or apply the central ideas. Your main goals in a lesson like this will be to do the following:

- Challenge students to develop a deeper understanding of one or more important concepts (or principles)
- Then *apply* this new understanding in some way

We believe that deductive lessons like the one conducted by Ms. Vargas are refreshing alternatives to lectures because they clearly focus on the *big ideas* within a subject and because students are *actively engaged* in the analysis of these main ideas. We'll see that effective deductive lessons are highly interactive, with students challenged to connect important new ideas (e.g., a working

definition for *culture* and a consideration of the dimensions of Spanish/other cultures) with their own previous experiences.

Figure 8.1 displays a suggested planning template for the Deductive Concept method. As you read through this template, think about how each part of Ms. Vargas's lesson on culture/cultural artifacts fits within the different stages. We'll then move on to discuss the planning process in more detail.

Focal Point 2: Initial Planning: Choosing and Articulating the Concept

Why Teach Concepts?

In an educational sense, concepts are especially important for a number of reasons. First, they help all of

---

Prelude

- Rationale (with connection to national standards)
- Performance Objective
- Materials and Lesson Aids

Enactment

- Hook: An attention-grabbing question, statement, quote, demonstration, skit; as always, possibilities are endless.
- Student Aim: Your statement of purpose for a deductive lesson will be fairly direct. Present a definition of the concept(s) or principle(s) involved. Display this definition prominently (e.g., on the board, overhead, computer program slide). Ask questions to check for initial student understanding of the definition; focus especially on key words or phrases.

Development

1. Investigation of Examples/Nonexamples
   a. Share examples (perhaps nonexamples if possible) of the concept with students. This can be done in a full-class or peer-group setting.
   b. Challenge students to investigate (especially compare and contrast) examples with a mix of specific and open-ended Trigger questions. Be sure to refer to the concept *rule*. Ask students to *test* the rule as they investigate.
   c. If possible, elicit further examples from the students
2. Application
   a. Conduct a brief activity or provide an assignment that challenges students to apply (i.e., actually *use*) the concept, fulfilling your Performance Objective(s).
   b. Again, elicit further examples from students if possible.
- Culmination
   1. Wrap-Up: Review, or challenge *students* to review, the main ideas generated. Be sure to address the "So what?" question: Why is this concept important?
   2. *Leap:* What new ideas or insights relate to the concept? What's in store for the class; how will we use the important idea that we've investigated?

Assessment and Evaluation Plan

- Assessment products (What will students produce in this/a later lesson?)
- Evaluation (How will you evaluate this product, e.g., with a scoring rubric?)

FIGURE 8.1 Deductive Concept Lesson Planning Template

us to make sense of the many things that we experience. Second, they represent some of the central, defining ideas in each discipline. Because these ideas are so essential in understanding every subject, it makes sense to occasionally teach lessons in which students are challenged to develop a deep and flexible understanding of important concepts.

We have already introduced just some of the exciting recent findings regarding perception, memory, and thinking. The pioneering research in concept formation and attainment was done primarily by Jerome Bruner, Jacqueline Goodnow, and George Austin (1967). David Ausubel (1963), Robert Gagne (1965), Hilda Taba (1966), and a host of other educators have contributed much to our understanding of thinking (and teaching) at the conceptual level. To summarize some of these important research findings, human beings actively perceive and process several million bits of information during a normal day, and our brains have developed mechanisms to help us sort information so that we are not overwhelmed by the task. One way that each of us deals with this constant flood of sensory input is by placing pieces of information into the ever-changing set of schemata (pl. for "schema"—generalized constructs; bundles of information with distinct features or characteristics) that constitute each person's frame of reference. This processing allows each of us to make sense of sensory input at a much quicker pace.

At this point, concepts come into play as we attempt to understand human thinking from a cognitive (and constructivist) perspective. There are many definitions for the term *concept*, but the most appropriate definition for our purposes is *a word that conveys a set of categories that allow us to classify objects or ideas.* We might also think of a concept as *a word or phrase that activates a schema or a set of schemata* (e.g., impressions of a tree, religion, school). Many writers have used the words *concept* and *schema* to mean virtually the same thing, but we'll invite you to remember this important distinction: A concept is a word or phrase that *activates* a schema. Think of it this way: The concept (word) is like a *light switch* that turns on a select set of *wiring* within the mind (a schema or a set of schemata). Also keep in mind that many different types of sensory inputs can activate a schema. For proof of this, think of sights, smells, and sounds that trigger a flood of memories and images in your own mind.

Since our personal set of cognitive structures allows each of us to make sense of the pieces of information that we perceive, it will be important for teachers to consider the nature of concepts when introducing new ideas to students. Because concepts represent some of the big ideas within any subject area and form the building blocks for principles, clear communication and shared

understanding of concepts are essential to effective teaching and learning. In the next few paragraphs, we will briefly review the nature of concepts.

Book, inertia, glasnost, truck, reptile, chair, war, poetry, isosceles triangle, characterization, middle class, metaphor, pollination, and *insanity* are all examples of concepts. Each of these words activates a schema that allows us to form a mental image of an object, event, or process without having to reprocess and analyze every piece of sensory input that we experience. We have seen that each individual constructs meanings for objects and events based on previous experiences. As a result, if several people try to define concrete or abstract concepts from *lion* to *love,* there would be considerable individual differences. In an educational setting, helping students to reach shared understanding of even seemingly simple concepts is vital and can present major challenges.

Our opening scenario hints that within any culture, people have shared certain experiences and, as a result, may have similar frames of reference that they use to understand certain objects and events. It is not surprising that individuals from the same culture often share meanings for some concepts. This allows them to communicate with each other without giving long, complex explanations. If a person states, "I saw a small animal with four legs, a tail, two ears, and brown fur," the creature in question could be a squirrel, a mongoose, a woodchuck, a cat, a dog, or a rabbit. But if the person says, "I saw a brown tiger cat today," most of us would be able to identify and produce an image of the object with more clarity.

Because each of us has had certain unique experiences, no two people will have *exactly* the same image of the brown tiger cat. One person might associate the cat with a striped kitten that she had as a child. Another person might think of an adult tiger cat that lives in the house next door. Although the images may not be exactly the same, the *conception* of cat allows the two people to focus on the same type of object without a lot of further explanation. When information sharing breaks down, it is often because two or more people taking part in the conversation do not have shared meanings for the same concepts. Many of the communication problems that occur in classrooms can be attributed to this effect, underlining the importance of students sharing common experiences in learning about concepts. This is especially true with concepts that are process oriented or highly abstract.

Discussion 2 Initial Planning: Choosing and Articulating the Concept

Obviously, one of the first major steps in planning a Deductive or Inductive Concept lesson is to choose a concept to serve as the central focus. Within any subject area, there are hundreds if not thousands of important concepts that connect to each other in myriad ways. Your first challenge is to choose concepts that are important enough to serve as a central focus and then to think carefully about how to define the concept and how to challenge students to investigate this *big idea.* The following discussion of the nature of concepts should help you to think through this process. Remember that many of these considerations will apply whether you choose to teach the concept deductively or inductively (inductive teaching will be our focus in Part 2 of this module).

Concepts have certain *critical attributes,* or essential features, qualities, or characteristics that establish a certain degree of *sameness* between two examples of the concept. Mammals, for example, share the ability to control their internal body temperature. A critical attribute of democracies is that citizens are allowed to vote or otherwise express themselves. In probability and statistics, a permutation is a situation in which the order of events matters, a combination is a situation where the order of events doesn't make a difference. These critical attributes must be present in order to distinguish an *example* of a concept from a *nonexample.* It is important to recognize that a concept may have only one critical attribute or several that work in conjunction.

Critical attributes (like events in a permutation) often have to be presented in a certain pattern or sequence so that they can be placed into specific conceptual definitions. The order in which these critical attributes are presented creates the concept's *definition* or *rule.* If we took off in an airplane and observed land, water, and a surrounding body, we may have observed either a lake or an island. The concept rule for a lake would be a body of water surrounded on all sides by a land mass. The concept rule for an island would be a body of land surrounded on all sides by water. If what we observed was a land mass surrounded on three sides by water, we would know that it was not an island, but a peninsula. Of course, we have used a simple concept and concept rules to illustrate a point. If a river enters a body of water, it is no longer surrounded on all sides by a land mass. Is it now a lake? The point of this last question is to remind you that even simple concept rules can be challenged on various points.

Along with critical attributes, many concepts can also have *noncritical attributes.* These are features, characteristics, or qualities that are variable or not essential parts of the concept. In our lake example, whether the lake contained salt water or freshwater would not affect the concept rule. The same goes for the size of the lake, its depth, or its shape. In the mammal example, the presence of hooves, a tail, or a certain color fur are examples of noncritical attributes. It is important to recognize that concepts may have a number of noncritical attributes, or none at all.

Types of Concepts

Concepts can be classified in several different ways, and it will useful for you to keep these categories in mind. A *concrete concept* refers to that which we can experience through the five senses. An *abstract concept* refers to that which we cannot experience or perceive directly through our senses. Another way to look at concepts is to categorize them as *conjunctive, disjunctive,* or *relational.* A *conjunctive concept* has a single set of characteristics or qualities that a person must learn in order to identify it. In contrast, a *disjunctive concept* requires a learner to identify two or more sets of alternative conditions under which the concept can and will occur. It often has an *or* in its definition. For example, a *citizen* could be defined as *a native or naturalized member of a state or nation who owes allegiance to its government and who is entitled to its protection.* As the definition indicates, there are different conditions under which the concept can be fulfilled.

While disjunctive concepts may be difficult for students to understand, *relational concepts* are often more challenging to teach. This type of concept requires a student to form a comparison between objects, events, or qualities; you'll find that it often makes sense to introduce two to three relational concepts together so that they can be compared and contrasted. Waste, pollution, and symmetry are all examples of this type of concept. Waste, for instance, has to be viewed in relation to its source, to the people who produce it, and to whether it has any value after it has been discarded. If you throw away an aluminum can, is it, in fact, a waste product? Although it may be to some people, environmentalists would consider the can a resource, because it is a recyclable product that could be used over and over again. If the value of such cans goes down to the point where it is no longer economical to collect and process them, are the cans waste again? In teaching relational concepts, it is obviously crucial to describe relationships between the concepts involved.

Concepts can obviously be classified in many different ways. The examples discussed here are meant to help you think about some of the ways in which you might go about teaching concepts in the classroom and why the teaching of concepts should be a vital part of instruction in any subject. When choosing which concepts to teach and how to teach them, there are several questions that you should consider:

1. Is the concept considered significant enough to serve as the central focus for a lesson? Do subject-matter specialists and state/local learning standards suggest that the concept is an important one?

2. Why would your students need to learn about the concept? Does the concept have relevant real-world connections that make it significant for your students?

3. Is there sufficient agreement on the critical attributes and the concept rule to have a basis for designing a lesson plan? Can clear and specific guidelines that reflect the essential characteristics of the concept be obtained from resource materials?

Once you have decided that a concept is important enough to teach, you should then ask yourself a series of questions that can help you plan a *concept lesson* (remember that these questions should be considered whether the lesson will be taught deductively or inductively). As you plan any concept lesson, consider these questions:

1. What is the name most commonly associated with the concept (example: *democracy*)?

2. What is the concept's rule or definition (example: *government in which political control is shared by all citizens, either directly or through elected representatives*)?

3. What are the critical attributes of the concept (*shared political control, participation of citizens*)?

4. What noncritical attributes are associated with the concept (*elected representatives*)?

5. What are some interesting, learner-relevant examples or cases of the concept that can be used during the lesson (*ancient Athens; nineteenth-century constitutional monarchies; modern United States*)?

6. What are some contrasting nonexamples that will help clarify and illustrate the concept (*Europe in the Middle Ages; Nazi Germany; modern China*)?

7. What are the most interesting, efficient, and thought-provoking media that can be used to teach the concept (*speech excerpts; case studies; interviews with local elected officials*)?

We suggest using these questions as an initial planning template for teaching concept lessons. Once you have answered them, you will have established a Rationale and direction in teaching a concept to your students.

Teaching at the conceptual level can be very powerful; learning a concept can provide your students with a useful lens for understanding new ideas and making real-world connections. Developing an understanding of concepts like democracy, for example, would enable students to better understand a wide range of historical and cultural events.

In short, teaching concepts makes sense because people naturally think in conceptual terms. Just as important, understanding concepts can help students make sense of the major *principles* within each knowledge domain. As we have noted, choosing one or more relevant concepts will be the first step in planning such a lesson. The list of potential concepts is almost endless, regardless of which subject you teach. Read through the list of potential concepts in Figure 8.2, and think about the images that each generates. Would there be some educational value in teaching any of these concepts within your subject matter area?

Focal Point 3 **Deductive Concept Method Markers**

Now let's turn our attention specifically to teaching concepts deductively. The method markers described here will help you to understand what makes this approach different from other constructivist methods that we'll introduce.

- In conveying the Student Aim, you will clearly *define the concept(s)* for your students.

- During the Development, you will challenge students to *investigate examples and possibly nonexamples of the concept(s)* in order to better understand the critical attributes (i.e., essential characteristics) of the concept.

- Later in the Development, you will invite students to *apply the concept* in some way, possibly through an activity, to *test* and deepen their understanding of this important idea.

---

pattern energy logic organic/inorganic imperialism citizenship observation symmetry rhythm integration existentialism migration literacy racism evolution revolution cycles nonviolent protest isolationism density motion manifest destiny natural selection genre relationship community tangram observation unit permutation gene pool compromise fertility frontier algorithm competition acid/base inference hero/villain surface area love (Petrarchan/Platonic) rebellion responsibility freedom tendon/ligament/cartilage dispersal mechanism(s) youth catalyst reciprocal terrorism coalition equation popular sovereignty hypothesis research treaty health exploration diversity environment electric circuits classism blockade cape joints/sockets plot mass buoyancy patriotism supply/demand feudalism functions perpendicular zone defense cubism self-determination

FIGURE 8.2 Examples of Concepts from a Range of Disciplines

- The Culmination will include some discussion of the *implications* of the concept. Why is this idea important, and how will we as a class use it in future lessons?

Keep these distinctive features in mind as we explore the deductive concept method in depth in the sections that follow.

Focal Point 4 Up Close: Planning and Conducing a Deductive Concept Lesson

Before taking a closer look at planning Deductive Concept lessons, we'd like to remind you once again that this method, like all of the others that we'll introduce, is incredibly flexible. There are countless ways to effectively conduct a Deductive Concept lesson. Our guiding suggestions are meant to help you to begin the planning process and to think about what you'll need to do to conduct lessons like this successfully.

Discussion 4 Up Close: Planning and Conducting a Deductive Concept Lesson

Prelude: Rationale

Let's use our opening scenario as an example of an engaging Deductive Concept lesson. Ms. Vargas is most concerned with helping her students to gain a deeper understanding of *culture* as a concept and to help them to learn to apply the concept. Notice that she was also, in a subtle way, trying to gain greater insights into her students' initial understanding of the elements of culture (you'll see that ILPE-type Trigger questions can be an important part of any constructivist classroom experience). Our Spanish teacher might have written a Rationale like this: "Stu-dents will develop a deeper understanding of culture as a concept by first considering a provided definition, then comparing and contrasting cultural artifacts from modern-day Spain, and finally by applying the definition to their own school culture. This experience will enhance critical-thinking abilities, help to develop group communications skills, and connects to INTASC Standards 1, 3, 4, 5, 6, 7, and 8." As in any well-conceived Rationale, Ms. Vargas has articulated, for herself but also for a substitute teacher or administrator visiting her class, some important reasons to do the lesson this way. In her Performance Objective, she gets more specific about what her students should be able to do as a result of this experience.

Performance Objective

Performance Objectives focus on what students should be able to do to show you what they've learned.

Again, the important caveat: We can't always (in fact, usually) predict exactly what students will learn; the process of learning is far too complex (thankfully) to be predictable. But writing Performance Objectives is a vital part of the planning process, because they focus you as the teacher on the importance of *student doing* and because they connect directly to the assessment of student learning. With this in mind, let's consider a possible Performance Objective for Ms. Vargas's lesson: "Students will be introduced to concept definitions for *culture* and *cultural artifact* early in the lesson and will then be challenged to consider the dimensions of culture by brainstorming examples of the 'ways of life' of groups of people. Later in the lesson, students will apply these concepts by articulating, in a group setting, a list of at least ten defensible cultural artifacts reflecting something about Carver High School culture" (preparation, product, and criteria). Once again, note that our spotlight teacher has articulated an interesting, and potentially highly challenging, way for her students to *show what they've learned,* the essence of a Performance Objective.

Materials

One of the most challenging aspects of planning concept lessons is to think about what examples and nonexamples might convey the main concept and its attributes (more on this when we move on to the enactment of the lesson). In our Spanish example, Ms. Vargas had to think carefully about what cultural artifacts would accomplish this and then to actually assemble these props. Listing these materials would certainly help her to consider how she might introduce the examples and in what sequence.

Now that we've taken a closer look at the Prelude, on to the Enactment of a Deductive Concept lesson, where the guiding question becomes: How can you challenge your students to *actually experience* your chosen concept?

Enactment: The Hook

As in any lesson, an effective Hook can set the tone for what is to come later. Anything is possible. Your Hook can consist of something elaborate (e.g., a skit written by you or the students and performed by volunteers) or something as simple as a truly challenging, open-ended question. We do suggest that the Hook for any concept lesson connect in some way to the main concept.

In our opening scenario, Ms. Vargas began her lesson with some music and a related, straightforward question ("What do you think of when you hear the word *culture*?"). In doing this, she subtly established one *dimension* of culture (music/the arts) that students might focus on later and gained some important initial insights into some of the background experiences of her students (the varied "cultural" foods enjoyed by her students; Maria's connection to the Cinco de Mayo parade). In addition, the teacher established an interactive, thinker-friendly tone for the rest of the lesson. Once again, our general advice is to *get your students involved in each of your lessons as soon as possible,* either through questions or activities. Through years of experience, we have found that breaking the ice in this way helps to engage students for the entire class period.

In conducting either a Deductive or Inductive Concept lesson, another option is to somehow share interesting examples of the concept *as a Hook.* In fact, providing a brief inductive intro to a lesson that is predominantly deductive can be very effective. For example, an English teacher introducing poetry of the Romantic era might read an intriguing example and challenge students to analyze it. An art teacher wishing to introduce Impressionist painting might invite students to examine a set of prints showing examples and nonexamples. A chemistry teacher introducing *indicator* as a concept might conduct a series of eye-catching demonstrations in which solutions dramatically change color upon mixing and then invite students to make observations and predictions about what might happen next. In each of these examples, the teacher would be creating some sense of wonder and anticipation and introducing dimensions of the main concept. This engagement is what you should hope to accomplish in the early minutes of any concept lesson.

Student Aim

As constructivist methods go, Deductive Concept lessons are fairly structured. This is reflected during the Student Aim phase of the lesson. Your most important goal at this point is to clearly share your concept rule (i.e., definition) with the class. In our example, Ms. Vargas displayed definitions for *culture* and *cultural artifact,* read these to the students, and asked a clarifying question to make sure that they understood a key phrase. Remember that *showing* and *stating* these definitions will help you to reach both visual and auditory learners. We also highly recommend a visual display of the concept rule, because students will be referring to this definition throughout the lesson; place the rule on the board, on a computer slide displayed on a TV screen, on a handout, and so on.

In planning a lesson like this, think carefully about how you'll define the concept(s) for your students. Obviously, it's vital to make the definition as understandable as possible. If it is important to use certain terminology in the concept rule, plan questions that would allow you to check for student understanding before moving to the next phase of the lesson. When planning concept lessons, it's useful for *you* to think in terms of *concept rules* and *critical* and *noncritical attributes,* but remember that these terms can sound needlessly complex and intimidating to students. Instead, get used to discussing *important features, qualities,* or *characteristics* when investigating concepts with your students.

After introducing your concept rule(s) (that can be working versions open to increasing complexity across time), we would suggest planning a transition statement of some kind to let the students know that they will now be applying the rule as they investigate a set of examples. This could be something as simple as Ms. Vargas's statement, "Let's talk about what this means and why it's important in Spanish."

Development: Investigating and Applying the Concept(s)

What really sets a Deductive Concept lesson apart from teacher presentations is that students are actively involved in the investigation of examples and later in the application of the concept. This is the phase of the lessons where you challenge your students to *become* scientists, historians, mathematicians as they think critically about the concept, the examples, and why these are important.

One of your biggest planning considerations, as we mentioned earlier, will be to choose and collect *examples* that students will find intriguing. Obviously, the nature of your examples will depend on your concept. Ms. Vargas shared a wide variety of cultural artifacts with her class. In this case, as could be the case with concepts from just about any discipline, your *examples* might consist of actual, concrete objects or pictures of objects. In math lessons, examples could include geometric figures or manipulatives, various types of problems, or statistical data. In English or history lessons, pieces of text shown on an overhead screen or distributed on slips of paper could serve as examples. In many of the example lessons that we'll describe, videoclips or recordings could be used to illustrate the concept. In physical education lessons, a teacher might demonstrate two or three different techniques for passing a basketball, making a block, or doing a high jump and challenge students to compare and contrast the *processes* involved. Again, the possibilities vary as widely as concepts do.

Once you decide on the examples that you might share, we would suggest planning a series of questions that will challenge students to observe the examples closely ("What do you notice about ____?"), compare and contrast them ("How are these alike? Different?"), and connect them to the concept rule ("Are these examples of ____? How can you tell?"). Questions that challenge students to consider the broader meaning/implications of the examples are important at this point as well. For example, Ms. Vargas asked her students what the various artifacts might indicate about Spanish culture; questions like these can challenge students to think more deeply about the meaning of what they are experiencing.

Remember that the analysis of examples can take place in a full-class or small-group setting. If you have enough examples to share, a brief (even five-minute) peer-group event at this point in the lesson can be very effective; this can provide each student with ample opportunities to *experience* the examples. If you do this, ask each group to compile a list of observations and tentative conclusions about the examples (e.g., "Are they examples of this concept? Why/why not?") that your students can share when the class reconvenes. Again, planning appropriate questions for this phase of the lesson is a must. Chances are that it will take time and effort to collect the examples that you share. Make sure you get the most bang for the buck by challenging students to investigate them thoroughly.

Following the investigation of examples, we would advise you to plan a brief activity or discussion that will challenge your students to apply the concept and meet your Performance Objective. In our example, Ms. Vargas subtly showed her students just how *generative* the concepts could be by challenging them to consider artifacts that might show something about a culture that they are all a part of. (Side note: This could be revealing on a number of levels, as one of your authors has found when conducting this lesson in a college classroom.) This application could involve individual or group writing or performing, problem solving (e.g., "Can you use the quadratic equation to find ____?"), or brainstorming (e.g., "Where have *you* experienced evaporation, condensation, and sublimation, and how did these processes impact you?"). The application phase is important. It serves as another check on student understanding and challenges students to extend the ideas involved beyond the walls of the classroom (see the sample lesson plan and Figure 8.3 for additional examples of this). Again, questions that challenge students to generate their own additional examples of the concept are very effective at this point.

Culmination

As you plan the Culmination for a Deductive Concept lesson, think about how you might provide an effective Wrap-Up. We would recommend some type of review of the concept and the dimensions of the concept that were investigated during the lesson. As in any lesson, you might plan on reviewing the main ideas yourself and/or asking reviewing questions that could challenge the students to provide a recap.

We feel that it's especially important in the *Leap* to ask the students why they think that the concept is important. Then you might ask them to apply the concept in a new way. Finally, let them know how you'll be using the concept in the future (once again addressing our "So what?" question). For example, Ms. Vargas might let her students know that they would be investigating additional cultural artifacts throughout the school year, thereby expanding their understanding of the cultures of Spanish-speaking countries.

As a constructivist teacher, remember that you'll regularly want to challenge your students to generate questions that they have regarding classroom experiences. Another option in the Culmination of a Deductive Concept lesson is to invite students to complete an ILPE-like one-minute essay ("One thing I'm wondering about Spanish culture is _____"). Always look for opportunities to gain insights into your students' thinking. Working techniques like this into lesson Culminations is an interesting, efficient way to do this.

Assessment and Evaluation

Like lessons featuring any constructivist approach, the Deductive Concept method includes multiple opportunities for you to informally assess the learning of students through watching their actions and listening to their comments. Formal assessment could come through the collection and evaluation of something that the students *produce* during the application phase or through a reflective assignment (e.g., a reflective paper, journal entry, even a research project) that they might complete after the lesson. As you plan your own Deductive Concept

---

Mr. Kondo and his junior American lit class are in the early stages of a unit that he has entitled "The Voice(s) of America," which will focus on the investigation of literature written by authors from disenfranchised cultural groups within our country. Mr. K. begins today's lesson with an enthusiastic reading of the Langston Hughes poem "Theme for English B." He then asks students to respond to the poem by asking open-ended Trigger questions: "What is the author telling us? How would you describe his life at this point? What words would you use to describe some of the words in the poem? Does he feel he's an American? How can you tell? *Could anyone else have written this poem in the same way? Why?*" Students debate their viewpoints vigorously; they spend several minutes debating elements of the poem before Mr. Kondo begins guiding the lesson a bit more directly. The teacher provides students with a definition for what he calls *authentic voice: words written in such a distinctive, original way that the reader feels that only that author could have written that particular piece. The writer conveys knowledge, passion, and genuine concern regarding the subject.* After a brief discussion of the definition, Mr. Kondo asks students to read three additional poems, and the class discussion focuses on the degree to which each reflects authentic voice. He then asks his students to write (and later share) a poem that reflects *their own* authentic voice.[2]

FIGURE 8.3 A Glimpse Into A Constructivist Classroom

lessons, we invite you to consider assessment products that you might evaluate.

Focal Point 5 When Should You Use the Deductive Concept Method in Your Classroom?

We believe that both Deductive and Inductive Concept lessons can serve as challenging, thought-provoking alternatives to lectures or complements to the Interactive Presentation (see Module Twelve). Even though constructivist classrooms are far more interactive and student-centered than more traditional classrooms, you will still have occasion as a constructivist teacher to introduce new ideas in your subject area. The frequent use of the Deductive Concept method is an effective, interactive way to do this.

We would suggest considering both deductive and inductive methods whenever you have a need to introduce and challenge students to *apply* important concepts and/or principles. On these occasions, one consistent question will be whether to use a deductive or an inductive approach; this is a question that we'll challenge you to consider throughout this module. We'll see that inductive methods would generally be considered to be more discovery-oriented and student-centered. But, for a number of reasons, we suggest a mix of deductive and inductive lessons. Consider the variety of learning style preferences among your students, for example. Random learners find great challenge and appeal in inductive experiences, but more sequential learners are most comfortable with deductive lessons. A mix of inductive and deductive lessons will likely allow you to connect to a range of learners, while at the same time frequently nudging all students out of their learning comfort zones. Deductive lessons are often especially appropriate when concepts or principles are completely novel and especially complex (although we'll see that inductive lessons are *certainly* useful when you introduce ideas that are likely to be new to your students). When choosing either a deductive or inductive approach, do consider the ability of your students to connect their own previous experiences to the central concept.

■ TIP FOR TECHNOLOGY INTEGRATION

The Internet can provide students with unique opportunities to experience concept examples as part of Deductive or Inductive Concept lessons. During the Development stage of a lesson, you might direct students to one or more Websites that feature pictures, text excerpts, audio or video segments, and so on that they might analyze individually or in peer groups as part of the testing or discovery of a concept.

■ ROUNDUP ■

Deductive Concept lessons can serve as engaging alternatives to didactic presentations. Even though most of our educational experiences have been deductive in nature, the format that we have suggested here is highly interactive and intellectually engaging. Lessons like this typically focus on one or more concepts that are big ideas within your discipline, ideas that can be used by the class later to understand events, processes, and so on. They feature an early presentation of a concept definition by the teacher, followed by the active investigation of a set of examples and nonexamples and the application of the concepts to potentially real situations.

Use the Deductive Concept method as a lecture alternative, especially when you wish to challenge students to learn and apply a central concept or principle that might be utilized in future lessons. There are several keys to planning such a lesson effectively. First, think carefully about how you might define the central concept(s); use the guiding questions that we have posed earlier to help you through this process. Referring to Bloom's Taxonomy (Module Five, Part 1) can help formulate your questions. Consider how you might share examples (and possibly nonexamples) of the concept(s) and whether you will do this in a full-class or small-group setting. As in any lesson, write your main Trigger questions into your lesson plans. Anticipate possible Probes. Our experiences have shown us that this will help any teacher challenge students to carefully investigate the examples and to think deeply about why the concept is important. Finally, do challenge students to apply the concept during the final phases of the lesson and in future lessons.

Take a look at the flowchart in Figure 8.4. Then read the sample lesson plan that follows. It will alert you to just a few more of the many possibilities for Deductive Concept lessons.

■ DEDUCTIVE CONCEPT SAMPLE LESSON PLAN ■

Unit Title: The American Legal System (Intended for: middle school social studies class)

Prelude

Rationale

(Combines What? Why? Justification); Introducing and deductively analyzing the concept *law* will challenge

1 = define concept or principle

A = B

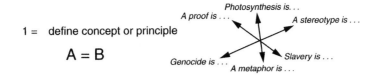

A proof is . . .
Photosynthesis is. . .
A stereotype is . . .
Genocide is . . .
Slavery is . . .
A metaphor is . . .

2 = compare and contrast

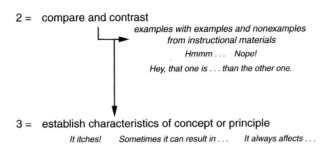

examples with examples and nonexamples
from instructional materials
Hmmm . . . Nope!
Hey, that one is . . . than the other one.

3 = establish characteristics of concept or principle

It itches! Sometimes it can result in . . . It always affects . . .

4 = elicit more examples from students

"I read somewhere that . . ."

5 = culmination: *reestablish definition of concept or principle*

A = B + implications

If this happens when that happens, then . . .

©2001 Ina Claire Gabler

FIGURE 8.4 Deductive Concept Method Flowchart

students to consider both the nature of laws in the United States and the ways in which laws impact our lives and serve to pique student curiosity as to how laws originate at the local, state, and federal levels. The experience will enhance the critical-thinking abilities of the students involved and connects to INTASC standards 1, 3, 4, 5, 7, and 8.

Performance Objective

(Combines Preparation, Product, Criteria): After being introduced to the main concept, students will decide and state verbally whether they believe each of a set of examples is a law. Then, working with a partner, students will describe in writing at least three examples of laws not previously mentioned in class.

Materials and Lesson Aids

Humorous filmclip featuring a bumbling police officer writing a ticket

Enactment

Time Estimate   Main Ideas/Concepts, Questions, and Teaching Methods

5–6 minutes   *Hook:* Let's start the lesson by watching a film of something that happened on a street in Rock Island last week. Keep a close eye on the policeman. See if you can figure out what he's doing and why he's doing it (play a movie scene in which a policeman gives a man a ticket while a bank robbery takes place behind him).

- Did this really happen on the streets of Rock Island?
- What was the policeman trying to do? Why?
- What was going on in the background?
- What were the bank robbers doing? (Breaking the law!)

1–2 minutes   *Student Aim:* This little scene leads us to the main focus of the lesson.

- What is a law? In the United States, we could define *law* this way (write on chalkboard): *A rule of conduct laid down and enforced by a person or group with official authority and that carries some penalty for being broken.*

5–6 minutes   *Development:* Investigating Examples (Teacher presents/discusses initial examples)—Let's talk about some examples of what might impact our lives as citizens.

- Why are all of you in school today (allow multiple responses)?
- What would happen to your parents if they didn't enroll you in school (list compulsory schooling law: children must attend school until the age of 16)?
- When you or your mom or dad are driving to the store, can they go as fast as they want to? Why not? What else do they have to do as they drive (list traffic laws)?
- What do your parents have to do by April 15 every year? Why (list paying state and federal taxes)?

7–8 minutes | Challenge students to determine why each example fits the definition of *law*. Now, let's talk about why each of these examples fits our definition of *law* (connect to critical attributes by comparing/contrasting examples; ask Probes/Redirects).
- What rule(s) is involved?
- What was this law intended to do?
- Who was responsible for making this law?
- What would happen to a person who breaks this law?

Discuss noncritical attributes through examples: the level at which the law was passed (federal, state, local) the body that enforces the law (local/state police; FBI) whether the law involves money

4–5 minutes | *Applying the Concept:* Let's talk for a few minutes about some other situations that may involve laws. For each example, let me know whether you think a law is involved (ask Probes/Redirects in discussing examples).
- Obeying the "No Swimming" signs along the Mississippi River
- Paying credit card bills on time
- Giving money to charity at holiday time
- Seeking shelter during a tornado
- Wearing seatbelts/motorcycle helmets

88–10 minute | Place each student with a partner to generate new examples:
- Now I'd like to give you a chance to talk about laws with your partner. In the next five minutes, write down as many examples of laws as you can.
- Be ready to share your ideas with the class—I'll be around to help each group.

5 minutes/as time allows | Call on groups to share ideas; ask Probes/Redirects.
Culmination
- Today, we've introduced laws—what they are, and what they're designed to do.
- Who can tell us what a law is (review concept rule; use examples generated by students to illustrate each critical attribute; ask Probes/Redirects)?

Leap

I'm wondering what YOU would like to know about laws. Let's do a one-minute essay (hand out index cards). Please finish this sentence for me: When it comes to laws, I'm still wondering about _____.

Assessment and Evaluation

In a future project assignment, the teacher might ask groups of students to investigate the origins of national, state, or local laws of interest, with a special focus on how the laws originated, how they were enacted, how they are enforced, and how they impact the lives of citizens.

◼ HANDS-ON PRACTICE ◼

Try your hand at planning a Deductive Concept lesson using this self-instruct planning sheet. Answering each of the following questions will help you to think through each phase of the process.

Step One: Selecting a Concept

1. What is the name most commonly associated with your concept(s)?

2. What is the concept's rule or definition? This may be a working definition open to expansion down the road.

3. What are the *critical attributes* (i.e., essential characteristics) of the concept?

4. What are some of the noncritical attributes (i.e., nonessential features) associated with the concept?

5. What are some interesting, learner-relevant examples or cases of the concept that can be used during the lesson?

6. What are some contrasting nonexamples (if any) that will help illustrate the concept?

7. What are the most interesting, efficient, and thought-provoking *media* that might be used to illustrate the concept?

Step Two: Planning the Lesson

Now add the details to complete your lesson plan. Think about what you *might* say/do/ask during each phase of the lesson. Refer to the template below to remind yourself of the Core Components and method markers.

Prelude (for teacher reference)

- Rationale (with connection to national/state standards)
- Performance Objective
- Materials and Lesson Aids

Enactment (student engagement)

- Hook
- Student Aim
  Concept definition
- Development
  Investigation of examples and nonexamples

- Application of the concept to new/problematic situations
- Establish critical and noncritical attributes of the concept
- Culmination
  Wrap-Up: What did the students learn?
  Leap: How will they use these important ideas?

Assessment and Evaluation

What will students produce to show you what they've learned?

How will you evaluate this product?

REFERENCES

Ausubel, D. (1963). *The psychology of meaningful learning.* New York: Grune & Stratton.

Bruner, J., Goodnow, J., & Austin, G. (1967). *A study of thinking.* New York: Science Editions.

Gagne, R. (1965). *Psychological principles in systems development.* New York: Holt, Rinehart, & Winston.

Joyce, B., & Weil, M. (1980). *Models of teaching.* Englewood Cliffs, NJ: Prentice-Hall.

Taba, H. (1966). *Teaching strategies and cognitive functioning in elementary school children.* San Francisco: San Francisco State College Press.

■ OVERVIEW: SCENARIO DEPICTING AN INDUCTIVE CONCEPT LESSON

As a high-school math teacher, Chuck Morgan's philosophy is to challenge his students to become mathematicians. In keeping with the vision put forth by the National Council of Teachers of Mathematics, Mr. Morgan consistently challenges his students to work through math-rich problem situations and to later apply what they've learned.

Today's geometry lesson is no exception. As Morgan's third period class begins, he flashes a scanned photograph of a modern downtown building on the large monitor in the corner of the room.

"I took this picture on one of my trips downtown last summer," the teacher begins. "What do you notice about this building?"

Students eagerly provide a range of responses. They note the color of the building, its huge size; Mia mentions "some unusual shapes" within the design.

"Great. Let's all take a look at the shapes that Mia pointed out. How would you describe these shapes?" asked the teacher. He receives a flurry of answers; students note straight lines, curves, connections between figures, different-sized figures. They begin to compare some of the angles within the various shapes. After many of these answers, Mr. Morgan asks Probe questions that challenge students to expand on what they've said.

"Excellent observations. Keep these in mind as I show a few more pictures," continues the teacher. "Please tell the class what you notice about each." Over the next five minutes, he displays several colorful pictures in succession: a close-up of the leaf of a tropical plant that includes some unusual venation, an M. C. Escher print, an intricate ceramic tile mosaic from a European cathedral. Morgan accepts three to four observations for each picture and asks a few Probe and Redirect questions (see Modules Four and Five) to pull new students into the conversation.

The teacher thanks students for sharing their observations, then tells them, "Today, we're going to investigate some of the shapes that we've seen here, to see what we can learn about them. We're going to work in groups of four. Over the next ten minutes, I'd like each group to examine a set of figures that I've drawn on poster board." He holds up a set of fifteen drawings, each on a six-inch square sheet, for the students to see. "Your challenge is to make as many observations about these figures as you can and to arrange them in groups, based on their similarities and differences: how they are alike, and how they are different." Mr. Morgan reviews the directions, and the students begin their investigation.

There is a hum of focused conversation in the room as the teacher moves among groups. He pauses to listen to the interaction and occasionally asks questions ("How are these two examples different, Carolyn?"; "What do you mean when you say the angles are 'wide,' Dave?"; "If you had to place these figures into groups based on their characteristics, how would you do it?"). After ten minutes, Morgan asks the groups to begin sharing their observations. The teacher lists these ideas and frequently asks follow-up questions. He then asks the class, "How did you group the figures, based on their similarities and differences?"

It turns out that the some of the groups had arranged the figures differently. Mr. Morgan asks each group to defend its system for grouping the shapes. One of the groups had categorized the figures based on whether they were open or closed; another used the presence or absence of curved lines as their main criterion. The teacher noted that each of their grouping systems made sense, but that "for our purposes today, let's look at the way that groups 1, 3, and 4 arranged the figures. If we were to group the figures like this" (showing the figures placed in three groups on a scanned slide on the monitor) "what would you say are the main characteristics of the figures in this group?"

The students volunteer observations as Morgan lists the similarities provided. His questions become more focused as he challenges the students to closely examine the examples ("What does this figure have that this one doesn't, Emily?"; "What makes this figure unique among all of the examples?"). Finally, he notes that the students have "discovered all of the important characteristics. Now, if you had to describe the figures in this group in one sentence, how would you do it?" Brian provides an initial response; Joanna quickly adds something to it. With the help of further guiding questions from the teacher, other volunteers define the figures in the first group as "closed two-dimensional figures formed by line segments that connect at only at their two endpoints, with no indentations inside the outermost boundaries of the figure."

"Does anyone know what a figure like this is called?" asks Mr. Morgan. A couple of students offer possibilities. The teacher lets the class know that such figures are known as *convex polygons*. The class is then able to define the figures in the second group, which Morgan labels as *concave polygons*. Mr. Morgan then tells them, "I'll keep you in suspense about the figures in this third group. We'll investigate them a little later in the course."

"Now, to learn a little more about convex polygons, I'd like to challenge each group to solve a riddle involving Pattern Blocks," says the teacher enthusiastically (the students had used Pattern Blocks before and were somewhat familiar with them). Each group is given a separate riddle (e.g., "There are eight blocks total. The three smallest blocks exactly cover the largest block. There are three different colored blocks. Which blocks are in this bag?"). Each group has five minutes to solve its riddle. The class ends with Morgan asking the groups to describe in writing how they solved their riddle and what they discovered about their set of polygons as they worked.

■ FOCAL POINTS AND DISCUSSIONS

Focal Point 1 What Makes the Inductive Concept Method Distinctive?

As young children, we learned some of life's most important early lessons by actively investigating the world around us. We all learned to walk, eat, throw a ball, communicate with others, and ride a bike through trial and error, doing something one way, observing the results, thinking about patterns, making adjustments, and trying again. In working through these learning experiences, we were actually using *inductive reasoning,* which we have defined as the *process of observing objects or events, recognizing patterns, and making generalizations based on observations.* In our opening scenario, Mr. Morgan challenged his geometry students to work through just such an active thinking process as they *discovered* convex polygons. Some of the most important lessons in your life have been learned inductively, and inductive reasoning serves as a foundation of all disciplines, particularly science and mathematics. For these and a number of other important reasons, we urge you to make inductive learning experiences regular events in your classroom.

Discussion 1 What Makes the Inductive Concept Method Distinctive?

In an inductive approach, students experience a number of examples and nonexamples and develop a pattern of critical and noncritical attributes (see Part 1 of this module) based on their experiences. It is important to note that unlike the deductive approach, teachers do not give students the concept name or rule at the beginning of the lesson. Instead, it is up to the *students* to generate (in a sense, to *discover*) the concept rule based on their experiences and analysis of (non)examples. For this reason, inductive lessons can be not only very challenging intellectually but empowering and fun for your students. (See Module Four.)

At this point, you might be asking yourself, "Why should inductive lessons be regular events in my classroom?" We would argue for the frequent use of inductive methods for a number of reasons. As a teacher, one of your main tasks will be to help your students develop an understanding of important new ideas within your discipline. A constructivist learning perspective would lead us to believe that you can't simply tell students everything that they need to know. As we have noted, there is a mountain of evidence that indicates that students never *truly understand* much of what teachers tell them and that they forget most of what they are told within a short time. As teachers, we must provide students with every opportunity to grapple with new ideas, constructing meaning through the interaction of their current frames of reference and elements of the new experience. Inductive concept lessons can provide exactly this type of challenging classroom experience. You are pushing your students to think historically, scientifically, mathematically as they try to make sense of complex, problematic situations. Also keep in mind that the interactive nature of inductive lessons allows us, as teachers, to gain insights into the meanings that our students attach to newly introduced ideas.

Most of us would also agree that teaching students *how to think* is more important than covering subject matter. Deductive and inductive concept teaching, when done effectively, can promote the development of critical-thinking abilities to a much greater extent than asking students to listen passively to teacher presentations or lectures. Although debate continues over the extent to which students might transfer such thinking abilities from one context to another (e.g., from a classroom situation to the real world, or from one discipline to another), experience has convinced us that students *can* apply inductive reasoning skills developed in the classroom to new situations. The potential for inductive experiences to help students develop thinking abilities is perhaps the most important reason for their inclusion in the classroom. As educator Bruce Joyce (1980) once put it, "We need to [challenge students to] reinvent the wheel once in a while, not because we need a lot of wheels, but because we need a lot of inventors."

Inductive methods are especially challenging intellectually since there is so much emphasis on the ideas generated by students themselves. We believe that another reason for providing frequent inductive experiences in the classroom is that they promote students *taking ownership* of ideas. Helping students to develop and later apply their own working definition for a concept such as

freedom, for example, might aid them not only to connect with their personal experiences but to *feel* a sense of ownership of the ideas produced, a powerful educational and motivational factor in the classroom.

Figure 8.5 displays a suggested planning template for an Inductive Concept lesson. As you take a look at the various stages of such a lesson, think about how Chuck Morgan followed such a path in his geometry lesson. We'll then take a closer look at what goes into planning Inductive Concept lessons.

Prelude

- Rationale (with connection to national/state standards)
- Performance Objective
- Materials and Lesson Aids

Enactment

- Hook: Start with an attention-getter that is somehow related to the concept. One option is to begin with one or more intriguing examples of the concept.
- Student Aim: Unlike the Aim for a deductive lesson, state your purpose for an inductive lesson almost mysteriously ("Let's see what we can learn by investigating these objects/events").
- Development
  1. Investigation of examples/nonexamples
     a. Share examples (and perhaps nonexamples) of the concept with your students in either a full-class or peer-group setting. When utilizing a more guided approach, tell the students whether each example is *positive* or *negative*.
     b. Challenge your students to first observe, then compare and contrast the examples by asking open-ended questions (e.g., "What do you notice about these?"; "How are they alike/different?")
     c. As students experience the examples, begin asking progressively more focused questions that deepen their analysis of the examples (e.g., "What do all of the objects/events in this group have that those in this group don't?").
  2. Discovery of the Concept
     a. Once your students have grouped the examples based on their critical and noncritical attributes (i.e., characteristics), challenge them to name the concept (optional) and to articulate the concept rule based on these attributes.
     b. Question students in order to get them to "test" their concept rule (e.g., "Is this true for each/this example?"). When using a more guided approach, confirm (and possibly adjust) the concept rule generated by the students (e.g., "I would add this to our definition").
  3. Application
     a. If possible, elicit further examples of the concept from your students.
     b. To fulfill your Performance Objective, conduct a brief activity or provide an assignment that challenges students to test/use the concept.
- Culmination
  1. Wrap-Up: Review, or ask students to review, the main ideas generated. Again, focus on the "So what?" question. Why is this an important concept/principle?
  2. Leap: How can we use the *big idea* that we've discovered today?

Assessment and Evaluation Plan

- Assessment products (What will students produce in this/a later lesson?)
- Evaluation (How will you evaluate this product, e.g., with a scoring rubric?)

FIGURE 8.5 Inductive Concept Lesson Planning Template

Method Markers

You'll find that the features described here combine to make the inductive teaching method one of the most thought-provoking approaches that we'll investigate. As you explore the specific method markers described, try to envision how inductive lessons are different from those that are taught deductively and what experiences an inductive lesson in *your* subject area might include.

- The Student Aim will be fairly open, indicating only the general direction the lesson will take. As the teacher, you *will not define or even hint at what the concept(s) is/are* during the early stages of the lesson. In effect, your Student Aim will *challenge the students to discover/articulate the concept(s).*

- During the Development, you will invite students to *investigate examples and possibly nonexamples of the concept,* making observations and looking for patterns. As the teacher, you'll facilitate this process by asking a sequence of *broad Trigger questions.*

- By asking *progressively more focused Trigger questions,* you will challenge students to *name, define, and apply the concept* later in the development. Establish (non)critical attributes.

- As in the deductive approach, the Culmination will include some discussion of the *implications* of the concept. Why is it important, and how will we use this "idea" in future lessons?

Please keep these important features in mind as we take you through the process of planning and conducting inductive lessons.

Up Close: Planning and Conducting an Inductive Concept Lesson

In planning and conducting inductive lessons in our own classrooms over the past several years, we have been heavily influenced by the work of Jerome Bruner (1967) and Hilda Taba (1966). Our suggestions for planning and conducting such lessons are based in part on their pioneering work.

Guided and Unguided Induction

In suggesting a series of stages in the Enactment section of inductive lessons, we'll make a distinction between *guided* and *unguided* approaches. You'll see that there are two differences between these two approaches: In a guided lesson, the teacher exerts more control over the interaction by asking more focused questions, *and* she directs students toward a more precise, pre-determined

definition of the concept(s) or principle(s). You'll also see that there is no absolute boundary between the two approaches. In fact, we believe that it is more useful to think of inductive lessons as falling on a continuum from guided to unguided, with wide variation in between. As we describe guided and unguided induction more closely, ask yourself which approach Chuck Morgan was taking in his geometry lesson.

Up Close: Planning and Conducting an Inductive Concept Lesson

Prelude: Rationale

At this point, let's transport ourselves back to Chuck Morgan's classroom as we discuss planning and conducting inductive lessons in depth. In his geometry lesson, the teacher challenged his students to carefully analyze a set of examples in order to articulate a definition for convex polygon, a concept that they would then use extensively in this math course. The Rationale for his lesson could look like this: "Through the peer-group analysis of a set of geometric figures, students will articulate an appropriate concept rule for convex polygons and later investigate this concept in more depth by solving polygon riddles through the use of Pattern Blocks. This experience will help students develop abilities related to analytical thinking, critical thinking (as they share and defend their agreed-upon 'system' for grouping the blocks and consider other grouping arrangements), and group communication skills. This lesson connects directly to INTASC standards 1, 2, 3, 4, 5, 6, and 7." As we'll see in the following section, the Performance Objective that you write for a lesson like this will be closely linked to your Rationale.

Performance Objective

Performance Objectives for inductive lessons usually link directly to the discovery/articulation or application of the concept. We would urge you to think about what you might ask students to do to show you that they understand and can use the concept principle rule. In his math lesson, Mr. Morgan challenged his students to investigate convex polygons in more depth by solving complex riddles involving their properties. His Performance Objective might have looked like this: "After comparing and contrasting fifteen varied geometric figures, students will articulate an acceptable definition for convex polygons. In a peer-group setting, they will then solve at least one riddle involving Pattern Blocks, recording in writing how they solved the problem and at least five observations of the polygons involved." A Performance Objective like this clearly conveys how the teacher might assess what students have learned. As you plan your own inductive lessons, think carefully along these same lines.

Materials

Just as in deductive lessons, one of your biggest planning challenges will be to assemble a set of concept examples and nonexamples that students can investigate. As you do this, think carefully about what physical objects, pieces of text, pictures, songs, and so on exemplify important concept attributes (more about this in the following sections). In conducting his geometry lesson, Mr. Morgan would likely have to create several sets of figures (computer graphics might help here), as well as assemble enough Pattern Blocks and write (or find in a resource) accompanying riddles. Again, this might sound like hard work, but the payoff comes when students are provided with an exciting, thought-provoking experience. Consider also that once you assemble a set of examples for a quality inductive lesson, chances are that you can reuse these materials in coming years.

Let's move on to the Enactment section of inductive lessons. What suggestions can we offer when it comes to the planning and *conducting* of these exciting lessons?

Enactment: The Hook

In inductive lessons, an intriguing possibility is to *start* the lesson by sharing one or more examples of the concept or principle, as we noted in Part 1 of this module and in Module Four. If you choose to do this, we suggest being intentionally cagey about what you have in store for the lesson. You're merely inviting students to investigate something interesting and to share their observations or reactions with you and their classmates. Eye-catching science demonstrations are especially effective in this way, as are pictures, songs, poems, written or recorded speech excerpts, and actual objects (props). The possibilities range as widely as *concepts* do. As an avid film historian, one of your authors is especially fond of using movie clips as Hooks for concept lessons. We have also enjoyed a great deal of success by asking students to perform and then analyze skits with subtle examples of the concept embedded in the lines (try writing such a skit for an inductive lesson).

In our opening math lesson, Mr. Morgan shared a series of interesting scanned photographs with his class and asked a series of open-ended questions about them. Not only did this introduce the central concept in an engaging way but it also sent some other subtle but powerful messages to the class (i.e., this concept extends beyond the walls of our math classroom, and it might be worthwhile to investigate it).

Of course, you have a great many options in planning a Hook for an inductive lesson. For example, we have found that open-ended questions that somehow relate to students' experiences are very effective. But whatever you choose to do as part of your Hook, remember not to get *too* specific about what the examples are and how they relate to your main concept. Leave this open enough for the students to discover later in the lesson.

Student Aim

As we have noted, your goal in inductive lessons is to challenge your students to analyze examples and in a very real sense discover the main concept/principle(s). It follows that your stated Student Aim for such a lesson should be open and indirect, especially when compared with a deductive lesson. For example, in his polygon lesson, Mr. Morgan simply told his class, "Today, we're going to investigate some of the shapes that we've seen here to see what we can learn about them." Such a statement can provide students with a basic feel for what you're going to do *without* directing their thinking to any great extent.

We have found that it's possible to lend a little mystery to inductive lessons by carefully planning the Hook and Student Aim. Most students seem intrigued by the openness of these lessons, and we have discovered that even learners who feel comfortable with more direct, deductive approaches will buy into inductive methods once they become a familiar part of your teaching repertoire.

A Student Aim like the one that Mr. Morgan used in his geometry lesson can serve as a nice transition to the heart of an inductive lesson: the investigation of concept examples.

Development: Investigation of Examples and Nonexamples

The key to designing an effective inductive lesson is to plan each phase of the lesson so that it builds on the previous phase, with each step gradually guiding students toward an understanding of the concept. A crucial point in any inductive lesson comes with the introduction of examples (and possibly nonexamples) of the concept or principle. Of course, the nature of your examples will depend completely on your main concept or principle, but the possibilities are just about endless. Anything, from sentences (as in an English or foreign language grammar lesson) to demonstrated dance steps to historic photos can serve as examples. When planning how and when to introduce your examples, ask yourself the following questions:

• Will it be most effective to introduce the examples in a peer-group or full-class setting? If your examples consist of a set of objects or sections of text and several *sets* are available (as in our polygon lesson), we suggest that you begin the example investigation in a peer-group setting, even for just a few minutes. This will allow each student to experience the examples and share observations to the greatest extent possible (and you can circulate around the room, listen, and ask questions, as Mr. Morgan did). If your examples consist of film clips, a series of demonstrations, or similar one-of-a-kind examples, you will probably need to conduct your initial investigation as a full class, although you can ask students to share ideas regarding an experienced example in peer groups.

• Will you introduce examples one at a time, inviting students to respond to each, or can they investigate an entire set at once? Many of the same considerations that we mentioned in the previous point apply here. With demonstrations, videoclips, or unique props, it's best to ask students to respond to a series of examples one at a time. In this case, we suggest listing their observations on the board/overhead so that you might compare and contrast them later.

• Perhaps most important, what might you ask students as they investigate the examples? Remember that the Inductive Concept method is as interactive as any constructivist approach. This part of the lesson should feature a great deal of student–student interaction, especially if you are utilizing a more unguided approach, and you can set the stage for this interaction with the right sequence of questions. During this portion of the lesson, we suggest planning a *broad-to-focused sequence.* Start as our math teacher did by simply inviting students to share initial impressions (e.g., "What did you notice about _____?"). Move on to questions that focus on specific, important features (e.g., "Take a look at line 3. What do you think she meant when she said _____?").

As you write an inductive lesson plan, we suggest getting specific about the sequence in which you'll introduce your examples and the sequence of questions that you *might* ask throughout the development. Remember that in doing this you're not trying to script yourself; as you conduct the lesson, you may find yourself veering away from your plans, especially if a student raises an interesting point that's worth pursuing. But, in observing hundreds of student teachers over the years, we've found that planning the main Trigger questions in advance has a huge positive impact on the quality of interaction in lessons. If you're a beginning teacher, you'll ask more questions, and better questions, if you plan in advance (see Module Five and sample lesson plans throughout *Invisible Teaching* for examples of this).

As this part of the Development unfolds, you should guide the students (to some degree) with increasingly focused questions. Move the students from making general observations to analyzing specific features to grouping the examples based on similarities and differences. Then comes what we call the *aha!* moment in an inductive lesson: when your students actually discover the concept.

The Discovery

In a well-planned and conducted Inductive Concept Lesson, your students will eventually reach that aha! moment. They'll connect enough of the pieces in the puzzle to recognize what your concept is and how it might be described in words. Your questioning will help them do this.

By this point in the lesson, your questions are becoming more specific. For example, after investigating the examples in peer groups and sharing and defending the various ways in which they had arranged the figures into categories, Mr. Morgan asked his students to take a closer look at the way that student groups 1, 3, and 4 had done this. He asked them about the main characteristics of the figures in these categories and then how the students "might describe the figures in this category in one sentence." As a class, the students generated the definition, with the help of further questions from their teacher, but the key here is that *the class* arrived at the definition, based on their analysis.

Note also that Morgan asked the students if they knew what figures like this are called; this is the kind of clinching question that you'll want to ask in an inductive lesson, perhaps even before the students articulate the concept rule. They may know the right label or term for the concept, especially if this main idea has some familiarity. The teacher may have to provide the words, as the math teacher did in our example (not many novice geometry students could have come up with *convex polygon,* to be sure!). Our advice here is to ask students to provide the right word for the concept, but be ready to supply the label, especially if the term is new to the class or especially technical ("We call figures like this _____").

Back to a question that we posed a few pages back: Was Chuck Morgan's lesson guided or unguided induction? In some respects, it's a trick question. We would say that the lesson is *fairly* guided, because the teacher determined in advance what the concept was, which figures were examples and which were nonexamples, and what important attributes should be included in the definition. But he did offer his class some latitude in deciding how the rule would be phrased. We have found that challenging your class to provide a *working definition* for a concept, as Morgan did here, can be very powerful educationally. *Their definition* can be used and tested in later lessons ("Based on what we know now, is there anything we should change in our definition of _____?").

One more note before moving on. Remember that you have discretion, as a constructivist teacher, over how much to guide any lesson, particularly an inductive one. If students struggle in their analysis of the examples, you can step in to ask more direct guiding questions. If their analysis takes off in exciting, unanticipated directions, you might back off and do less guiding than you had planned.

The development of any Inductive Concept lesson ends with some challenge to test and apply the concept/ concept rule. In most cases, this is that point at which you challenge students to show you what they've learned, fulfilling the Performance Objective(s). In many cases, you can begin this application process by simply asking the class to brainstorm additional examples of the concept ("What else have you seen that fits our definition?"). In our math lesson, Mr. Morgan developed a novel way to do this, inviting the class to solve engaging riddles in order to make additional discoveries related to the polygons. Remember that your challenge to apply the concept could come in the form of an in-class or take-home writing assignment or something that takes place during future class sessions. We are particularly fond of ending class sessions with application-type questions for students to consider for the next day. Try this approach as a way to buy into your students' time away from your classroom.

Culmination

As in a deductive lesson, it's important to plan a *Wrap-Up* that conveys the importance of the concept. It's generally very effective to ask students to review the main ideas generated, at least partially as a final check on their understanding of the concept(s). We would also advise either asking or telling the students directly why the concept is important and asking them to relate the concept or principle to real situations (the *Leap*). For a Look Ahead, you could ask or tell your students *how they might use these ideas in future lessons.* As always, inviting your students to generate questions that they have regarding the concept can provide you with insights into their thinking as well as guiding questions for future lessons.

As you can see, inductive lessons tend to be even more student-centered than deductive lessons. The challenge is for the students to participate in an in-depth analysis of the examples and to (frequently) name and articulate the concept. As teachers at the middle, high school, and college level, we have found inductive lessons to be incredibly challenging and empowering for students, and they can be a refreshing change of pace in any classroom. Inductive lessons are often more challenging to plan and conduct than deductive lessons, but we have found that the result is well worth the effort.

Assessment and Evaluation

Just as in a Deductive Concept lesson, a formal assessment and evaluation event could take place either in the application phase of the lesson or immediately following the application (see the sample lesson plan at the conclusion of this module for an excellent example of this). As you plan your own inductive lessons, we invite you to consider the many possible assessment *products* that you might challenge students to generate.

Focal Point 4 When Should You Use the Inductive Concept Method in Your Classroom?

It's important to note that, like any lesson, a concept lesson should not stand alone in your classroom. Lessons like these will serve to effectively introduce new concepts and begin the process of analysis. Follow-up discussions and activities will provide students with additional opportunities to construct meaning for the concept and to connect it with other ideas. These follow-up lessons will be essential in developing a more complete understanding, so consider inductive and deductive lessons to be part of a series of classroom experiences. Use these methods frequently when introducing new ideas. Remember that concepts are the vital building blocks for high-level thinking and are particularly important in understanding the major principles in any discipline. Using these strategies may push you, as the teacher, to consider the most important themes, or big ideas, within your curriculum. This is a vitally important process, lest students become lost in the information provided in the classroom, losing sight of connections to their own world. Once introduced, major concepts can be used to help students make connections between important ideas. Inductive lessons are often challenging to plan, so a mix of deductive and inductive lessons is most realistic when planning time is considered. In thinking about students' preferred learning styles, using a mix of deductive and inductive methods will allow you to reach more students more effectively.

■ TIP FOR TECHNOLOGY INTEGRATION

Teacher- and student-designed computer programs can provide students with a medium for sharing their *understanding* of concepts. As a teacher, challenge students to complete such projects on systems that allow them to extend their understanding of central concepts.

■ ROUNDUP ■

Inductive Concept lessons challenge students to investigate examples and nonexamples of a concept or principle, analyze their similarities and differences, and ultimately to discover the main idea and articulate and test

Ms. Wagner's sixth-period U.S. history class has embarked on a unit focused on race relations and the Civil Rights movement. Students enter the room today to the sound of Bob Dylan's *Blowin' in the Wind.* They had analyzed the lyrics the day before, when they learned that the song was written about the Civil Rights movement. The teacher starts this lesson by inviting students to listen and respond to video excerpts of speeches by Malcolm X and Martin Luther King; she asks them to compare and contrast the tone of the speeches and the content and lists students' ideas on the board. Minutes later, the teacher challenges students to analyze video excerpts that include authentic footage of protests held across the South during the early 1960s. Ms. Wagner asks broad questions at this point in the lesson ("What happened in this scene?"; "What were the people involved doing?"; "Why do you think they did what they did?"; "What is the response of the authorities?"), then asks the group to begin comparing and contrasting the events and to connect to comments made in the speech excerpts. The teacher then challenges the class to put the pieces together by asking, "How would you describe the approach used by the people who wanted to change things in the South?" With the help of further guiding questions from the teacher, the class develops a working definition for *nonviolent protest: an attempt to achieve desired social change through mass, organized, lawful, passive resistance designed to raise public awareness.*[3]

FIGURE 8.6 A Glimpse into a Constructivist Classroom

a definition for it. We consider the Inductive Concept method to be a quintessential part of a constructivist classroom. In effect, you're challenging your students to *become* historians, linguists, scientists, mathematicians as they directly experience concept examples and develop and utilize critical-thinking abilities to make sense of complex situations. Done effectively, inductive lessons provide students with excellent practice in developing reasoning patterns, presenting and defending clear statements of position, and listening to and challenging the ideas of others. Our experiences have shown us that the frequent use of the Inductive Concept/Principle method can have an intellectually invigorating, empowering effect on students. We urge you to make frequent use of this method in your own classroom as an alternative to didactic teacher presentations.

Remember that there are several keys to conducting effective inductive lessons. Grab the attention of your students early in the lesson. Sharing an intriguing example or two of the concept early on is a good way to do this. Think carefully about what examples of the concept to share, in what sequence, whether the investigation of the concept should take place in a peer-group or whole-class setting, and what questions you might pose along the way. Remember to start with broad questions that will challenge *your students* to analyze the examples. Again, the real beauty of inductive lessons is that students are doing the thinking and discovering. Your questions should become progressively more focused as you guide students toward the concept. Carefully consider how *much* guiding you'll do and what type of concept rule you'll want the students to articulate. Finally, consider how you might challenge your class to apply the concept during the final phases of the lesson, and in future lessons. See the Inductive Concept Flowchart in Figure 8.7 for an encapsulation of this method.

■ INDUCTIVE CONCEPT SAMPLE LESSON PLAN ■

Unit Title: Characterization in Novels, Short Stories, and Poems (Intended for high school literature class)

Prelude
Rationale
(Combines What? Why? Justification): Using a guided inductive approach focused on an analysis of two characters within the poem "Daddy" will allow me to challenge students to articulate broad, working definitions for *flat* and *round* characters that can then be applied to other written works as the unit progresses. This experience will enhance the group communications skills and critical-thinking abilities of my students and connects to INTASC standards 1, 3, 4, 5, 6, 7, and 8.

Performance Objective
(Combines Preparation, Product, Criteria): After completing a visual representation of one of the characters in the poem, students will explain elements within their drawings and support decisions made by citing excerpts from the poem. Then, after articulating definitions for flat and round characters, the learner will provide at least one example of each character type from a written work or film and defend that choice.

Materials and Lesson Aids

1. Copies of the Sylvia Plath poem "Daddy" for the entire class.

2. One piece of construction paper for each pair of students.

1 =   compare and contrast examples and nonexamples
of a concept or principle
from instructional materials

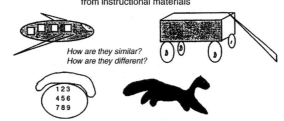

How are they similar?
How are they different?

2 =   establish characteristics of examples and nonexamples

Which attributes are constant?   Which attributes are variable?

mobility   human controlled   *materials   machines or animals*

nonexample

telephone doesn't carry a product or person somewhere else

3 =   guide student expression of the concept or principle

characteristics ————————➤ $A = B$ Transportation is . . .

animate or inanimate   moves people and things

4 =   elicit student examples of the concept or principle

spaceships   *submarines* with characteristics
camels   *elephants*

5 =   culmination: $A = B$ ——➤ ! ?

reestablish the concept definition with implications

transportation has shrunk the world   increases the need for fuels   delivers people and goods

increases peace?   changes the nature of war

© 2001 Ina Claire Gabler

FIGURE 8.7 Inductive Concept Method Flowchart

---

3. One set of colored pencils for each set of students.

Enactment

Time Estimate	Main Ideas/Concepts, Questions, and Teaching Techniques
5–6 minutes	*Hook:* I'd like everybody to think about one of your favorite books or movies. (pause)

• Who were your favorite characters in the book or movie that you picked (survey class for ideas; ask Probes/ Redirects)?
• Why did you pick this character?
• Did you like/dislike this character? Why?
• Does this character remind you of anyone that you know? Yourself?

• How is your character like _____?
• What did the author/film director do to introduce this character to you?

3–4 minutes   *Student Aim:* Today, we're going to learn something about how writers introduce characters to us. I'm going to read a short poem to you—it's called "Daddy" and it was written by Sylvia Plath. The poem involves two characters, the narrator and her father. As I read the poem, try to imagine what each of the characters might be like, based on what the author tells us.

Read "Daddy" out loud.

8–10 minutes   *Development:* Investigating Examples I'd like to challenge you to think about the two characters in the poem! You're going to work with a partner. I'd like you and your partner to talk about what you've learned about one of the characters—I'll tell you which one.

Then, I'm going to give you five minutes to draw a visual representation of your character. You can draw what you think the person might actually look like or use symbols to convey something about the character. Be ready to share your drawing with the rest of the class (assure students that their drawings don't have to be artistically perfect.).

Arrange students in pairs; provide each pair with a piece of construction paper and set of colored pencils.

Potential questions addressed to groups:
- Do you like the poem? Why/why not?
- How did the poem make you feel?
- What's the significance of the title? How does the narrator feel about her father?
- Does she say anything that's confusing? Which line(s)?
- What did the author do to introduce the character to you?
- Why would you draw _____ this way?
- What does _____ in your drawing symbolize?
- How could you explain _____ when you share your drawing?

6–8 minutes

Discovering/Defining the Concept: Ask groups to volunteer to share their drawings. Ask questions, including those listed above; probe/redirect as groups share their ideas. Guide students toward concepts through the following questions:
- How is _____'s drawing similar to _____'s? How are they different? Why might you see these similarities/differences?
- What does Plath tell you about the narrator? Her father? How does she tell you these things (list student-generated ideas in *father* and *narrator* columns)?
- Which character do you feel that you know better? Why?
- Which is better developed? Why/how?
- Which character seems more complex? Why?

- Which do you feel more emotionally attached to? Why?
- What devices does she use to describe the father? Do we ever really get to know him? (What is a stereotype? How are stereotypes used here?)

5–6 minutes

To summarize what we've done, what words could you use to describe the narrator character (refer to list—complex/developed; know motivations; emotional attachment; less predictable)?
- What is the father like (refer to list—more one-dimensional; stereotypical; more predictable)?
- Has anyone heard the terms *round* or *flat* character before? Which might apply to the father? To the narrator?

Challenge students to articulate working definitions of round and flat characters. Establish (non)critical attributes of the concepts.

5 minutes/as time allows

Applying the Concept

Again, think back to a favorite book, short story, or movie. Pick a character from your choice. Is the character flat or round? Why do you think so (get a range of responses from students; compare/contrast examples; probe/redirect)?

Do you think that there might be degrees of *flatness* and *roundness*? Why?

Culmination

Wrap-Up
- What are some ways in which authors introduce us to characters?
- What are some purposes for which characters can be used?

Leap
How could you apply the concept of round or flat characters to your own personal experiences?

Look Ahead
Tomorrow, we'll start to explore a favorite short story of mine and use what we've learned about flat and round characters as we try to find meaning in the story.

Assessment and Evaluation

As a written assignment, ask students to choose a character from a favorite written work or movie. In a three- to four-page reflective essay, challenge them to describe the character, based on what the author tells them, and to label the degree of *flatness* or *roundness* of the character. Remind them to justify their choice by using the class definitions and supporting evidence from the book, film, and so on.

■ HANDS-ON PRACTICE ■

Try your hand at planning an Inductive Concept lesson using this self-instruct planning sheet. Answering each of the following questions will help you to think through each phase of the process.

Step One: Selecting a Concept

1. What is the name most commonly associated with your concept(s)?
2. What is the concept's rule or definition?
3. What are the *critical attributes* (i.e., essential characteristics) of the concept?
4. What are some of the noncritical attributes (i.e., nonessential features) associated with the concept?
5. What are some interesting, learner-relevant examples or cases of the concept that can be used during the lesson?
6. What are some contrasting nonexamples (if any) that will help illustrate the concept?
7. What are the most interesting, efficient, and thought-provoking *media* that might be used to illustrate the concept?

Step Two: Planning the Lesson

Now add the details to complete your lesson plan. Think about what you *might* say/do/ask during each phase of the lesson. Refer to the following template to remind yourself of the Core Components and method markers.

Prelude (for teacher reference)

- Rationale (with connection to national/state standards)

- Performance Objective
- Materials and Lesson Aids

Enactment (student engagement)

- Hook (consider possible introduction of examples)
- Student Aim (open-ended)
- Development
  Investigation of examples and nonexamples
  Discovery of the concept
  Application of the concept
- Culmination
  Wrap-Up: What did the students learn?
  Leap: How will they use these important ideas?

Assessment and Evaluation

What will students produce to show you what they've learned?

How will you evaluate this product?

ENDNOTES

1. Thanks to Deanna DeBischopp, Augustana College Class of 1998, and Carolyn Carter, Augustana College Class of 2000, for their contributions to this scenario.
2. Thanks to Sarah Knoblauch, Augustana College Class of 2000, for her contributions to this scenario.
3. Thanks to Eric Turley, Augustana College Class of 1998, for his contributions to this scenario.

REFERENCES

Ausubel, D. (1963). *The psychology of meaningful learning.* New York: Grune and Stratton.

Bruner, J., Goodnow, J., & Austin, G. (1967). *A study of thinking.* New York: Science Editions.

Gagne, R. (1965). *Psychological principles in systems development.* New York: Holt, Rinehart, and Winston.

Joyce, B., & Weil, M. (1980). *Models of teaching.* Englewood Cliffs, NJ: Prentice-Hall.

Taba, H. (1966). *Teaching strategies and cognitive functioning in elementary school children.* San Francisco: San Francisco State College Press.

CONSTRUCTIVIST METHODS

Section C

Constructivist classrooms are both *active* and interactive places. As we've seen in describing a number of techniques and methods, constructivist teachers place great emphasis on what we might call classroom discourse, which is the respectful and purposeful exchange of ideas between teachers and students and among the students themselves. Such discourse is the focus in classroom discussions.

You may have noticed that some teachers consider a discussion to be a one-way stream of words from the teacher *to* students. *Our* approach to discussions is much different. We define a *discussion* as *the verbal investigation or consideration of a question by a group of people.* Discussion is also *a conversation with a purpose.* In the three modules that follow, we'll introduce three distinctly different types of discussion methods, the *Directed,* the *Exploratory,* and the *Reflective.* You'll see that each method is highly versatile but that each is characterized by specific goals, a specific type of structuring question and resulting pattern of interaction, and a specific conclusion or outcome. These methods are not necessarily discrete, but exist on a continuum.

When using any discussion method, let the class know that you'd like them to participate, that it's a time to express opinions and contribute new ideas. Teach *them* the differences between Directed, Exploratory, and Reflective Discussion methods. This meta-awareness often motivates students because you are including them in the "inside story" (see Module Two, "Resocializing").

For successful discussions, students should have an appropriate understanding of the topic to allow them to speculate and form opinions. Second, students can't be expected to discuss issues with which they are completely unfamiliar. You will frequently have to furnish some type of prerequisite information, unless students have some experience with the issue/topic in another setting. You can also help ensure the success of a discussion by asking students to complete an interesting reading assignment beforehand, by conducting a lesson (e.g., a concept lesson, see Module Eight) that will set the stage for the discussion, or by doing a short presentation, a skit, a film clip, or activity during the lesson Hook. Think about yourself as a student. Wouldn't a lesson Hook featuring an interesting videoclip or a teacher-planned skit performed by classmates pique your curiosity and possibly make you feel more willing to participate? (See Module Four.)

We have found that the right physical setting can also promote classroom interaction. Arranging desks in a circle, giving students the opportunity to look directly at one another, can facilitate interaction. This often makes an amazing difference (See Module Two, Part 1.). Usually, it's a good idea to seat yourself in the circle of chairs, at eye level with your students, especially when conducting Exploratory and Reflective discussions. If you stand over the group or position yourself in front of the classroom, students will tend to look to you for a response after every comment that they make. Students in any setting will not speculate on issues if they feel that they will be embarrassed by making an incorrect or half-conceived answer. Remember that your stu-

145

dents must feel secure enough to take chances, and this will depend largely on your questioning and the response from you and their classmates (see Module Two, "Resocializing"). These suggestions help to create a thinker-friendly community.

We invite you to use Figure C.2 to compare and contrast the three discussion types. As you experience and practice each method, remember that there are no absolute boundaries between them; much will depend on questions and ideas that you and your students spontaneously generate. At this point, start to consider ways in which you might use each discussion method in your subject-matter area, and continue to think in these terms as we introduce each discussion method in detail.

Discussion Type	Nature of Discussion	Teacher Preparation	Nature of Structuring Device	Interaction Pattern	Role of Students	Role of Teacher
Directed	Structured investigation; analysis of a focused question; decision somewhat predetermined by teacher	Lists points he/she wishes to raise and writes questions designed to help students understand each point	Highly focused; provides a direction for interaction		Reach new levels of understanding by responding to focused questions	Guide: poses a series of focused questions that help students reach new insights; asks frequent Probes/Redirects.
Exploratory	Brainstorming: investigation of (1) alternatives, (2) pros & cons, (3) implications; decisions made by students	Plans open-ended questions by anticipating possible areas of student response	Extremely broad/open-ended, designed to *include* peripheral topics, alternative explanations		Free thinkers: generate ideas *and* new questions in an open setting	Moderator: sets initial direction; asks occasional Trigger, Probe, and Redirect questions
Reflective	Decision making: investigation of a value-based question	Plans potential questions based on implications/issues connected to main question	Somewhat focused: challenge students to make/defend a *best* decision.		Decision makers: struggle with debating a question that has no *right* answer	Moderator: aids flow of discussion; challenges students to justify/support decisions

◀▶ interaction strong in both directions
◀┄▶ interaction less emphasized

FIGURE C.2 Classroom Discussion Methods

The Directed Discussion Method

Overview: Scenario Depicting a Directed Discussion

Focal Points and Discussions

What Makes the Directed Discussion Method Distinctive?

Directed Discussion Lesson Planning Template

Directed Discussion Method Markers

Up Close: Planning and Conducting a Directed Discussion

When Should You Use the Directed Discussion Method in Your Classroom?

Tip for Technology Integration

Roundup

Directed Discussion Method Flowchart

Directed Discussion Sample Lesson Plan

Hands-On Practice

■ OVERVIEW: SCENARIO DEPICTING A DIRECTED DISCUSSION

For the past two weeks, Ida Jackson's senior American and British literature class has been engaged in a unit on satire. They started by investigating a wide range of more recent examples of satire, from literary works to political cartoons, even excerpts from an episode of *The Simpsons*. As one of the newest teachers in the English department, Ms. Jackson is excited about teaching this topic for the first time. She recently told a colleague how happy she has been with the results of introducing more recent examples of satire first. "They've been a really effective hook for the rest of the unit," she noted cheerfully. One of her most effective lessons so far came early in the unit. Students inductively analyzed a series of text excerpts from satirical pieces and articulated a working definition of satire for the class: "A humorous and/or serious convention, intended for a specific audience, used to ridicule a particular person or situation for purposes of raising awareness or causing social change." The class has been using this definition as they have investigated other examples of satire.

The class is now in the process of investigating works from earlier historical periods. Ms. Jackson is determined to connect works of literature to events taking place at that time. To prepare for today's lesson, her students (most of them, anyway) have read Jonathan Swift's *A Modest Proposal* as well as a brief overview that the teacher has written as a homework assignment describing relations between Ireland and England during the early seventeenth century. As the second period bell rings, Ms. Jackson flashes a recently published political cartoon (focused on school violence and gun control issues) on the large computer monitor in the front corner of the classroom. "What message do you think this cartoonist was trying to send the public when he drew this?" she asks the class.

Hands fly in the air as her students offer comments; school violence seems to be an issue that concerns these soon-to-be graduates. There is some debate among those in the class over exactly where the cartoonist stands on Second Amendment rights. For a few minutes, Ms. Jackson moderates a fairly heated discussion over specific features of the cartoon. A couple of students express some concern over the content of the cartoon. Monica pointedly tells the class, "I'm not sure it's right to publish a cartoon that's supposed to be funny about such a serious issue!"

"Monica raises an outstanding question," says Ms. Jackson to the group. "Should people use humor to express their opinions about serious issues? Is this justified?" Several students offer opinions, both pro and con. Ms. Jackson promises the class, "We'll focus on this issue specifically in tomorrow's lesson; it's an important question. And it certainly connects to the piece that we read for today, *A Modest Proposal*. What general reactions did you have to that piece?" The students reactions range from "outrageous" to "funny" to "cruel" to "totally gross." "His suggestions don't sound all that bad to me!" says Brian to a chorus of laughs.

Ms. Jackson asks a few questions to check on the students' understanding of the history of the period, based on their reading of the overview. She then asks the class to "keep these points in mind as we discuss *A Modest Proposal* in depth. It's a piece that most of us agreed was funny, that deals with issues like hunger, poverty, and homelessness, about as serious as issues get. Our main question for the next several minutes is this: *Who or what does Swift seem to be ridiculing here, and how does he accomplish this?*"

Over the next twenty minutes, the teacher asks a sequence of focused questions that guide students through an analysis of the text. Ms. Jackson asks questions about specific passages ("Why do you think he opened the piece this way?"; "What point do you think he was making when he mentions admirable boots and fine gloves for ladies and gentlemen?"; "Who or what was he criticizing in mentioning 'the papacy'?") that connect directly to the main question. Slightly broader questions like "What is the significance of the title?" and "What is the intended audience for this piece, and how might they have responded at that time?" also elicit a range of responses from the students. Ms. Jackson asks numerous Probe and Redirect questions; the focused nature of the questions results in a largely teacher-student–teacher-student interaction pattern.

Fifteen minutes before the end of class, Ms. Jackson returns to the main question: "So who or what was Swift ridiculing in this piece? And how did he do it?" Several students contribute to a summary of the points raised. "You did a terrific job analyzing the text!" says Ms. Jackson enthusiastically. "I want you to remember these points when we move on to writing our own pieces of satire later this week. Today, we're going to conclude by writing a one-minute essay in response to two questions: How does *A Modest Proposal* compare to other pieces of satire that we've seen? And would you change anything about our definition for satire based on our discussion today? We'll share our responses when you're done writing."[1]

■ FOCAL POINTS AND DISCUSSIONS

Focal Point 1 **What Makes the Directed Discussion Method Distinctive?**

Welcome back from Ms. Jackson's lit class. You have just taken part in what we call a Directed Discussion. Directed Discussions are designed to serve as highly interactive substitutes for more teacher-centered methods (e.g., lecturing). As the facilitator of this type of discussion, your main goal will be to utilize a sequence of focused, thought-provoking questions to guide students through a series of points in addressing a structuring device in order to arrive at new insights with regard to this main, guiding question.

Discussion 1 What Makes the Directed Discussion Method Distinctive?

Think about Directed Discussions this way: It's almost as if you're guiding your students up a complex, winding, wooded path, with a destination that is too far away to see from the start. You begin the journey with a major initial question. At each important point along the path, you'll ask a secondary question that will guide the group a bit further along. As you near your destination, students begin to put the pieces together; they come closer and closer to a more complete understanding of that big question. Then, daylight, you emerge at the end of the trail; you return to the structuring question, which the students can now fully address. They have met each of the intellectual challenges that they faced on the path.

Depending on how you plan them, you'll see that Directed Discussions can feel like very interactive concept lessons, especially if students are challenged to compare and contrast objects, events, pieces of writing, types of problems, or other examples. Directed Discussions can be planned to include deductive or inductive elements (See Modules Four and Eight.). There will be much less teacher *input* of new information in a discussion like this as compared to a concept lesson. Again, your main goal will be to challenge your students to arrive at higher and higher levels of understanding through your questions (you'll be *asking*, not *telling*).

Remember that in a constructivist classroom, teachers will be challenging students to develop deep understanding of new ideas almost every day. Using Directed Discussions is a thought-provoking, interactive way to do this. As the discussion leader, you will be guiding your students to new insights by *making the connections themselves rather than by spoon-feeding them predigested bits of information.* This is a vitally important distinction. We'll see that topics chosen for Directed Discussion are usually focused and well defined, especially since, to a large degree, the conclusions that students reach will be somewhat predetermined by you. For this reason, heavily value-laden topics are not appropriate for Directed Discussions because you play a strong leadership role and shouldn't be perceived to be pushing your students toward a certain values position (more on this in the following sections).

Take a few minutes to explore Figure 9.1, a suggested template for Directed Discussions. Remember that there

---

Prelude

- Rationale (with connection to state/national standards)
- Performance Objective
- Materials and Lesson Aids

Enactment

- Hook: Your attention-grabber should connect to the main focus of the discussion and help to establish a context for the lesson.
- Student Aim: Statement of purpose for your discussion is conveyed through the initial posing of the structuring device (an option—display this main question on the board, overhead, etc.)
- Development
    You pose a sequenced series of challenging Trigger questions.
    Students reach enhanced levels of understanding as they discuss each main point introduced by your secondary questions.
    You probe and redirect to engage each of your students and to push student thinking to higher cognitive levels.
- Culmination
    1. Wrap-Up: Pose the structuring device once again. Students can now *answer* the structuring question completely.
    2. Leap: How will they use/apply these new insights in the future?

Assessment and Evaluation Plan

- Assessment products (What will students produce in this/a later lesson?)
- Evaluation (How will you evaluate this product, e.g., with a scoring rubric?)

FIGURE 9.1 Directed Discussion Lesson Planning Template

are countless ways to implement each of our constructivist methods; in general, Directed Discussions will follow this path.

Focal Point 2 Directed Discussion Method Markers

Now let's focus on the features that make the Directed Discussion unique among the three discussion methods. We'll see that this is the most highly structured of our three discussion methods, but that the design of such lessons will challenge students to reach new levels of insight as they struggle (in a positive way) to address new ideas and thought-provoking questions.

- As you might expect, the Student Aim will be fairly structured and specific. After establishing the context for the discussion in your Hook, you'll establish the Aim by *posing the structuring device as a question.* Note that the structuring device is posed almost rhetorically at this point; this question will not be fully answered until you reach the Culmination.

- During the Development, you'll pose a *sequence of focused Trigger questions* that will challenge students to come to new levels of understanding with regard to a series of teacher-determined points as they explore the parameters of the structuring device.

- As students struggle (in a cognitive sense) with each of the secondary Trigger questions, they begin to reach new levels of insight with regard to the main question (i.e., structuring device). The entire development features a *teacher-student-teacher-student* interaction pattern, with the teacher asking focused Trigger questions and frequent Probes and Redirects.

- During the Culmination, the students *answer the structuring question* as the discussion comes full circle.

In the sections that follow, we'll discuss each method marker in detail as we walk you through the process of planning and conducting Directed Discussions.

Focal Point 3 Up Close: Planning and Conducting a Directed Discussion

Remember that Directed Discussions can last from a few minutes to about one-half hour, depending on a number of factors. From our opening scenario, you can see that Directed Discussions are highly interactive and can be among the most engaging of constructivist teaching methods. The teacher–student interaction pattern will allow you as the facilitator to ask literally dozens of challenging questions that can involve each student in the classroom. At this point, let's take a closer look at what it

takes to plan and conduct such discussions, focusing closely on composing engaging questions (See Module Five.).

Discussion 3 Up Close: Planning and Conducting a Directed Discussion

Prelude: Rationale

Once again, let's consider our opening scenario as we investigate the Directed Discussion method. Ida Jackson's ultimate goal is to challenge her students to carefully analyze the text of Swift's *A Modest Proposal,* to analyze it as a piece of satire, and to consider just how this author has used satire to criticize both people and institutions of his time. The teacher might have started her planning process by writing a Rationale (see Module Three) like this: "Through the guided analysis of *A Modest Proposal,* students will apply much of what they have learned about satire to discover who and what one author was ridiculing during an historical period and how he accomplished this. This experience will enhance a wide range of critical-thinking and verbal communications skills and connects to INTASC Standards 1, 3, 4, 5, 6, 7, and 8." In the next section, we'll see how Ms. Jackson could utilize a Rationale like this to articulate her Performance Objectives.

Performance Objective

Performance Objectives for discussions usually describe how students might show you, as the teacher, that they can address the structuring device. Obviously, the statements that students make during the discussion can show you this. We would also recommend, whenever possible, that you ask them to produce something (e.g., a written statement) that will provide further evidence that they've learned something from the discussion. Ms. Jackson challenged her class to address two questions in writing and let them know that they would be creating *their own* piece of satire soon. One of her Performance Objectives (see Module Three) might have looked like this: "After analyzing a recent political cartoon for content and intent, students will analyze and discuss who and what Swift was satirizing in *A Modest Proposal* and how he accomplished this. Students will then individually address two specific questions in writing in appropriate detail." Ms. Jackson has specified what students will do to show what they have learned from the discussion (and note that student responses to these questions could serve as springboards into a lesson tomorrow or later in the unit).

Materials

Although discussions will often include activities, they are often less activity oriented than other lessons (e.g., concept lessons). The materials that you utilize for a discussion will often be used during the Hook or for reference *as* the discussion is progressing. Our satire lesson is a case in point. Ms. Jackson used an interesting (and to the students timely) political cartoon, as well as her brief historical background piece and the text of *A Modest Proposal.* When thinking about materials you might use for any discussion, always consider providing something concrete (like a piece of text) that students can *talk about.*

Let's now take a look at the actual enactment of a Directed Discussion. What do you need to do to engage your students in a worthwhile exchange of ideas?

Enactment: The Hook

Our classroom experiences have shown us, time and time again, that an effective discussion Hook can make a world of difference. Intuitively, this makes perfect sense. In any discussion you'll want your students attentive, truly interested in your topic, and *willing to share their ideas about it.* We have found that using a Hook that's unusually visual, funny, or controversial seems to work well for discussions. As you might expect, *getting students involved as quickly as possible* is a must. Breaking the ice early with some kind of interaction can set the stage for engaging discussions.

Although Ida Jackson's Hook (the political cartoons and accompanying questions) didn't connect *directly* to Swift's text, it offered a number of advantages. It certainly got the students' heads back into the topic (satire) effectively; it connected satire to a current issue (school violence) that they cared about; and it gave them an opportunity to debate viewpoints and raise questions. We would note that students will raise important, insightful questions like Monica's *if given these opportunities* (this very question was raised by a student during the actual lesson on which this scenario is based). Our spotlight teacher took advantage of Monica's question to springboard into her planned analysis of the text. Look for opportunities like this when conducting discussions of any kind.

As in any type of lesson, we will also remind you that the sky's the limit when it comes to Hooks. Pictures, demonstrations, poems, quotes, newspaper headlines, intriguing problems, daunting questions, film clips, even jokes or a teacher costume can all accomplish your goals during this part of the lesson (see Module Four). It needn't be elaborate or showy, but plan a Hook that'll *get 'em involved and get 'em thinking.*

Student Aim

In each of our three discussion methods, the Student Aim is most clearly expressed by the nature of the structuring device, or main question, that you plan. Recall our *definition* for discussion: *The verbal investigation or consideration of a question by a group of people.* As this implies, this main question is really the heart of your discussion. We have found that the planning for classroom discussions *usually begins* with the writing of an effective structuring device (as we'll see, *the nature of the structuring device will dictate your choice of discussion method*). Your structuring device, and what you say immediately *before* posing it, will convey to students not only the topic for the discussion but also the type of interaction that the discussion will feature. The structuring device will say a lot about what you will ask students to do in the coming minutes.

We see in Modules Ten and Eleven that Exploratory and Reflective Discussions, which are *highly* student centered, feature open-ended main questions that allow students to move in any number of directions as they think carefully and share their ideas. The structuring device in a Directed Discussion is designed to begin a focused discussion, to a certain extent excluding peripheral topics and alternative explanations. Ida Jackson asked her class, "Who or what does Swift seem to be ridiculing and how does he accomplish this?" This is a question that has some definite right answers and establishes a direction for the discussion. Consider another example. These three questions might be posed to begin a Directed Discussion in a history classroom:

1. What were the main causes of the Civil War?

2. How was the doctrine of states' rights a cause of the Civil War?

3. How was the right of secession a cause of the Civil War?

Which question would be the best structuring device for a Directed Discussion? Remember that the degree of focus in your structuring question depends on your goals in conducting the discussion. Question 3 is obviously the most focused. Question 2 or 3 might be appropriate for a Directed Discussion. Question 1 is probably not appropriate, since it is too broad and calls for students to make values-oriented decisions in choosing the main causes for the war. We'll see that such a question would be better suited for a Reflective Discussion, because it allows for greater student freedom to make and defend decisions based on supported individual beliefs.

The following questions might serve as effective structuring devices for Directed Discussions. The questions indicate the kinds of topics that are appropriate for a discussion like this. See whether they provide you with clues on Directed Discussion topics that could connect to the first units that you might be asked to plan.

1. How is the theme of _____ reflected in this poem/story?

2. Why does this type of collision provide support for Newton's first law?

3. Given this information, how can we show that _____ (when completing a proof or demonstrating a problem-solving approach)?

4. How does the study of logic lead to a better understanding of literacy?

5. Shown are two circles that intersect at *R* and *Q. PQR* is a straight line and *PM, PN* are tangents to the circles. Prove that *PM = PN*.

6. How can we use limits/matrices to find _____ (e.g., the optimum price for product X)?

7. Which government policies helped to cause the stock market crash of 1929?

8. What changes in trading patterns should have been expected in the United States and Mexico after the NAFTA treaty was ratified?

9. Now that we know parental genotypes, what are the potential genotypes of any offspring?

10. How does the author use (literary element) in this story?

11. How has the artist used (light/shading/color/shape) to achieve a desired effect?

12. How did this person (e.g., Pythagoras/Britt/Balinsky) derive this theorem?

13. How do bones and muscles work together to allow your body parts to move?

14. How does the author use a _____ metaphor to convey meaning in this passage?

15. How are tenses formed in regular and irregular French verbs?

16. What can we learn by investigating the arrangement of colors on a color wheel?

17. What trash disposal method has been shown to be the safest environmentally?

18. What can the various symbols used in *The Great Gatsby* tell us about Fitzgerald's intended message?

19. What are the main differences between *familiar* and *formal* sentence structure in German?

20. What can these sculptures tell us about the artists and about the cultures in which they lived?

21. What can we conclude about the early and late works of Hemmingway by comparing *For Whom the Bell Tolls* with *The Old Man and the Sea*?

22. In Spanish, how are pronouns used to refer to prepositional phrases?

Again, how you phrase your structuring device can have a big impact on your discussions, so think carefully about what you'll ask students to consider. As far as the Student Aim is concerned, we would also recommend alerting students to the importance of this main question with a questioning *preface.* For example, Ms. Jackson invited students to "keep these points in mind as we discuss *A Modest Proposal* in depth. Our main question for the next several minutes will be _____." In making this statement, she clearly emphasized the importance of the question and reminded the students to consider points they had already raised.

Development: Investigating the Structuring Device

You've planned that enticing structuring question. Now what? Once you have articulated the structuring device, decide what points you need to make to help your students reach an understanding of this guiding question; what will they need to know to answer the structuring device? Then think carefully about what Trigger questions you might ask to enable your students to reach an understanding of your main points. In our satire discussion, Ms. Jackson walked students through a careful analysis of the text with a planned sequence of questions. She called their attention to the title, opening paragraph, and to especially interesting lines within various sections. Notice that her Trigger questions weren't too *leading;* she clearly challenged the students to do the analyzing as they put the pieces together in coming to a better understanding of the guiding question.

In planning your questions, it is often effective to relate the known to the unknown. Asking students, for example, to compare and contrast the conveying of tenses in French and English verbs, a familiar science process with a new one, or the elements of ancient and modern cultures can help them come to a greater understanding of the unknown.

Let's consider another planning example. Suppose that a United States history teacher had decided to discuss the right of secession as a cause of the Civil War. In planning this lesson as a Directed Discussion, this teacher should sequence focused questions that will lead logically to the idea that the right of secession was a cause of the war. Consider the following sequence of points that the teacher would want raised through questions concerning secession:

1. Sovereignty rests with the people, as stated in the Declaration of Independence.

2. The states represent the people.

3. The union represents the states.

4. Hence the people acting through their sovereign state government can dissolve the union.

Each of these propositions could be expressed in question form, put by the teacher and considered by students. Each question would require a significant amount of discussion before it was understood. When actually conducting the planned questions, the students exercise some degree of control over the direction of the discussion, because the teacher cannot move to the next point until the answer to the present question is understood.

Ordinarily, you'll need to ask additional questions to help students understand your main points. These questions will include Probes and Redirects as you continually check on the understanding of each student regarding each point in the argument. Also note that the questions asked in Directed Discussions involve both lower- and higher-cognitive-level processes. Many of the questions asked initially involve knowledge and recall. The entire discussion is directed at analysis and then synthesis in the collective insights offered by the class as a group. Responses to specific questions in the examination of the structuring device involve analysis as students sift through what they know to find justification for the assertions that make up the argument. The entire discussion, if well planned, will challenge students to think critically at each stage, as students move toward a deeper understanding of your main question.

Multiple examples can help illustrate each of your main points and can make your discussion interesting, relevant, and fun. "How is this similar to this?" questions are often a mainstay of Directed Discussions. For example, if Ms. Jackson's students had seemed confused at any point in the discussion, she might have asked them to refer back to a previously analyzed piece in order to aid their understanding of an important point. *Remember that the key to a truly interactive discussion is to plan your main questions in advance.* Because these discussions are fairly fast-paced, it's difficult to articulate effective questions on the spot; you risk clumsy questioning and too much teacher talk if you don't think carefully about the questions that you'll ask. We also recommend directing as many as half of your questions at specific students in the class and to ask abundant Redirects, to engage as many students as possible in the discussion. On many occasions, we have observed teachers conduct Directed Discussions in which a few students provide most of the answers to the main questions. Don't fall into this trap.

Again, remember that your students do not answer the structuring question immediately. You will generally state (or ask) the structuring device rhetorically at the start of the discussion and return to address it toward the end. The real learning in this type of discussion comes in the *process* of analysis that comes in answering the structuring device and Trigger questions. For example, a math teacher might pose the following problem: "Given this diagram and these conditions, prove that segments *A* and *B* are equal." The problem itself is entirely novel to students. Solving it will involve a student analysis of the situation

and then sorting through knowledge associated with related experiences and a selection of various known definitions and theorems. As such, the overall problem involves analysis and application, yet experience shows that certain students may have the splash of inspiration that allows for a quick solution. If this should happen, you should conduct the discussion in such a way that the inspired student doesn't reveal the answer prematurely, perhaps allowing the student to play a large part in explaining the process (again, direct a large number of your questions to help prevent premature disclosure). In this way, the rest of the class has the opportunity to engage in higher-level thinking.

In addition, there may be more than one way to solve the problem, and the discussion may allow for investigation of alternative solutions. Students do leap ahead and lag behind. It will be important for you to diagnose which students are following your thought processes and to what degree. When group members do leap ahead, take care to require students to make the logical steps that they have followed clear to others within the class; that is, ask students to justify their responses. Those students lagging behind will often catch up during the descriptive process that comes with the answering of your questions.

When you conduct Directed Discussions, remember that brief digressions from the main questioning sequence are useful *at times* for further developing your main argument or for providing illustrations or examples. We recommend that you keep these digressions to a minimum, lest the main points become lost in a more open format. As always, it's important to seize a teachable moment if a student raises an insightful question that you hadn't anticipated; discuss the question/point raised, but try to return to your main line of questioning. In addition, you may find that you have to digress to teach or reteach a certain point if students are confused, so your involvement in the discussion will depend largely on how the class responds.

At least two additional topics should be considered when planning Directed Discussions, *pacing* and *teacher feedback*. The pace of Directed Discussions should range from deliberate to moderately rapid. The questions asked do not as a rule require an inordinate amount of pondering, yet much more thought is required than in a drill and practice-type recitation. Extending your wait time (See Module Five) will be important in this type of discussion, as always. If an answer is not forthcoming, redirect to another student, or break the question into smaller parts to simplify it. Occasionally, Directed Discussions break down because none of your students can make the next logical step in the argument. Again, you can help students over these sticky points with miniteacher presentations (two to three minutes) or a series of simpler questions. Overall, the tempo for a Directed Discussion will usually be quicker than for an Exploratory or Reflective Discussion.

We have briefly discussed teacher feedback to student response (Modules Two and Six). To reiterate, one key is to recognize and sometimes compliment correct answers without heaping so much praise on students that your replies are meaningless. (Side note: One of the authors once supervised an enthusiastic student teacher who gave students a cheery "Super!" after virtually every response. It didn't take long before students began to tune her out completely.) Of course, not all responses will be correct. Some will be incorrect, some partially correct. For these answers, let your students know that part of the answer is correct, and tell them that part of their answer is incorrect. It is often advisable to initiate another question to correct the questionable portion of an answer without causing embarrassment or a loss of face to the student who offered the original response. Truly insightful answers should be praised openly. Let students know *why* their answers are excellent (or even super). Again, encouraging students to make their thinking process explicit and to discuss these processes is an effective way to help them develop critical-thinking skills. In general, feedback that is explicit and moderately positive will encourage participation and contribute to the social atmosphere of any classroom.

In conclusion, pacing and teacher feedback are important to the success of Directed Discussions. Keep the tempo *fairly* quick. Reinforce answers in a positive way, and let students know why certain answers are partially incorrect, correct, or outstanding. Assure them that misconceptions (rather then "wrong" answers) are an important part of the thinking process. Take care that confusion does not occur regarding what aspects of student answers are acceptable.

Again, we emphasize the important point: Because teachers play a strong leadership role in Directed Discussions, this method is not appropriate for coming to decisions on value-laden issues. In our society, individuals are free to value what they wish. *Never* put your students into the position of being railroaded into a values position that they find repugnant. Such issues are better saved for a more open (Exploratory or Reflective) Discussion in which students can present and defend a values position of their choice.

In summary, remember that the development of a Directed Discussion features the use of a planned sequence of questions in the consideration of a structuring device and the utilization of Probe and Redirect questions in involving everyone in higher-level cognitive processes. Be careful about the introduction of tangential topics unless they are closely related to the issues at hand. If a student does interject with a truly insightful question, be sure to address it, but attempt to keep this kind of discussion focused.

Culmination

You've conducted a Directed Discussion. During the Development, your students have raised a number of thought-provoking points as they addressed your questions. What do you do to bring the discussion to an effective Culmination? Challenge students to return to and *answer* your structuring device. Restate your major question and ask your students to put the pieces together as they provide a detailed class response. We recommend involving a number of students in this *Wrap-Up* process. Use Probes and Redirects that will challenge the group to respond fully.

You should also reiterate the importance of the lesson by reviewing how these ideas connect to your main unit focus, to topics or ideas discussed earlier in the course, and/or to important events taking place beyond the walls of the school. This process could include a review of ideas introduced in past lessons and/or previewing future lessons. As in the *Leaps* that you might plan for any lesson, we have found that it is often incredibly effective to *leave students with a question to think about for next time.* Whenever possible, challenge your students to extend their thinking outside of your classroom. Try to buy into their time away from your classroom.

In meeting your Performance Objective at some point in the Culmination, challenge your students to apply what they've learned during the discussion. Can they write a sentence or paragraph or participate in a conversation using their new knowledge of Spanish pronouns, for example? As time allows, or on the next day/class session, challenge your students to put their new insights to work.

Assessment and Evaluation

There is a wide range of possibilities for both informal and formal assessment events in connection to Directed Discussions. These discussions provide you with multiple opportunities to listen to student responses, comments that can provide valuable insights on their thinking. For example, think about Ms. Jackson's satire lesson. Throughout the discussion, her students are revealing their thoughts regarding not only *A Modest Proposal* but about both historical and current events connected to this general topic. It is possible (even desirable) to use discussions as a springboard for research projects and other assignments. As with any constructivist lesson, think about what you might ask students to produce during or after your Directed Discussions to show you what they have learned and how they might apply their new knowledge.

Focal Point 4 **When Should You Use the Directed Discussion Method in Your Classroom?**

The Directed Discussion is one of the most versatile teaching methods that we introduce in *Invisible Teaching*. Because you have an opportunity to introduce and encourage discussion of new ideas, and students interact with both you and one another, this type of lesson is a welcome alternative to a straight teacher lecture in any subject-matter area, from art to calculus. This kind of discussion is valuable when used in conjunction with activities and demonstrations as well, as it allows you to walk students through a process, questioning them at each step. As a result, you'll find that Directed Discussions can be used at any point in a unit, from beginning to middle to end. They also serve well in *applying* and *reviewing* previously introduced ideas, as the suggested structuring devices described here will imply. Discussions of this type are useful in helping students review for an exam or a quiz and in summarizing and connecting the main points generated in a concept lesson, Interactive Presentation (Module Twelve), or activity. As a result, your Directed Discussions might vary from five to thirty minutes, depending on when they are used.

At this point, it is important to start to visualize what your fifty-minute (or longer) class period might look like. Based on what you've learned about learning, it should be obvious that you cannot lecture for fifty minutes (or more than ten minutes) without the risk of losing (and probably boring) most of the students in your classroom. All students need the opportunity to process the new ideas that you will introduce, and this is difficult if they are consistently in the role of passive listener. During *each* class period, allow your students to apply, analyze, and, in general, reflect on what they've learned. As one example, you might begin with a concept lesson, move into a peer-group activity, and end the period with a brief Directed Discussion. In this way, each of your students will be given some opportunity to consider important new ideas. Such variety in methods will be especially important if you are teaching in a setting that features block scheduling and class periods of eighty to ninety minutes.

As you might imagine, providing different kinds of settings for cognitive processing will have a number of advantages in terms of reaching students with diverse preferred learning styles and previous experiences. As with every method that we'll introduce, our general advice is not to overuse Directed Discussions, even though the method *is* so versatile. Give your students frequent opportunities to participate in more open discussions (i.e., Exploratories and Reflectives) and activities that allow them even greater freedom to direct the interaction, express their own views, and generate their own questions. Keep our general advice in mind: *Use a wide variety of methods to connect with the diverse learners in each class.*

■ TIP FOR TECHNOLOGY INTEGRATION

Programs like HyperStudio and PowerPoint can be used to enhance what we would call the visual quality of Directed Discussions. We have integrated (and observed other teachers integrate) these programs by using them to display the structuring device and Trigger questions on large monitors visible to the entire class. Then, as points

---

Mr. Nelson's European history class has been investigating life in the Middle Ages. The unit has included a look at the sometimes mythical world of castles, quests, crusades, knights, ladies of the court, and has included multiple connections to literature. But the teacher is also determined to promote an understanding of the actual living conditions of the time. The class enters the room today to the sound of monks chanting; as the bell rings, their teacher appears, dressed in a monk's robe. He reads an authentic (and somewhat terrifying) account of the Black Death, written by a witness in the thirteenth century. Mr. Nelson then poses the structuring device for the discussion: "*How did the Black Death spread to kill 25% of Europe's population?*" The teacher then asks a series of focused Trigger questions, many of which challenge students to apply what they had recently learned: "How would you describe living conditions in a typical medieval city at this time?"; "How would you describe the sanitation?"; "What would garbage and rotting food attract?"; "What parasites do rats and other mammals often carry?" (here the teacher shares a microscopic picture of a flea to multiple *yuks* from the class); "What main foods consumed by people at that time would the rats be attracted to?"; "How else could fleas spread disease to humans?"; "How would the city population respond to the spread of the death?" As the students respond to (and sometimes debate) answers to the questions, Mr. Nelson writes agreed-upon responses on the board. Twenty-five minutes after reading the account of the Black Death, Mr. Nelson once again asks the structuring question, and the students review the sequence of conditions and events that led to the rapid spread of the Black Death.[2]

FIGURE 9.2 A Glimpse Inside a Constructivist Classroom

are introduced through the discussion, the teacher can list these below each trigger question. The advantages? The visual display of the questions can include color and motion; the discussion can be further enhanced by the display of pictures, maps, even videoclips.

■ ROUNDUP ■

Directed Discussions are used to develop an argument or point of view. They are initiated with a focused, convergent structuring question that is posed during the Student Aim. The teacher then asks a series of focused Trigger questions that challenge students to come to an enhanced understanding of a number of secondary points. Have your main and secondary questions written into your lesson plan, ready to develop the argument. There may be times when you won't use all of these questions, but have them ready just in case. As with each of the methods that we have introduced, we will provide you with a sample lesson plan that will illustrate the kind of sequential questioning (See Module Five, Part 2.) that is part of planning a Directed Discussion.

The boundaries of Directed Discussions are largely maintained by sticking to the predetermined set of key questions that form the framework for the argument being developed. The basic communication pattern is teacher–student, but student–student interaction is often fruitful in developing the argument. As always in a constructivist classroom, allow student-initiated digressions if you feel that valuable points are being made. Directed Discussions are concluded by a restatement of the structuring question and a review of the key points being made (remember that this reviewing can be done by you or your students). Try to avoid pushing for the resolution of values-laden issues in a discussion like this, because students may feel that they are being pushed into positions they may find objectionable.

We feel that there are several keys to conducting effective Directed Discussions. Obviously, an interesting topic and an engaging structuring device are vital. Plan your structuring device and secondary questions carefully. Make these questions thought provoking without being leading; as in each of the constructivist methods that we introduce, your ultimate goal will be to challenge your students to do the thinking rather than providing them with bits of information. Also consider each of our earlier recommendations for effectively questioning students; this type of discussion is as interactive as any method you'll ever use, and your asking of thought-provoking questions and encouraging interaction will be crucial. As we discuss in "Resocializing" (Module Two), it will take time for your students to warm up to discussions

of any kind. Be patient when conducting your discussions. Figure 9.3 provides a flowchart for the Directed Discussion.

■ DIRECTED DISCUSSION SAMPLE LESSON PLAN ■

Unit Title: Weather and Climate (intended for high school physical science class)

Prelude

Rationale

(Combines What? Why? Justification): By challenging students to analyze and compare and contrast three demonstrated science phenomena, I will create an opportunity to help students to understand air pressure and its impact on living and nonliving things in a challenging, interactive way. This experience will help students to develop their ability to reason scientifically and connects to INTASC standards 1, 2, 4, 5, 7, and 8.

Performance Objective

(Combines Preparation, Product, Criteria): After observing each phenomenon, students will articulate at least five observations related to each event. Then, after comparing and contrasting the events, students will verbally describe the related causes for each phenomenon and write at least three additional examples of the effects of air pressure on living and nonliving things.

Materials and Lesson Aids

1. Hot plate
2. 3–4 empty pop cans
3. bowl of ice water
4. candles
5. water tray
6. large and small glass jars/glasses
7. matches
8. 2 flasks
9. a hard-boiled egg
10. 3 balloons

Enactment

Time Estimate	Main Ideas/Concepts, Questions, and Teaching Methods
8 minutes	*Hook:* Who can tell us what an observation is (possible: using the senses in perceiving an object or event)?

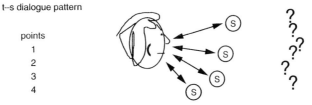

1 = structuring device: question as Aim

intention ⟶ to arrive at a teacher-determined insight

STOP

Detour

What are the hidden causes of . . . ?

2 = questions elicit predetermined main points in instructional materials

t–s dialogue pattern

points
1
2
3
4

?
?
?
?
?
?

3 = compare and contrast main points

elicit, do not tell, predetermined insight based on compare and contrast
of main points

⬭ + ▯▮ + ⬭○ + △ = insight

4 = culmination: students answer structuring device question

elicit implications of insight

If . . . then . . .
Only . . . because . . .

FIGURE 9.3 Directed Discussion Method Flowchart

I'm going to start this lesson by asking you to observe something—watch closely as I place a jar over this burning candle (candle/tumbler demo).

What observations can you make? What did you see/smell/hear/feel (list observations; possibilities: candle went out, smoked; water filled glass; glass felt hot)?

3 minutes

Second demo: Let's watch a second event and compare it with what you just saw!

I've been heating a pinch of water in these cans (3–4 cans placed on a hot plate).

What do you predict will happen if I pick a can up and turn it upside down in water (probe: get students to justify predictions)?

Let's try it—make as many observations as you can (can demo).

What did you see/smell/hear/feel (possible observations: can was crushed quickly; can cooled down; water filled can; sound of can crushing)? Anyone surprised?

Student Aim: Posing Structuring Device as a Question

10–12 minutes

I'd like to address an important question in the next few minutes: *How can we explain these two events?*

Development: Addressing the Structuring Device through a Sequence of Focused Questions

First of all, how are these two events similar? How are they different?

Similarities	Differences
heat involved	can crushed; glass wasn't
air heated	different heat source (flame)
water moved	water cold in 2nd demo
bubbles from can/ glass	
temp. extremes	

Does anyone think that they have an explanation for what happened, a hypothesis (list student explanations)?

Does air have weight? How do you know (balloon example)?

How much air is above us (about 600 miles!)?

What impact does all of that air have on the earth's surface?

List Conclusions as They're Reached

1. We live at the bottom of an ocean of air.
2. The air above us presses down on anything on the earth's surface (air pressure).

   What happens to air when it's heated (it expands!—flask/balloon demo)?

   What happened to the air in the glass, and in the can, when it was heated?

   How do we know that some of the air escaped (the bubbles!)?

3. Heated air expanded in can/glass; some air escaped.

   What happened to the air in the glass when the flame went out?

   What happened when the can hit the ice water?

4. Cooling air contracted in can/glass.

   Why did the water move into the glass? the can (extend wait time; allow for multiple responses)?

   What role did air pressure play in these events?

   What did the air pressure do to the can?

5. Air pressure pushed water into the glass/can and crushed the sides of the can.

Culmination: Revisit the Structuring Device

3 minutes	*Wrap-Up* Knowing what we now know, how could we explain these two events (encourage students to explain both events; account for similarities and differences)?
3 minutes	*Leap* • Can you think of other ways that air pressure impacts us on the earth's surface (encourage students to share examples)? • We've seen that the weight of this ocean of air affects us in many different ways. • I'm going to leave you with one more example: Think about why this happens. Egg/flask demo (light a match, quickly drop it into a flask, cover the flask with a hard-boiled egg)

Assessment and Evaluation

For tomorrow, write a one to two-page reaction paper explaining why you think the egg moved into the flask.

■ HANDS-ON PRACTICE ■

Plan a Directed Discussion by using the template below. Refer to Module Three for the Core Components of a lesson plan, and review Module Eight for detail on this type of discussion.

Prelude (for teacher reference)

• Rationale (with connection to national/state standards)

• Performance Objective (remember to be specific about what your students should be able to *do* to show you what they've learned)

• Materials and Lesson Aids

Enactment (student engagement—what you might say/do/ask at each stage of the lesson)

• Hook

• Student Aim

   Initial posing of the structuring device (How will you phrase this main question?)

• Development

   Student consideration of a sequence of Trigger questions helps them to understand a series of important points (What *are* the main points that they'll need to discuss?)

How will you phrase each of these Trigger questions?

- Culmination

Wrap-Up: What will you say/do/ask to help students *answer the structuring device?*

Leap: How will students use/apply these ideas in the future?

Assessment and Evaluation

What will you ask students to produce during/after the lesson to show what they've learned?

How will you evaluate this product?

ENDNOTES

1. Thanks to Joanna Kluever, Augustana College Class of 2000, for her contributions to this scenario.
2. Thanks to Creston Fenn, Augustana College Class of 2002, for his contributions to this scenario.

Module 10

The Exploratory
Discussion Method

Overview: Scenario Depicting an Exploratory Discussion

Focal Points and Discussions

What Makes the Exploratory Discussion Method Distinctive?

Exploratory Discussion Lesson Planning Template

Exploratory Discussion Method Markers

Up Close: Planning And Conducting an Exploratory Discussion

When Should You Use the Exploratory Discussion Method in Your Classroom?

Tips for Technology Integration

Roundup

Exploratory Discussion Method Flowchart

Exploratory Discussion Sample Lesson Plan

Hands-On Practice

OVERVIEW: SCENARIO DEPICTING AN EXPLORATORY DISCUSSION

As a high-school science teacher, John Rizzi believes, first and foremost, in challenging his students to *do* science. During their ecology unit, for example, his biology students undertake an authentic investigation of a nearby pond and stream, completing a detailed chemical analysis of the water and studying the organisms native to both habitats. Later in the unit, they begin to apply ecological concepts they have learned in order to understand the interactions of living things in these and other ecosystems. Taking an interdisciplinary approach, Rizzi believes, makes these experiences more meaningful and *impacting* to his students. As they have investigated the influence of human activities on the biosphere, the teacher has integrated literature, songs, and poetry with their experiences and has challenged students to take a close look at (and possibly change) their own lifestyles in light of what they've learned.

On this Wednesday morning, Mr. Rizzi's third-period Biology I students enter the room to the strains of a song called *Out in the Country,* recorded by the rock group Three Dog Night in the early 1970s. The teacher invites his students to "listen for clues as to how the song's writer feels about the natural world." As the song ends, he invites students to share their thoughts on the lyrics. Many share environmental concerns that they have expressed during previous lessons, concerns which they felt were reflected in the song. Some of the comments are remorseful. In others, the teacher senses an admirable kind of *let's take action* spirit that he finds in many of today's students.

"We're almost finished with our ecology unit, and I'd like to give everyone a chance to apply some of what we've learned to our lives today," Mr. Rizzi tells the class. "I'm going to invite all of you to go back in time for a few minutes. The year is 1854. The United States government has made an offer to a Native American tribe in what is now Washington state to buy tribal land. The tribe's Chief Seattle has written a formal reply to the people of the United States, which I'd like to read to you now. As you listen, you might want to close your eyes and see what images come to mind as you hear his words."

With that, the teacher begins to read the haunting verses of the document that has come to be known as *Chief Seattle's Reply.* For the next three minutes, there is an unusual hush in the normally busy room as the students listen. They are seated in a large circle; some are looking at classmates; many have closed their eyes as the teacher invited them to do. Mr. Rizzi reaches the end of the text and changes his tone slightly as he says, "Back to the present day. I'd like to invite you to share your ideas

about what we just heard. We're going to have an open, Exploratory Discussion. Feel free to reply to each other; there's no need to raise your hands. I'd also encourage you to focus on specific comments made by Chief Seattle in his reply" (he passes copies of the text around the circle of students). "Our main question is this: *As American citizens living at the start of a new century, what can we learn from the words of Chief Seattle?*"

It doesn't take long for the exchange of ideas to begin; at the outset, a few of the more outspoken students offer comments, but then others join the conversation. Mr. Rizzi, who has taken a seat within the circle of chairs, is silent for the first few minutes as he inconspicuously records student comments on an overhead transparency. Many of the initial comments are fairly broad ("His people seem so much closer to nature"; "Their pace of life is so much different!"). Students begin to build on one another's comments; when Luke mentions, "His people seem to have a whole different set of values," Michelle asks him what he means and Kristin and Jeff jump in with examples. Amy mentions Chief Seattle's use of the word *savage.* "I think he's mocking us when he says he's a savage," she says confidently.

"I've always wondered exactly what he means when he says that," relates Mr. Rizzi. "What do others feel about what he means when he uses the term *savage?*" A number of students offer opinions. Some agree with Amy. Others offer the opinion that he has a completely different meaning for the word. "He's actually proud of the fact that he's a savage!" states Ken at one point.

Mr. Rizzi nudges the discussion in a related direction by asking, "What view of the role of technology do people in the two cultures have?" Immediately, Nate says, "People in our culture have tended to rely on technology too much, and it gets us into trouble." A number of students share opinions on this and offer examples. "It makes you wonder what 'progress' really is!" states Laura at one point.

"The scary thing about this is that he's telling us what our future will be!" offers Diana in a somber tone.

"What predictions does he make, and are they accurate?" asks the teacher. Students mention a number of specific passages; as a final question, the teacher asks, "How do you think he might feel if he could see his land today?" The student replies seem heartfelt.

"Excellent discussion!" offers Mr. Rizzi. "I'd like to recap some of the ideas that you've shared" (he does this briefly as he turns on the projector and displays the notes he has taken on the overhead transparencies). "*Chief Seattle's Reply* has had a big impact on my life. He urges us to teach our children that the earth is their mother. In the last ten minutes of class time today, I'd like you to meet in your regular lab groups to consider two questions: How *can* we teach future generations that the earth is their mother? And what would you be willing to change about your own way of life in the future as a result of hearing Chief Seattle's words?"

■ FOCAL POINTS AND DISCUSSIONS

Focal Point 1 What Makes the Exploratory Discussion Method Distinctive?

A quick question as we begin our look at a second discussion method. How is the discussion that Mr. Rizzi conducted different in form from Ms. Jackson's discussion of satire?

Some of these differences will jump right out at you. The nature of the questions asked by the teacher is vastly different in the two discussions. The Exploratory Discussion is perhaps the most student-centered of our discussion methods. When you think *Exploratory Discussion,* think *brainstorming* or *freethinking,* with a definite purpose. In Exploratories, students respond to an extremely open, broad structuring device (question); they have wide latitude in determining the direction of the discussion and in deciding just how the structuring question should be addressed. For these reasons, we have found Exploratory Discussions to be highly empowering for students who are used to being told what and how to think by teachers. The format allows students to use their imag-

ination and creativity as they share and comment on one another's ideas.

Discussion 1 What Makes the Exploratory Discussion Method Distinctive?

The ultimate goal in most Exploratory Discussions is for *students* to identify alternatives in responding to that main, structuring question. An Exploratory Discussion might, for instance, be used to identify alternative methods for solving a problem, explaining an event, or interpreting a piece of literature or artwork. Exploratory Discussions differ from the other two types in that no true resolution of the structuring question is necessary; the list of pros and cons, alternatives, implications, or ideas/suggestions is considered the resolution. These discussions are often used to begin a series of lessons or to challenge students to apply new ideas after a series of classroom experiences. As we will see, Exploratories provide teachers with a valuable tool for gaining insights into student experiences related to a new topic and for connecting elements within the topic to events relevant in students' lives.

Figure 10.1 displays our suggested template for planning Exploratory Discussions. This will provide you with a global feel for the stages in these discussions. As you look over the template, think about how Mr. Rizzi might have gone about planning each phase of his lesson.

Prelude

- Rationale (with connection to national/state standards)
- Performance Objective
- Materials and Lesson Aids

Enactment

- Hook: As an option, couple your attention-grabber with the structuring device
- Student Aim
    Use the structuring device preface (i.e., set up/contextualize the main question)
    Pose the structuring device as a question
- Development
    Students brainstorm in response to the structuring device
    Teacher facilitates discussion with wait time, Trigger questions
    List pros and cons as desired
- Culmination
    1. *Wrap-Up:* Students/teacher recap ideas generated
    2. *Leap:* How will students use/apply these ideas in the future?

Assessment and Evaluation Plan

- Assessment products (What will students produce in this/a later lesson?)
- Evaluation (How will you evaluate this product, e.g., with a scoring rubric?)

FIGURE 10.1 Exploratory Discussion Lesson Planning Template

Exploratory Discussion Method Markers

These method markers make Exploratory Discussions unique and will help provide you with an initial schema (a construct with discrete characteristics) for planning and conducting them. Of the three discussion methods, you'll see that Exploratories are the most unstructured, but they do have a definite purpose and direction.

- The Student Aim conveys the general direction of the discussion. Once you establish a context for the discussion in your Hook, you'll convey the Student Aim by *posing an extremely broad, open-ended structuring device as a question.*

- As the Development unfolds, the teacher takes a step back to promote a *student–student interaction pattern.* Students are given the widest possible freedom in determining how they will address the structuring question. As an interesting option, initial student brainstorming can take place in peer groups to promote maximum engagement of all students. List pros and cons as desired.

- As the Exploratory Discussion facilitator, you will ask *occasional, additional questions to gently guide the exploration in new directions.* In acting as facilitator, you'll ask these additional questions only as needed.

- During the Culmination, you should challenge students to *return to the structuring device* by reviewing the main ideas generated.

Already you should have a sense that Exploratory Discussions are quite a refreshing departure from many of the methods used in classrooms today. Depending on your purposes, these open exchanges of ideas can be fairly brief (e.g., five minutes) to about one-half hour (after which time, we've discovered, students have usually done about all the brainstorming they can). Keep these method markers in mind as we discuss the planning and conducting of Exploratories in the sections that follow.

Focal Point 3 **Up Close: Planning and Conducting an Exploratory Discussion**

Prelude: Rationale

Let's return to the Exploratory Discussion conducted in John Rizzi's biology class as we provide you with our best advice for planning and conducting truly student-centered discussions. A discussion like Mr. Rizzi's, if effectively done, could challenge students intellectually and affectively on a number of levels. The discussion is a terrific example of what we would call *interdisciplinarity* (a hallmark of constructivist classroom experiences). *Chief*

Seattle's Reply could be analyzed as an historical primary source document, as a cultural artifact, even as a piece of literature. It connects to the values systems held by people of two different cultures and would certainly cause most young people to take a closer look at their own actions and their environmental effects. There is also a powerful connection to ecological concepts and principles and to the impact of technology on society and the environment. Rizzi might have written a Rationale like this as part of his planning process: "During an open discussion focused on possible lessons learned through the reading of *Chief Seattle's Reply,* students will apply what they have learned regarding the environment and the impact of technology on the environment to the analysis of an historical and cultural text. This experience will enhance a wide range of critical-thinking abilities and verbal and small-group communications skills and connects to INTASC Standards 1 through 7." When using the Exploratory Discussion method, do be sure to have a clear, compelling Rationale that describes a good reason for *doing* the discussion and convey this to your students. You don't want them to come to believe that Exploratories are nothing more than informal chats with no real purpose.

Performance Objective

How could you, as a teacher, accurately assess what students had learned as a result of an experience like the biology Exploratory? Student *comments* made during the discussion would certainly indicate a great deal about the cognitive and affective connections that they made. Toward the end of this lesson, the biology teacher asked his students to respond to two thought-provoking, summative questions. A possible Performance Objective for this lesson: "Following a reading of *Chief Seattle's Reply,* students will brainstorm lessons that American citizens living today might learn from the text. In a peer-group setting, students will then respond in writing as a group to two questions designed to assess the impact of the discussion and will later share and defend these written responses in a full-class setting." We believe that it's essential to challenge students to *apply* ideas generated during Exploratory Discussions soon after the discussion takes place. Again, this is the best indicator of the true impact of the discussion. As you plan your first Exploratory Discussions, consider ways in which you might invite students to use ideas brainstormed by the group.

Materials

As educators, we firmly believe that you can't have a meaningful discussion in a vacuum. Your topic and structuring device, which flow from the subject matter that you invite students to investigate, must be compelling and (you hope) relevant to your students. For example, in conducting the discussion described in the opening scenario in both high school and college classrooms, one of the authors can attest to the profound impact that *Chief Seattle's Reply* has on most students. As far as materials are concerned, *pick something interesting* as the focus for Exploratories. Ask yourself, "Will my students *want* to discuss this? How *might* they respond?" Once you've chosen your material, then ask yourself, "How will I use these materials before and during the discussion?" Mr. Rizzi made an important choice—he read the text for the students, believing that this might have the biggest impact, and he distributed copies of the text so that they might refer to it during the discussion. When thinking about your materials, remember your visual and auditory learners.

Because of their format, and the fact that students have a lot of control over the direction of Exploratories, consider a peer-group activity in the context of these discussions. Let students read, manipulate, or otherwise investigate your materials after you pose the structuring device then share their ideas in a full-class setting, much as you might do in a concept lesson. More on this important option as we turn to the Enactment.

Enactment: The Hook

Throughout *Invisible Teaching*, we have discussed the dozens of options that you have in trying to *hook* your students. As we mentioned in the Directed Discussion module, it's doubly important to involve your students early when conducting any discussion. This is especially true in Exploratories, the most open kind of discussion that you'll conduct.

John Rizzi's Hook (the song and accompanying questions) certainly established a theme for the discussion. In this case, the song featured a writer expressing some of the same feelings about nature as Chief Seattle conveyed in 1854. In essence, the reading of *Chief Seattle's Reply* served as a *second* Hook, since it came before the class launched into the true exploratory part of the lesson. The message here: Try make your Exploratory Hooks especially novel and inviting in an effort to create that thinker-friendly environment. Again, don't feel as though you have to rely on a gimmick to interest or entertain your students. Your goal isn't to entertain them; it's to open their minds for the discussion. Our experiences *have* shown us that even something relatively simple (e.g., music, a picture, a puzzling problem, a quotation) can capture the imagination of your students, lend a bit of mystery and anticipation to the lesson, and pave the way for the honest sharing of ideas.

Student Aim

Again, the structuring device that you plan for any type of discussion conveys much about the Student Aim. In fact, *the nature of the structuring device will dictate which discussion method you choose for a lesson.* Remember that your planning for discussions will often *begin* with your articulation of this main structuring question, because it has such an impact on what you hope will take place during the rest of the discussion.

Exploratory and Reflective Discussions are especially student-centered. As a result, we have some special advice regarding the Student Aim for lessons that feature these methods. Think about how you might preface the structuring device. What might you say to set up this main question? Because you want to promote student–student interaction (you want students to listen to and respond to each other directly), our advice is to *let them know this.* Plan a statement that lets them know that the *big question* is on its way. For example, Mr. Rizzi told his class, "I'd like to invite you to share your ideas about what we just heard. We're going to have an open, Exploratory Discussion. Feel free to reply to each other; there's no need to raise your hands." He also reminded them to refer to passages in the text as they shared their ideas. With this straightforward statement, the teacher conveyed exactly what the students would have the freedom to do during the discussion. This will be vital in your first student-centered discussions, since *many students aren't used to sharing ideas with each other regarding anything academic.* Notice also that he told them directly that they'd be doing an Exploratory Discussion. Our advice is to teach your students the difference among the discussion methods that you'll use (many of the teachers with whom we've worked do this at the middle and high school levels with great success). The advantage is that as soon as you say *Directed, Exploratory, or Reflective,* you establish a set of expectations for everyone, and your student-centered discussions will take off with much less prodding from you. (See meta-awareness in Module Two.)

The Structuring Device

So you've thought carefully about how you'll set up your structuring device. Now it's time to consider how you might phrase that crucial question. Because your goal in conducting an Exploratory Discussion is to investigate alternatives, implications, advantages/disadvantages, and so on, the structuring device must be an inviting, open-ended question or statement. These broad questions or statements are designed to *include* peripheral topics and novel or creative explanations. As the following examples illustrate, Exploratory structuring devices are much less focused than those used in Directed or Reflective Discussions. You'll see that some of the examples are specific to certain unit topics, while others are more generic and adaptable to a range of topics. Our purpose is to encourage you to *think about the possibilities.*

1. (Science; following a teacher demonstration) "What are some possible explanations for what we've seen?" Or, "What questions do you have regarding what we just experienced?"

2. "What are some alternatives to the Bush budget proposals in 2001?"

3. "How have women's roles in our society changed since World War II?"

4. "What are the environmental implications of locating an industry in a small, remote town like ____?"

5. "Given *ABC* with segment *AB* = segment *AC,* how many ways can we show that *S* = *C*?"

6. "What are some *possible* interpretations of this text (e.g., poem/story/letter/speech)?"

7. "In what ways can the technology of a time period affect the literature of that era?"

8. (Given this situation within this novel/play/short story/historical context) "What possible actions could this person take?" And/or "What would be the advantages or disadvantages to each course of action?"

9. "How would your life be different today if ____ had/hadn't happened (e.g., the Confederacy had won the Civil War; ____ had been elected president)?"

10. "How does building design reflect prevailing values during a period in time?"

11. "What are the advantages and disadvantages of continued research in genetic engineering on human stem cells?"

12. "What impacts did the events of September 11, 2001 have on life in the United States? How lasting might these impacts be?"

13. "What factors are important in passing controversial legislation/ writing a good poem/ preventing disease/ designing a successful game plan, etc.?"

14. (In a unit on *Pygmalion*) "What would be some possible implications of Eliza Doolittle learning proper English?"[1]

15. "What song lyrics and/or dance steps could you use to convey to someone else how you went about solving this equation?"

16. "What are some *possible ways* to solve this problem? What are the advantages and disadvantages to each method?" (In a history or government class: "What are some possible ways to ensure the solvency of Social Security and other OASDI programs for the next fifty years?")

In brainstorming for possible Exploratory topics in your subject-matter area, try variations on these questions. Note that these broad structuring devices emphasize generation of a set of alternatives, rather than the stating and *defense* of values positions (i.e., you're asking students to brainstorm possibilities rather than make and defend a *best* decision). Topics that challenge students to state and defend positions are better suited for Reflective Discussions in which your students defend a point of view. These topics and issues can often be explored initially in this Exploratory format, as long as you do not push for a true resolution to the issue, problem, and so on by requiring students to defend a particular point of view.

Development: Student Brainstorming in Response to the Structuring Device

You've carefully planned your structuring device, and you've posed it as you conduct your first Exploratory in class. As the discussion facilitator, what should you do next?

You want to encourage students to share their ideas, possibly taking certain intellectual risks as they do this. You want them to listen carefully to their classmates and to build on and at times challenge ideas put forth by peers. For these things to happen, you'll need extreme patience (especially in the first few Exploratories that you try). Extend your Wait Time I and II (see Module Five) until it *hurts*. We have found that it frequently takes a few minutes for these discussions to get rolling. Wait for those initial responses. In an effective Exploratory, each teacher question should be followed by several responses, as students build on each other's ideas. Be careful *not* to interject immediately if students don't respond to each other right away; even if your students give you that doe-in-the-headlights look at first, be patient and encouraging. In many cases, *restating or rephrasing the main question will promote interaction.* Try this if the discussion begins slowly.

Certain other questioning techniques will enhance and improve the quality of the student–student interaction. In planning Exploratory Discussions, try to anticipate general categories of student response in question form. Ask yourself where the students should or *might* go as they explore the topic, and have questions ready to guide the interaction *if necessary.* You will sometimes find that students will exhaust one area of alternatives without addressing other possibilities. If the group fails to address an important point, simply ask a secondary question to jump-start the discussion in a new direction (e.g., "We've looked at ____ as one alternative. Have you considered ____?"). Be sure to give your students every opportunity to bring up these categories before interjecting, because they should determine the direction of the discussion (i.e., *be careful not to turn your planned Exploratory into a Directed Discussion*).

In our example biology discussion, the students began to respond to each other without much *directing* from their teacher. You'll find that this will most often be the case, especially when you set the discussion up effectively and students are used to this method. It seems as though Mr. Rizzi did ask at least a few of his secondary questions ("What view of the role of technology do the two cultures have?") to challenge students to explore new dimensions of the text. Again, we have found in planning Exploratories that it's useful to *anticipate what students should/might explore and have secondary questions planned in case the discussion bogs down* (see the sample lesson plan for examples of this). Do remember that in the case of Exploratories, these additional questions are things that you *might* ask, not things that you *have to* ask.

Promoting interaction and encouraging depth of thought among your students can be enhanced by asking a few Probe and Redirect questions. We have found that the (limited) use of clarifying Probes is very helpful in Exploratories ("Can you tell us what you mean by ____?"). These questions are designed in part to check the degree to which a statement has been understood by others. *Reflective Probes* can help clarify student statements. To ask such questions, simply paraphrase all or part of the student's response; he will often clarify or add something to the original answer, and other students may build on these ideas. Reflective clarifying questions can be preceded by a phrase such as: "Did I hear you say . . . ?" Use clarifying questions yourself, and encourage students to use them as well if statements are unclear ("I'm not sure that I know what you mean. Could you say that in another way?").

As we have noted, it will be important for you to encourage students to compare and contrast statements made by members of the group. Asking Redirect questions can encourage this. Mr. Rizzi asked an effective Redirect in responding to Amy's comment ("What do others feel about what he means when he uses the term *savage*?"). Look for opportunities to do this when students make particularly insightful points. Try to keep as many students as possible engaged in the discussion; from time to time, you may want to direct questions toward individual students. Again, it will be important to strike a balance between necessary questioning and interfering with the flow of the discussion; too many teacher questions, even when open-ended in nature, will inhibit student–student interaction, so be careful.

Another subtle but important planning consideration is the physical setting. We have found that seating students so that they can see and respond to each other makes a huge difference (see "Resocializing," Module Two). If possible, seat students *and yourself* in a circle. This will help promote the student–student interaction that you're looking for. Sitting with the students sends the important message that they are responsible for leading the discussion with less direction from the teacher (our biology teacher enhanced his Exploratory Discussion by doing this). If the initial part of the discussion will take place in a peer-group setting (do consider this as an op-

tion), desks or seats can be arranged initially in pods or smaller circles.

Once students are used to Exploratories, another interesting option is to conduct two or even three discussions simultaneously, with students seated in smaller circles of eight to fifteen. The advantage to this approach is that more students have a chance to provide input; you can spend time with each group, asking occasional questions. However you decide to seat or group your students, we highly recommend remaining at eye level with them; don't tower over the group, as this will send the message that you are going to direct the flow of the interaction.

Besides facilitating the discussion, we suggest that you write the main ideas generated by your students on paper or on an overhead transparency. The collection of ideas can later be shared with the class (the benefit of using overhead transparencies) and saved and used in future lessons. Because the structuring devices are relatively unfocused, your students' contributions will not necessarily occur in a logical sequence. As a result, you may want to group random student contributions as you write them and later discuss possible emerging categories of alternatives. Especially toward the end of the discussion, make an effort to cluster student statements into categories of some kind. This can be accomplished by having you or your students summarize alternatives to the structuring question; this focusing is important when you do longer Exploratories ("Who can summarize the ideas that we've mentioned so far?").

One more issue before we move on to the Culmination: Remember that Exploratory Discussions can only succeed if students feel free to express themselves, knowing full well that not everything that they say will prove totally sensible. They must come to *trust* you as a teacher and as a facilitator of such open discussions. If students perceive the game to be one of finding correct answers, they are not likely to explore ideas no matter what you say, so take care to accept all student statements. When justifications are made, they should be done in a respectful and deliberate way, with patience and sympathy. It will be important for you to avoid the appearance of judging the value of contributions; remember that the value test of a contribution is logical, not personal. *Criticize ideas, not people* is an important critical-thinking rule to emphasize when conducting any discussion; model this kind of accepting, open-minded attitude for your students.

Culmination

Let's say that your first Exploratory Discussion has gone well. Your students found your main question interesting, and they responded to each other as they brainstormed a range of interesting ideas (some of these really surprised and impressed you—that's the beauty of doing Exploratories). How do you conclude a discussion like this?

First of all, it is sometime hard to tell when an Exploratory has run its course; this will be a judgment call on your part. Once you feel students have generated enough useful ideas (or when you run out of time), we recommend returning to the structuring device and reviewing, or asking students to review, the main ideas generated. Remember that you're not pushing for a specific *resolution* or best answer to the structuring question. In a sense, the list of ideas generated actually serves *as* the Culmination. Mr. Rizzi shared his overhead notes with his class as he recapped points made by the students; we have found that this practice is especially effective. In fact, students are often impressed with the variety of ideas that they can generate in a short time.

It's important to convey that your Exploratories have a definite purpose. In planning your Leap, let students know how you'll be using these ideas in the future and why they're important. In meeting his Performance Objective, John Rizzi challenged his students to respond to two questions in writing that conveyed both the importance and relevance of his chosen topic. Ask your students to do something to apply what they've learned in some concrete way, whether this happens during the same class period or in a future lesson. Get 'em to put those ideas to work!

Assessment and Evaluation

As with any of our three discussion methods, you might challenge students to produce something for you to evaluate *during* or *immediately after* the lesson. We have found that reflective or reaction-type papers are especially effective as a way to challenge students to think further about topics discussed (e.g., a response paper or journal entry would be ideal as an epilogue to John Rizzi's lesson). As you plan your Exploratory Discussions, think carefully about what you might ask students to produce during or after the experience.

Focal Point 4 When Should You Use the Exploratory Discussion Method in Your Classroom?

Exploratory Discussions serve several purposes and can range in time from a few minutes (brief brainstorming sessions) to about one-half hour. These discussions can serve as excellent introductions to entire units or to lessons in which you utilize other methods. For example, you might begin a class period with a brief Exploratory in which students generate alternatives and then focus or expand on one of their ideas in a Directed or Reflective Discussion. This approach is very useful in math and science classrooms ("What do we need to know to solve this problem?"; "What questions will we need to address before we begin this process?"). In these cases, the Exploratory can serve an ILPE-type purpose (See Module Seven), with the teacher gaining valuable insights into initial student thinking on a new topic. As a science teacher, one of the authors has found Exploratory Discussions to be incredibly valuable for challenging students to articulate initial explanations for events/teacher demonstrations (i.e., science phenomena). Teachers in other subjects can conduct brief Exploratories for the same purpose, asking students for initial responses to pieces of prose or descriptions of historical events. Remember that in a constructivist classroom, investigating *student-generated* questions is a central focus, and the Exploratory format is ideal for accomplishing this.

As we noted earlier, Exploratory Discussions can also serve to conclude a unit or a series of lessons by challenging students to connect new ideas to other concepts and principles; Mr. Rizzi's *Chief Seattle* discussion serves as an example. In a history class, a structuring device such as "What would your life be like today if ____ had/hadn't happened?" can cause students to think deeply about the significance of past events, making real-world connections between ideas discussed and their own experiences. In the same way, during a study of plays/novels/short stories, an English teacher might ask students to immerse themselves in a text to brainstorm *possible* actions that a character might take in a difficult situation.

For a quintessential student-centered Exploratory, try role-playing (see Module Four). Students can assume various roles that govern the arguments related to an issue. Role-playing can be carried out either in a whole-class or in a peer-group setting, in which peer groups engage in role-play simultaneously.

As you will see, each of the three types of discussions will serve to empower your students. Student-centered discussions can play a huge part in creating a thinker-friendly classroom environment. By using these methods, a teacher is sending a clear signal to each student: *Your ideas are important, and the people in this classroom care about what you think.* It is a message that is too often missing in classrooms at all educational levels. We have found that Exploratory Discussions are tremendously effective in promoting creative, outside-the-box thinking. For example, a student teacher working with one of the authors frequently invited his students to work in groups to complete different math problems that might be solved in various ways and then to design and perform skits or songs that conveyed to the rest of the class how the problem was approached.[2] Not only were these peer-group Exploratories fun for the entire class but the teacher found that students remembered and could later use problem-solving approaches much more effectively.

As part of their probability and statistics unit in Ms. Claypool's discrete math course, students have been conducting and discussing a variety of probability *experiments.* They have flipped coins, rolled dice, even played card games as they have collected and analyzed data and *discovered* a number of important concepts. Ms. Claypool believes that the collection and analysis of real data is the most effective way to learn to apply the principles of probability and statistics, and she is about to challenge her students to embark on their most ambitious project yet. The class had discussed the process of *polling* to some extent. At the outset of today's class, she presents them with a new challenge. "As you know, Central High is considering a name change for the school mascot. Dr. Wigglefence [the principal] knows that this class has some expertise in probability and statistics, so he has chosen us to poll the student body to discover what kind of mascot might be preferred. We need to start this process today by doing some brainstorming. Here's our main question. *"What questions or issues will we have to address in order to conduct the fairest and most complete student poll that we possibly can?"* For the next twenty minutes, the class brainstorms an impressive list of issues that must be resolved before the class can conduct its student poll (e.g., How many students should we question? How will they be chosen? What kinds of questions should we ask? How many? Should we ask open-ended questions? Or ask for the most popular choices and have a schoolwide vote?). In wrapping up the Exploratory, Ms. Claypool tells the class that they have anticipated many of the toughest issues facing pollsters and statisticians and that their next challenge will be to resolve each issue and actually conduct the poll.

FIGURE 10.2 A Glimpse Inside a Constructivist Classroom

■ TIPS FOR TECHNOLOGY INTEGRATION

- In the math classroom, a number of commercially available programs (e.g., Geometer's Sketchpad, Escher Interactive) can be used in conjunction with Exploratory Discussions. You can challenge students to experiment with various program functions (e.g., manipulating/discovering different types of tessellations) as they simultaneously share observations/results with classmates in response to Exploratory questions.

- Internet connections between schools create the potential for conducting *electronic Exploratories* between students in classrooms miles apart (in a chat-room-type arrangement). Teachers or students can post open-ended, Exploratory-type structuring devices, which can be responded to by students in various classrooms. Students can then respond to each other's comments, creating an electronic forum for student–student interaction.

■ ROUNDUP ■

The purpose of Exploratory Discussions is to allow students to brainstorm alternatives, implications, pros/cons, or other ideas in response to an open-ended structuring device. Exploratory Discussions are exceptionally student-centered; you should allow your students wide discretion in deciding how they'll respond to the structuring question. In these discussions, the teacher plays a facilitative role, asking occasional Probe and Redirect questions. Your main task as facilitator will be to ensure that the main question is "explored" in terms of both breadth and depth and that the discussion engages as many students as possible.

Remember our advice for conducting effective Exploratories. Plan a broad, inviting structuring device *and* possible Trigger questions that you might ask at some point in the discussion. *Be patient.* It may take a few minutes for the discussion to get rolling, but the interaction will usually take off if you extend your wait time and encourage the group. The right seating arrangement can help. Arrange the classroom so that students can see each other, and seat yourself at eye level with the group. Try to write ideas generated by the class (and possibly group these) so that they can be used or referred to later. Controversial or "hot" topics are most successful.

Exploratory Discussions can serve to empower your students and are very effective in allowing students to brainstorm ideas or questions that can be used later, all vital dimensions of the constructivist learning experience.

Take a look at the sample lesson plan that follows; it will help you to better understand what it takes to put together an effective Exploratory. The Hands-On Practice sheet will guide you through the process of designing such discussions. The flowchart in Figure 10.3 will also help you.

1 = structuring device: question as student aim

intention ———▶ examine two sides of an issue or controversy
without making a value judgment

*What are the advantages and
disadvantages of . . . ?*

What are the pros and cons of . . . ?

2 = elicit both sides of the issue or controversy

use questions or role-play based on instructional materials

S–S dialogue.
DO NOT LECTURE.
Steer discussion only
when necessary.

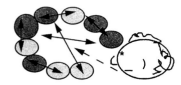

3 = organize points of view by headings

use board, overhead, etc.

PROs	CONs
1 ___	1 ___
2 ___	2 ___
3 ___	3 ___

4 = culmination: students answer structuring device

elicit implications without making value judgments

When . . . then . . . . If . . . then . . . . It appears that . . . when . . . .

© 2001 Ina Claire Gabler

FIGURE 10.3 Exploratory Discussion Method Flowchart

■ EXPLORATORY DISCUSSION SAMPLE LESSON PLAN ■

Unit Title: Biotechnology and Genetic Engineering (intended for a high school biology course)

Prelude

Rationale

(Combines What? Why? Justification): Participation in an Exploratory Discussion focused on the value of research in biotechnology will help students to understand that the scientific community and citizens will face a number of crucial ethical decisions in the future about how far such studies should go. Students will have an opportunity to consider the advantages and disadvantages as well as the implications connected with continued research. This experience will help students to develop important critical-thinking and ethical decision-making abilities and connects to INTASC Standards 1 and 3–7.

Performance Objective

(Combines Preparation, Product, Criteria): Students will first review some of the major trends in biotechnology research. Then, following a student-centered discussion, students will summarize at least four advantages and disadvantages of continued research in the field and will support each statement by referring to evidence from the discussion and supporting reading materials.

Materials and Lesson Aids

1. A collection of previously assigned readings/handouts focused on trends in biotechnology research.

2. Cartoon (featuring a dinosaur destroying a lab amid a group of shocked scientists)

Enactment

Time Estimate | Main Ideas/Concepts, Questions, and Teaching Methods

5–6 minutes | *Hook*
What do you think of when you see this cartoon (show cartoon on overhead)? What do the comments by the scientists show you? *Why* would a cartoonist draw this? What does this show you about the public's attitude toward scientific research? Are there some legitimate concerns about this research? Have you seen movies/TV shows or read articles that reflected some of these fears (discuss examples from readings)?

You've actually had a chance to extract DNA, splice it with restriction enzymes, even to do some cloning of your own. Let's review for just a minute: What is cloning? What do you start with? End with? In general, what did we do to the bacterial cells?

1–2 minutes | *Student Aim*
For the past four weeks, we've been talking about biotechnology, about some of the research trends, and what *might* happen in the future. Today, I'd like to spend some time talking about the future, what scientists *might* do, and perhaps what we should avoid doing. We're going to do an Exploratory Discussion, so feel free to respond to each other's comments without input from me. My question is this: *What do you see as potential advantages and disadvantages to continued research in biotechnology?*

Development

15–20 minutes | Student-centered discussion with teacher moderation.

Potential Trigger Questions
• How could we benefit in terms of agriculture/food production?
• Are fears within the public about *eating* genetically engineered products legitimate? Why/why not?
• What are the *possibilities* for treat-

ment of human disease? For enabling more successful organ transplants?
• What benefits could come from stem cell research? What dangers do you see in this?
• Could research provide us with ways to save endangered species? *Would this be a positive thing? Why?*
• What possible abuses do you see if research goes on at its current pace?
• Would you as a citizen favor any *restrictions* on research? If so, which ones?

3–4 minutes | *Culmination*
Wrap-Up: You raised a range of important issues today! These are issues that will definitely have an impact on us as citizens in the near future. Who can summarize some of the major points we addressed? (Probe/redirect, based on responses)
Leap: Tomorrow, we're going to look at a specific situation and a set of issues connected to biotech research. Before then, I'd like you to consider an important question: Would you, as a future parent, ever want to be given the opportunity to decide *in advance* on the sex and the physical attributes of your children? Explain.

Assessment and Evaluation

What was the quality of the discussion in terms of cognitive level? (Cite criteria.)

How thoroughly did the students explore various issues? (Cite criteria.)

How well did they justify their assertions? (Cite criteria.)

Did students ask thoughtful questions? (Cite criteria.)

■ HANDS-ON PRACTICE ■

Plan an Exploratory Discussion by using this template. Refer to Module Two for a look at the Core Components of a lesson plan, and review this module for detail on this type of discussion.

Prelude (for teacher reference)

• Rationale (with connection to national/state standards)

- Performance Objective (remember to be specific about what your students should be able to *do* to show you what they've learned)
- Materials and Lesson Aids

Enactment (Student engagement: What might you say/do/ask at each stage of the lesson?)

- Hook
- Student Aim

  Structuring device preface (How will you set up/contextualize your main question?)

  Posing the structuring device as a question (How will you *phrase* this main question?)

- Development

  Students brainstorm in response to the structuring device. (What will you do to promote this, e.g., through a special seating pattern; the use of reference materials?)

Teacher facilitates interaction with Trigger questions. (How will you phrase the questions that you *might* ask?)

- Culmination

  Wrap-Up: What will you say/do/ask to help students summarize the main points discussed?

  Leap: How will students use/apply these ideas in the future?

Assessment and Evaluation

What will you ask students to produce during/after the lesson to show what they've learned?

How will you evaluate this product?

ENDNOTES

1. Thanks to Rebecca Ayers, Augustana College Class of 1999, for this contribution.
2. Thanks to Nick Polyak, Augustana College Class of 1999, for this contribution.

Module 11

The Reflective Discussion Method

■ OVERVIEW: SCENARIO DEPICTING A REFLECTIVE DISCUSSION

The students in Mrs. Garcia's first period United States history class seem excited as they enter the classroom today. Over the course of the school year, they had come to expect the unexpected from their history teacher: interactive discussions, guest speakers, skits, group projects, even Mrs. Garcia, one of the other teachers, or a parent dressing up occasionally as an historic figure. Pocahontas, Thomas Jefferson, Henry David Thoreau, Susan B. Anthony, and the Marx Brothers had all made appearances this year. The desks are arranged in one big circle today, which is pretty common for this history class. Before the bell rings, two students talk briefly about what they might do today.

"We've got to finish talking about World War II today," offers Shannon to Nikki. "I wonder what she'll have cooked up."

"I'm not sure, but we'll probably go out with a bang," Nikki replies. "That's one thing I really like about this class. She asks us interesting questions and listens to our ideas."

Mrs. Garcia doesn't waste a minute as she stands in front of the circle of desks. "Let's go back in time," she begins, her voice bright with anticipation. "It's July, 1945. What's happening around the world in July, 1945?" She pauses for a few seconds as hands shoot up. "Alexis?"

"The war's almost over. Germany already surrendered," answers Alexis confidently.

"Who can add something to what Alexis said?"

"President Truman just took over," notes Jack. "They want to set up the United Nations."

"Everyone's listening to swing music and dancing," adds Sue to a few chuckles.

"We're, I mean the U.S., is closing in on Japan, but they haven't given up!" says Nikki.

"You're all right. Today, we're going to focus on Nikki's point and talk about what's happening in the Pacific," says Mrs. Garcia. "I'd like to welcome all of you to Washington DC for an important meeting of President Truman's closest advisors." She pulls on a string attached to the projector screen, which was lowered over the chalkboard, to reveal the words SECRET SESSION—PRESIDENT TRUMAN'S WARTIME ADVISORS.

"On these sheets I've got descriptions of the roles that you'll play in today's discussion. I've mixed them up randomly, so I'm not sure who will get what part." The students smile at each other—they had done lots of role-playing and found it interesting.

"When you receive your role, read it carefully. Each role will describe your character's initial point of view." Mrs. Garcia moves around the circle as she's speaking, handing each student a sheet of paper. When everyone has a role, she races through the attendance and waits for the students to finish reading. The room is unusually silent for about three minutes.

When everyone is finished reading, Mrs. Garcia continues. "Last night, you had a chance to read about a new and frightening weapon that's been developed, the atomic bomb. Your challenge today is to decide whether the United States should use the bomb to try to end the war in the Pacific. You're a group of the President's closest advisors, and he has entrusted you to make a decision today that could change history," she notes in a serious tone.

"Remember that this is an open discussion. Feel free to challenge each other's ideas, but remember that only one person speaks at a time. The President will be responsible for moderating. Who is President Truman?"

Nikki's hand shoots up to a mix of applause and chatter.

"All right. I'd like to call on the President to begin the meeting," Mrs. Garcia says. "The question before the council is this: *Should the United States drop an atomic bomb on Hiroshima, as suggested by the Joint Chiefs of Staff?*"

"Let's start the meeting. I'd like to start by asking for suggestions from the council," begins Nikki with an air of confidence. "Who has an opinion?"

For the next thirty minutes, the class of twenty-five debates the pros and cons of using the atomic bomb. Students speak as a range of characters: parents of servicemen in the Pacific, military officers, members of Congress, arms manufacturers, religious leaders, and Eleanor Roosevelt are all present at the meeting. The students rely on knowledge that they've gained during the World War II unit in stating their opinions and challenging each other with questions. Mrs. Garcia (who is the Secretary of State, she tells the group) challenges various students with occasional questions (What would happen if . . . ?; Is there another alternative to . . . ?; What else can you tell us about Mrs. Roosevelt's suggestion to . . . ?). But she relies on Nikki to moderate the discussion, and Nikki responds thoughtfully.

With fifteen minutes left in the class period, Mrs. Garcia reminds Nikki that the council needs to vote on whether or not to use the atomic bomb. The class has articulated three alternatives on which to vote, and Mrs. Garcia reminds the group that they can deviate from their character's original position if they believe they should do so. Nikki presents the alternatives and asks for a show of hands as the students make an individual decision. The class spends the last few minutes of class discussing their choice and reflecting on the discussion itself. Mrs. Garcia asks the group to write a brief essay for tomorrow in which they address three questions:

- What points did they consider as they made a decision? Why?
- What would they choose to do if they had served on such an advisory council, and why?
- Was the Truman administration justified in dropping an atomic bomb on Hiroshima? Explain and justify.

■ FOCAL POINTS AND DISCUSSIONS

Focal Point 1 What Makes the Reflective Discussion Method Distinctive?

You've just witnessed what we call a Reflective Discussion. In conducting Reflective Discussions, your main goal will be to challenge your students to express and defend their thoughts regarding complex, values-oriented questions or issues. Perhaps more than any other constructivist teaching method, there is an emphasis in Reflectives on helping students to develop their critical-thinking abilities. As we'll see, you'll be inviting students to consider an issue, search for and weigh evidence, listen and respond to the positions of others, consider multiple perspectives, and eventually make, share, and defend a final decision.

Discussion 1 What Makes the Reflective Discussion Method Distinctive?

These discussions occupy a place between Exploratory Discussions and Directed Discussions in terms of the degree of control that students have over the direction of the lessons. Reflectives share with Directed Discussions the characteristics of having a convergent, focused *structuring question* and a *specific resolution* to the question posed. They are similar to Exploratory Discussions in the degree of freedom that you'll afford your students over the flow of the interaction, even though the interaction is more focused. In Reflective Discussions, students are given opportunities to find ways to address academic problems and to make their own decisions, rather than being guided by the teacher through the process step-by-step, as in Directed Discussions.

Figure 11.1 shows our suggested planning template for Reflective Discussions. As you take a look at the stages, think carefully about what Mrs. Garcia did in each phase of her Reflective Discussion.

Prelude

- Rationale (with connection to national/state standards)
- Performance Objective
- Materials and Lesson Aids

Enactment

- Hook: If possible, connect to structuring device to help contextualize the discussion
- Student Aim
    structuring device preface (e.g., provide background information, provide students with ground rules for the discussion)
    Pose the structuring device as a question
- Development
    Students debate/share and challenge opinions in response to structuring device
    Teacher facilitates interaction with secondary questions, extended wait time
    List pros and cons as desired
- Culmination
    1. *Wrap-Up:* Students/teacher recap arguments; students reach resolution on structuring question
    2. *Leap:* How will they use these ideas? What will we do as a result of this decision?

Assessment and Evaluation

- Assessment products (What will students produce in this/a later lesson?)
- Evaluation (How will you evaluate this product, e.g., with a scoring rubric?)

FIGURE 11.1 Reflective Discussion Planning Template

Focal Point 2 The Nature of Values and Beliefs

We've noted that Reflective Discussions challenge students to use their *values* to make well-informed decisions on important questions/issues. Before continuing in our description of Reflective Discussions, we will pause to explain values in a bit more detail, relate them to the constructivist learning perspective, and suggest how teachers can best discuss values with their students.

As educational research has shown (see Module One), regardless of what tasks students are engaged in, their past experiences and, consequently, associated *frames of reference* will have an immediate impact not only on how certain material is learned but also on how it will be used later. Each of our *frames of reference* are profoundly affected by the values system that we have constructed through interactions with family, friends, and others within our culture and the larger society. We would define *values,* for the purpose of this discussion, *as the acts, customs, institutions, objects, and ways of behavior and thinking that members of a group of people view as desirable.* A *belief* is *a value that a person holds to be true.*

As soon as students decide that a particular solution to a problem is right or wrong, they are reflecting some value that they have learned in school or from family and friends. Clearly, some issues are more heavily value-laden than others. Values obviously have a profound effect on the way we see the world. Our system of values has an impact on how we perceive and interpret both past and current events. In an English class, students are making values choices when they state that the actions of a character in a story or play were justified. In geometry, a student selecting a method to complete a proof is making a values choice. Even the most mundane student tasks, such as listening and taking notes, are influenced by values and belief structures. In high-school classrooms, for instance, taking notes to get a higher grade will be seen as crucial by those students who plan to go to college. For students who see little value in school, taking notes may not be very important. Although it would be safe to say that most cultures have certain core values held by most members, individual values may differ significantly among people. The fact that people hold different values when it comes to certain issues is not necessarily bad, nor should the discussion of these values be avoided in the classroom.

Dealing with values in the classroom can be a challenging task for teachers. In fact, there is a great deal of talk today about *teaching* values in the classroom, but those doing the talking can mean vastly different things when they say this. For some, teaching values means telling young people *what to think,* in essence *what to value* (a process that we and others might call *values inculcation*). It is our position that, as teachers, we have an obligation to deal with values directly as part of the learning experience but that we do not have the right to press or impose our own values on our students.

The approach that we recommend, which would include the use of methods like Reflective Discussions, would be to challenge students to consider real, complex situations in which they and others will need to make difficult decisions that could be logically supported. As students work through these intellectually challenging classroom situations with the help of teachers and classmates, it is our belief that they will become better decision makers who are able to reason well at the highest intellectual levels (i.e., analysis, synthesis, evaluation). Methods like Reflective Discussions can cause learners to experience what we call *values disequilibrium,* a questioning of their own current values system and a possible change in this system based on experiences. In addition, by using procedures that achieve a thorough and balanced exploration when investigating values-laden issues, you can avoid conflicts with parents, peers, and school administrators. Like many of the constructivist teaching methods that we've introduced, Reflective Discussions can promote a valuable struggle in coming to understand complex situations *and make well-reasoned decisions.* That's what Reflective Discussions are all about.

In the previous module, we noted that we had found that Exploratory Discussions can be empowering to students. It has been our experience that Reflectives can have this very same impact. We believe that these discussions will help your students to develop some of the most vital thinking abilities that they'll need in the future, both in school and beyond. For this reason, we urge you to make Reflective Discussions regular events in your classroom, regardless of which subject you teach. Remember that the main idea behind this method is to take students' current beliefs associated with a topic and to challenge these beliefs with new information and perspectives on that topic. Your overall goal will be for students to express their values or beliefs, reconsider them in the light of new information, and either reinforce or modify them in light of new experiences. In order to further this goal, you present new information in a way that may create conflict or values disequilibrium (cognitive dissonance), that is, the clash of new ideas with current student values systems. The key is to spend the majority of the lesson in a discussion in which students take the leading role.

Focal Point 3 Reflective Discussion Method Markers

We've described some of the general features of a Reflective Discussion—now to get a bit more specific. In the sections that follow, we'll see that these discussions are highly student-centered but more highly structured than Exploratory Discussions. The method markers described here will provide you with an initial schema (a mental construct with discrete characteristics) for planning Reflective Discussions.

- The Student Aim for Reflectives is more structured and specific than in Exploratories. You'll set up the discussion in the Hook and then convey the Student Aim by *posing a focused structuring device that calls for a values-based decision as a question.* Although students may form initial opinions on this question, the structuring device won't be *finally* answered until the Culmination.

- As the Development proceeds, students will struggle with or debate the Structuring Device in a setting that features a high degree of *student–student interaction.*

- As the teacher, you'll moderate the discussion by asking *Trigger, Probe, and Redirect questions* (see Module Five) that will challenge students to carefully consider their position, its implications, and the implications of other possible positions. List pros and cons as desired.

- During the Culmination, you'll challenge each student to *make and defend a final, individual decision* regarding the structuring question.

Note the similarities and differences between the Reflective Discussion and the Directed and Exploratory methods. We'll focus on these characteristics as we discuss planning in the sections that follow.

Focal Point 4 Up Close: Planning and Conducting a Reflective Discussion

Like Exploratory Discussions, Reflectives are highly student-centered, but they are more structured in that they challenge students to make and defend decisions. So, just what will you need to do to successfully plan and conduct these discussions? This will be our guiding question in the following sections.

Prelude: Rationale

We'll focus on Mrs. Garcia's history lesson as we analyze the Reflective Discussion Method. Like all constructivist teachers, one of Mrs. Garcia's most important goals is to challenge her students to *live,* or directly experience, her subject. For example, as her students *do* history (through research, analysis of primary source documents, interviewing people who lived through important events, etc.), she feels that it's vital to challenge them to struggle through some of the same complex issues and questions

that people in various historical periods struggled through. This priority is certainly shown in this example Reflective Discussion. Her planning for the lesson might have started with writing a Rationale like this: "By participating in a role-play situation that challenges them to take and defend a position on an important historical issue, students will apply what they know about this historical context as they directly experience an authentic debate. This experience will help students to develop and enhance a wide range of critical-thinking and verbal communications skills and connects to INTASC Standards 1 and 3–8." Again, as with Exploratory Discussions, convey your *reason* for doing Reflectives to yourself and to your students. Writing a clear, compelling Rationale can help you to do this. Your Performance Objectives will flow directly from the Rationale. (See Module Three for the Core Components of a lesson.)

Performance Objective

We have noted that writing Performance Objectives for discussions can be tricky. Listening to student comments can certainly provide some of the best indications as to what they're learning through the experience. Asking them to do or produce something in which they apply what they've learned is something that we'd recommend. Again, *showing students that learning in your classroom is a generative process is vital.*

During or after Reflective Discussions, we would also recommend challenging students to think (and talk or write) about how the experience influenced their thinking. Mrs. Garcia accomplished this with her writing assignment. In planning this lesson, her Performance Objective might have looked like this: "Following a brief review of the historical context, students will participate in a role-play in which they are challenged to take and defend a position regarding the dropping of the atomic bomb on Hiroshima. Individually, they will then address three questions in appropriate detail in a take-home essay, the contents of which will later be shared in class." Note that in the case of Reflective Discussions, student *application* of the lessons learned (and carrying out the Performance Objective) could take place during the discussion itself, later in the class period, or still later in an assignment or individual or peer-group research project. Any or all of these assessment options could be expressed in your Performance Objective. As you plan lessons utilizing this method, think carefully about what you might do to challenge students to apply what they've learned and to reflect on how their thinking was influenced by the lesson.

Materials

The right materials and lesson aids can spice up any kind of discussion and lead to a lively exchange of *mean-*

ingful ideas. The materials that you utilize can vary as widely as discussion topics do. Text of all kinds, videoclips, political cartoons, data sheets, maps, prints/sketches, computer programs—almost anything can help you to provide students with the right context for intelligently considering your structuring question. For all three types of discussions, we have found that providing students with text to use *during* the discussion can make a tremendous difference. *Immersing* students into text of all kinds is vital, and using text during discussions can facilitate this.

When you conduct Reflective Discussions (and usually Directeds and Exploratories), you'll often want to *create controversy*. This can provide a kind of *cognitive jolt*. To accomplish this, you'll often want to utilize role-plays or debates (more on this in the following sections). If you choose to do this, some of your most important materials will include the role descriptions or debate guidelines that you'll need to distribute to students (again, further details to follow). In our history scenario, Mrs. Garcia had composed a wide range of roles for the class to play as they *became* President Truman's advisors. Each of these roles would need to be described on paper and distributed to the students. Your role-plays and debates might include other textual materials for students to use. Science, art, music, and PE Reflectives might include a wide range of other materials. Again, think carefully about what your students will need to *make their decisions*.

Enactment: The Hook

Now on to the actual conducting of the discussion: In planning your Reflective Discussion Hooks, think about what you might do to create controversy or convey the feeling to your students that some kind of a problem exists. In our history example, Mrs. Garcia asked some relatively open warm-up questions that *began* the process of taking students back to 1945. Then, she set the scene in a more definite way (and with a little flourish) by welcoming the class to a meeting of the President's advisors. In doing this, she was using the role-play *as* a Hook.

In planning the Hook for any of our three discussion methods, one key is to somehow connect to the problematic or challenging situation or question that will serve as the focus for the discussion. Doing this will let your students know that they'll be discussing something worthwhile; if you can convey a sense of urgency, drama, intrigue, or mystery in your Hook, it will be that much more effective. You can do this in any subject. For example, our glimpse into a math Exploratory in the previous module showed that a real application or situation can make just about any discussion topic feel more genuine.

Another overall goal for a Reflective Hook is to convey to students that *values* do come into play in the consideration of the main question/issue. Try to make them aware, early in the lesson, that this will be a difficult decision because of the possibly conflicting values that the people involved might hold. For example, Mrs. Garcia's students quickly found that there would be a wide range of defensible opinions on the question that their teacher posed. The conflicting values perspective can be conveyed through your initial questions to the students or through the use of an article, a set of algebraic/geometric proofs, a film clip, a series of photographs, a poem, and so on.

Student Aim

We mentioned in the previous module that since Exploratory and Reflective Discussions are so student-centered (and as so, outside the norm for most students) that you should set up or preface the structuring device carefully. Let your students know that they will have the freedom (and responsibility) to decide how they will go about debating the central question. We would suggest planning a statement to this effect, as Mrs. Garcia did for her discussion ("When you receive your role, read it carefully . . . . Remember that this is an open discussion. . . . I'd like to call on the President to begin the meeting"). Such a statement can, in a concise way, let your students know what the parameters for the discussion will be.

One of your biggest considerations in planning a Reflective Discussion will be how to phrase that main question. Structuring devices for Reflective Discussions usually take one of these general forms: *Does X have value? Is/was X justified? What should we/he/she/they do in this situation?* From these general examples, it follows that structuring questions/statements should have the two necessary characteristics:

1. They should provoke a defended stand on an issue letting students know what kind of decision they need to make.

2. They should also identify one or more intellectual activities (Bloom's cognitive skills; see Module Five) associated with your Rationale and Performance Objective for the lesson.

When planning your structuring device, be careful that the range of possible student responses is not so broad that you cannot deal with them in depth during a class period (although Reflective Discussions can span several class sessions if necessary). For example, the structuring device planned and posed by Mrs. Garcia ("Should the United States drop an atomic bomb on Hiroshima, as suggested by the Joint Chiefs of Staff?") clearly conveys what decision her students are being challenged to make and also *hints* that other possibilities might be open for consideration (e.g., If not Hiroshima, would some other target be suitable?).

Consider the example structuring devices that follow. Note that some are written generically so that you might adapt them to a range of topics, while others are examples plucked from specific lessons. Again, our intent here is to encourage you to consider the wide range of possibilities. Notice that although the structuring question is broader than in a Directed Discussion, it is important to provide some focus, as these examples illustrate.

1. "Is the poem provided an example of Romantic poetry? Why or why not?"

2. "Given the alternatives available to this community, what is the best possible solution to the solid waste controversy?"

3. "T. S. George has argued that industrialized nations should not expect developing countries to control their birthrates because they themselves do not control their rates of consumption. Is he justified in making this argument? Explain."

4. "Is it right for local school boards to decide what should or should not be read in public schools? Justify your viewpoint."

5. "Should the children of illegal aliens enjoy the same educational opportunities enjoyed by the children of American citizens? Why/why not?"

6. "What is the *best* hypothesis available to explain this phenomenon?"

7. "Given the different methods of proof that we have introduced, what is the best way to solve this problem?"

8. (After students read the beginning of a short story or historical vignette) "What do you feel is the most likely ending for this story? Why?"

9. "Given the economic and environmental positions outlined in the article, was the Clinton administration's position on logging in old-growth forests justified?"

10. "Given the information in this story problem, what is the best way to set up equations to find an answer?"

11. "Given the extent of the AIDS epidemic in large metropolitan areas, are school boards justified in distributing condoms in local high schools?" Explain.

12. (While analyzing pictures associated with a current or historical event) "What do you think the people in these pictures are thinking/feeling? Justify your viewpoint."

13. "With the data/information that we have, what is the best decision that we can make regarding _____? Explain."

14. "Given the evidence that we have, should we as a jury find Tom Joad guilty or innocent of murder? Why?"

15. "Was the Bush administration justified in calling for military tribunals to try suspects in the September 11, 2001 terrorist attacks? Justify your stand."

16. (After reading/discussing a story, novel, or film) "Was ___ justified in taking the action that he/she took?"

17. (In a foreign language class) "Given what you know about _____ culture, what would be the best response in this situation?" (What might you say using the language?)

18. (In a PE class) "Given this situation, what would be the best strategy for ____?"

When planning Reflective Discussions, try using a variation on one of these questions as you articulate your own structuring device. Note that it is often possible and desirable to connect Reflective Discussion topics with earlier student experiences, both within and outside the classroom. For this reason, Reflectives are often very effective when concluding a series of lessons or to culminate a major research project. Notice also that topics for Reflective Discussions often involve making interdisciplinary connections, a highly worthwhile goal from the constructivist perspective. It follows that in planning these discussions, you may have to do some cognitive stretching of your own in anticipating potential student responses.

Development: Students Debate Options, Make and Defend Decisions

We now move to the true heart of the Reflective Discussion. You have planned and posed an enticing structuring question. It's now up to the students to *consider* this question. How do you go about encouraging this? During a Reflective Discussion, *your* role is *not* to make your own value judgments or to push students toward given solutions, but rather to act as *mediator and facilitator* as students think deeply about the question or problem. Whenever possible, you should help students to challenge each other respectfully and to help them to look for flaws in reasoning. As you plan and conduct such a discussion, consider the following points.

First, think carefully about the present level of understanding and values of your students. Within your classroom, you should have a fair idea about how your students feel about certain issues. This serves as your starting point. Think back to previous lessons and determine where your students have demonstrated inconsistencies, disagreement, and confusion. For example, a math teacher may have noticed that some students always attempt to use a certain problem-solving method when confronted with a certain type of exercise. A social studies teacher might note that certain group members hold very biased views of some historical event or issue. An English teacher might have students who believe that a character in a book should have taken a different course of action. A science teacher might have learned that none of the group members recycles bottles and cans. Each of these examples shows ways in which you can gain insights into how your group members stand on certain issues.

Second, think carefully about some way to *promote a degree of disagreement or controversy*. You must begin the lesson by making students aware of the evidence that brings their values into question. As students face this evidence, you will help them to clarify their present beliefs and explain why they feel the way that they do. This clarification will be developed by having students outline values positions as clearly as they can while discussing the topic or issue with others in the group. But remember that Reflective Discussions shouldn't stop with mere values clarification. Once the students have clearly defined the problem and clarified their own initial views, plan on exposing any contradictions in logic and encourage others in the group to respectfully do the same. In doing so, students may gain a valuable sense of discomfort regarding their current viewpoints, otherwise known as *values disequilibrium.*

There are different ways to promote this feeling of values disequilibrium. If you are relatively sure that you have selected a topic on which students hold a range of opinions, you can structure the discussion in a straightforward way, posing the structuring device and allowing students to take the lead in expressing and defending their views. We have found two other techniques to be especially effective when it comes to creating values disequilibrium: You can set up a role-playing situation (as Mrs. Garcia did) or structure a formal or informal debate. We have found that both techniques can lead to a lively exchange of ideas and enhanced depth of understanding of the issues. In Figure 11.2, we have taken a more detailed look at role-playing, which we have found to be particularly effective in the context of Reflective Discussions. This section includes a number of important considerations that come into play whenever you plan and conduct role-plays. (See Module Four.)

Actual debating during a Reflective Discussion is also an effective option. There are a number of possible variations that you might try. In less formal debates, you can simply assign half of your students to a pro position and half to a con and open the discussion at that point. Another possibility is to formalize the debate a bit by splitting the class into teams, allowing team members to plan arguments then present their case with specific time limits, with some allowance for counterarguments. Formal debates have some advantages and some drawbacks.

There is some excellent opportunity for productive student–student interaction as the debate teams prepare arguments. During the presentation phase, be sure that students make some allowance for multiple spokespersons; we have observed many classroom debates in which more confident, verbally articulate students dominate the discussion. Set up team requirements that will ensure the involvement of each student. Other debate options include holding *simultaneous* debates in smaller peer groups and then convening the groups to discuss the results. This technique can work effectively in groups of four or six (e.g., three pro, three con).

Regardless of the format that you choose for the Development, play a moderating role as the teacher. After asking your structuring question/statement, let silence reign as students complete the necessary thought processes. If your extended wait time (see Module Five) fails to promote discussion, ask a few comprehension questions to determine whether or not students understand the structuring question. A few preliminary questions can serve to break the ice and promote interaction.

If the responses to your comprehension questions suggest that students do understand the question and the topic, restate your structuring device. If you conclude that student understanding is lacking, you may have to do some remedial teaching in the form of a minipresentation.

Above all, do not answer the structuring question yourself. If you become too heavily involved in the process of answering the question, little real student reflection will occur. If your students are still reluctant to address the question, you might consider soliciting individual reactions with *secondary questions* that toss a challenge to students, playing devil's advocate. Whether you choose to role-play or debate as part of the Development in a Reflective Discussion, remember that your role will be to moderate the interaction, ask appropriate questions, and make certain that as many students as possible stay involved. You want your students to interact with/debate each other to the greatest extent possible, so plan on intervening only to challenge students to think in more depth about certain points or to throw in a new twist that keeps the discussion moving.

To prepare for your moderating, try to determine possible student responses in advance. Note that in planning for Reflective Discussions, you must be prepared to react to many more lines of argument than in Directed Discussions. Plan for the most likely lines of inquiry, but, as when planning Exploratories, have secondary questions written and ready that will encourage students to investigate related ideas. If the discussion lags, or students do not take all facets of an issue into account, you can utilize these prepared questions. Consider these examples:

What IS "Role-Playing"?

We may describe role-playing as *the investigation of situations through placing students in another's position, challenging them to think about something, and then analyzing the process.*

Keys to Effective Planning: What Do You Need to Do to "Set Up" a Role-Play?

- Focus on a situation that is interesting, thought-provoking, problematic. These situations can be *real* or *hypothetical:* Create/recreate a scene from a novel, an historic event, a meeting designed to resolve an issue (any subject), a situation that your students could find themselves in (foreign language). If necessary, ask initial clarifying questions to make sure that students understand the situation (e.g., "What are the issues here? Why are they important? How might ____ feel about this?"). Controversy helps; create a situation that will promote debate and disagreement. Real situations with community connections are especially relevant ("What should our community do about ____?").

- You can ask your students to role-play real or imaginary people (e.g., historic figures, characters from novels/short stories). If you have time and opportunity, challenge your students to research the person that they'll play. It is often effective to spring roles on students when you introduce a situation (as Mrs. Garcia did in our scenario) to get a more spontaneous response. In either case, give students handouts that provide just enough background. Make suggestions about how the person could feel about the issue, but give students some space to inject their own thoughts. *It is often advisable to assign role-players to argue for a specific position.* Think about suggesting options within these role descriptions (should we do A, B, or C?), especially when role-playing is new to your students. Think carefully about whether you'll assign specific roles to students or hand roles out randomly. Try both approaches. An enticing role can draw out quiet students. It is also very effective to challenge students to argue from positions with which they disagree initially (create that cognitive dissonance). Do allow students to opt out of a role that makes them uncomfortable. (Never force students to take a values-based position.) Consider challenging a student to play a moderating role (once again, consider our history example, as one of Mrs. Garcia's students was chosen randomly to moderate the discussion as President Truman).

- Think carefully about the role that you will play as a teacher. It is usually advisable to take part in some way. If you feel that the situation will require extensive moderation (e.g., a high level of controversy; students who are inexperienced at role-playing), give yourself a role that will allow you to interject unobtrusively (e.g., the judge in a trial or the mayor at a town council meeting; Mrs. Garcia became the Secretary of State). If you trust that students will be able to carry on a healthy debate without much guidance, give yourself a more peripheral role.

- Allow students enough time for the role-play. Don't rush things. Challenge them to make some kind of decision (i.e., reach a personal resolution on that structuring device) during the Culmination of the lesson. Class consensus on the question may be possible, but don't push this. Taking some type of vote or trying to reach a consensus is one option but certainly not a requirement (consider a secret ballot if the issue is especially controversial).

- Spend time processing the role-play during the lesson *Wrap-Up* and in future lessons. Allow your students to step out of roles and discuss the experience, especially if they've been asked to argue from a certain perspective. Plan processing questions ("Was this a realistic situation?"; "Why IS this a difficult issue?"; "How did it feel to play ____?"; "What other solutions might have been considered?"; "How DO you feel about this issue?"; "How did this experience change your thinking?"). Challenge students to do a written response to the role-play, using guiding questions like these.

FIGURE 11.2 Suggestions for Effective Role-Playing

- If might is right in wartime, then wasn't dropping the first atomic bomb on Japan beyond moral scrutiny? Jose, what do you say to that?

- O.K., Penny, what if you were framed for a murder that you didn't commit? Would you still say the death penalty is a just practice?

- Let's say a hate group is sending false information over the Internet to stir up bigotry against people of your ethnic origin. Should that group be protected by free speech rights? Daryl, what's your view on that?

You can often *jump-start* the discussion by asking in this way about a new area for consideration: "We've spent a lot of time discussing _____. Have you considered what effect _____ has on the issue?". Do everything in your power to establish a student–student pattern. The intellectual benefits to students will be great. Once you establish a teacher–student pattern, it's hard to break, because students will look to you for a response after every comment. (Remember that this will probably be their tendency, at first. Be patient in waiting for students to address each other.) We discuss this and similar issues in more depth when we discuss resocializing students (Module Two).

If you need to ask secondary questions like these, your *response* to student comments at this point is crucial. Evaluating student replies, or asking Probe questions, will probably result in a teacher–student–teacher interaction pattern developing. In this case, the lesson will look more like a Directed Discussion, which is highly undesirable, given the nature of Reflective Discussion topics. The best thing to do is respond with Redirects and extended wait time ("What does the rest of the group think about Susanne's statement?").

We have found that student response to Reflective Discussions is usually highly positive; chances are that your Reflectives will take off as planned, if you set them up effectively. As in Exploratory Discussions, one final consideration is your planned seating arrangement for the class. A setup that allows students to look directly at each other always seems to promote interaction. Consider circular seating patterns especially. As a moderator, place yourself within this circle, where you can capture student ideas in writing and ask occasional questions.

Culmination

Reflective Discussions are often lively and fast-paced, and this makes them challenging to conclude. An effective Culmination, one in which you and your students reach some resolution to the main question, is essential. Students will quickly tire of discussions that seemingly never get anywhere. To the greatest extent possible, call on each student to formulate and express a *specific resolution* before the lesson ends. A consensus is often not achieved and is often not desirable, especially when you are discussing complex or emotionally charged issues.

For the *Wrap-Up*, you can provide a summary of main points or ask a student to do the same, but it is often effective to let each student express and justify his final point of view as a *specific resolution* with a brief statement. In the Leap, ask students to analyze their own thought processes ("Do you feel different about the issue now? Why?"). If you have asked students to play certain roles within the discussion format, it is a good idea to let them step out of these roles toward the end of the lesson to express their true views. Otherwise, the entire activity can become frustrating for the student, especially if she is asked to play a role with which she disagrees for the entire discussion.

In our history example, the teacher challenged her class to answer the main question in a couple of different ways. The presidential advisors stepped out of their roles to actually vote on the options that Mrs. Garcia had presented in setting up the role-play. (*Note:* the teacher had no idea, in advance, what the class's decision would be. This is part of the excitement that Reflective Discussions can create, for both the students and you). The class then had time to discuss the role-play itself and how it had in-fluenced their thinking—something else we would highly recommend. The teacher also challenged each student to *personally* reflect on the decision they had made by responding to three challenging questions in a written theme. You can often use ideas expressed by students in these written responses as a springboard into future lessons, a great way to challenge students to see the connections between their classroom experiences.

One final suggestion on a possible *Leap* for your students. If students have strong feelings about the issue/problem involved and it's a current issue, ask them to consider what *action* they might take to deal with the situation. Is there a person they might write to in order to express their opinion as a concerned citizen or consumer? Could they invite a local elected official or company representative to visit the classroom to discuss the issue? Could you encourage the class to undertake further research as a part of this process? Remember that one of your main goals as a constructivist teacher will be to help your students make connections beyond the walls of the classroom and to apply what they've learned to real situations. Look for opportunities to do this when you conduct Reflective Discussions.

Assessment and Evaluation

As we noted in the Performance Objective section, asking students to reflect on what they have learned and to produce something that might extend their thinking can make Reflective Discussions even more meaningful. We have found that asking students to provide a written response to Reflective Discussions can serve to deepen their thinking not only about that particular issue but also about the thinking processes that were involved in the discussion.

Focal Point 5 **When Should You Use the Reflective Discussion Method in Your Classroom?**

Regardless of your subject-matter area, we urge you to make frequent use of the Reflective Discussion method. These discussions promote complex thinking at the synthesis and evaluation levels and can make any topic more exciting and relevant to your students. Reflective Discussions can take place anywhere within a planned unit. They can serve as effective motivators toward the beginning of a unit, as you alert students to potentially new issues. These discussions are often effective when used following a Directed Discussion ("Now that you understand _____ in more detail, what decision would you make regarding _____?") or in conjunction with class research projects. Reflective Discussions are particularly effective near the end of a unit, or as a wrap-up to a series of lessons, because they challenge students to apply what they've learned to make sense of complex situations and make well-reasoned decisions.

Once again, think back to the suggestions that we made regarding promoting critical thinking. The Reflective Discussion method is ideally suited to the *context of justification,* when you challenge your students to consider what they know to make well-informed decisions, because they can help students pull the cognitive pieces together and to *use* what they've learned in a meaningful context. The implication in doing this is that there is a purpose for learning about a topic, that learning in your classroom is generative (i.e., what your students learn in your classroom will be useful for understanding events in the real world).

Conducting Reflective Discussions, which focus on students' viewpoints and insist on intellectual rigor, sends the message that you actually care about what your students think. This implied confidence in your students will strengthen positive affect in your classroom (see "Resocializing," Module Two) and help motivate the kids to take on new challenges.

■ TIP FOR TECHNOLOGY INTEGRATION

Taking a position, defending it, and reflecting on the process are a big part of the Reflective Discussion experience. We recommend the use of programs like HyperStudio or PowerPoint as part of this process. Challenge students to share their position on an issue and their de-

fense of it by developing and sharing a self-designed program with classmates. Projects like this can be done individually or in peer groups.

■ ROUNDUP ■

In your classroom, use Reflective Discussions to challenge your students to consider complex, challenging issues and problems, consider and debate possible solutions, and come to a final resolution that they can defend, based on logical reasoning and an analysis of their own values. This method is perhaps the ultimate one for helping students to develop their critical-thinking abilities. They are challenged to search for and weigh evidence; listen to and consider the positions of others; consider biases; and ultimately to make, state, and defend a final decision—all supremely important critical-thinking abilities. These discussions also challenge students to *use* what they have learned with regard to important topics, thus deepening and extending their understanding of central concepts and principles.

We believe that there are several important keys to conducting effective Reflectives. Obviously, a compelling topic, which students have some basic understanding of, helps. Your structuring device must invite some debate or consideration of options and call on students to make some kind of a defensible choice. You must plan the discussion so that you promote a lively exchange of ideas and ideally some degree of controversy or disagreement among your students; using role-playing or debate techniques can help you to do this. In addition, the Culmination to a discussion like this should call on students not

---

The students in Mr. Nemcek's Algebra I class have spent the last two weeks learning about matrices. In teaching each topic in each of his math courses, "Mr. N" tries to make as many of what he calls real-world connections as possible; and that is his goal in today's lesson. After the bell rings, the teacher conducts a brief review of some of the topics covered and then asks an unusual question: "How fair would an election be if the person setting up the election knew in advance who the winner would be?" The students look at him quizzically; many reply that it would be unfair, that it shouldn't be allowed, and so on. Mr. Nemcek then tells the class that they are going to use what they know about matrices to determine the fairest way to elect a president for the school math club. The teacher then explains three different approaches that the eleven members of the math club could use to choose from among four candidates for club president. As one option, all persons in the club could have one vote for their top choice. Option #2 would allow members two votes, which they could give one candidate or split between two. The third option would allow voters to rank candidates 3, 2, 1, 0 based on their preferences. Mr. N challenges the class to "use what they know about matrices to determine what they think is the fairest way to elect a president." During the ensuing discussion, utilizing different matrix options provided by the teacher, the students discover that if someone knew in advance how each voter felt about the candidates in order of preference, it would be possible to have three different winners, depending on which voting method is selected! With the help of occasional questions from Mr. Nemcek, the class debates the pros and cons of each approach and finally chooses what it feels is the fairest method through, ironically, a class vote.[3]

FIGURE 11.3 A Glimpse Inside a Constructivist Classroom

only to make and defend a position but to think carefully about the entire discussion process and how it affected their thinking.

As you conduct your first Reflective Discussions, we urge you to be as patient as possible and to skillfully use the questioning techniques that we have suggested. It might take some time for your students to become accustomed to this approach, but the benefits make the entire process worthwhile.

Take some time to explore the complete Reflective Discussion lesson plan that follows. We then invite you to use the Hands-On Practice sheet to plan *your* first Reflec-

tive Discussion. The flowchart in Figure 11.4 is another planning aid.

■ REFLECTIVE DISCUSSION SAMPLE LESSON PLAN ■

Unit Title: Probability in Your Life (intended for a high school Algebra II or probability and statistics course)[4]

1 = structuring device: question as student aim

intention ⟶ examine two sides of an issue or controversy
and arrive at a value judgment with justification

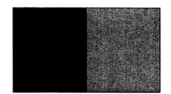

Which is the more effective . . . ?
Can we justify our point of view?

Do the detriments outweigh the benefits of . . . ? Why?

2 = elicit both sides of the issue or controversy

use questions or role-play based on instructional materials

S–S dialogue.
DO NOT LECTURE.
Steer discussion only
when necessary.

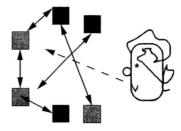

3 = organize points of view by headings

use board, overhead, etc.

PROs	CONs
1 ___	1 ___
2 ___	2 ___
3 ___	3 ___

4 = culmination: students answer structuring device

elicit value judgments with justifications   elicit implications

I think this is beneficial because . . . .   It's not moral because . . . .

© 2001 Ina Claire Gabler

FIGURE 11.4 Reflective Discussion Method Flowchart

Prelude

Rationale

(Combines What? Why? Justification): By challenging students to first assess the validity of a set of statistics and then to *use* this information to make a real-life, values-based decision, I will provide multiple opportunities for students to apply mathematical concepts in authentic contexts. This experience will help students to develop important mathematical reasoning and critical-thinking abilities and connects to INTASC Standards 1 and 3–7.

Performance Objective

(Combines Preparation, Product, Criteria): After analyzing a collection of statistical claims in a set of advertisements, the class as a group will brainstorm a list of concerns about the validity of any such claim. Then, in two large groups, students will prepare pro/con arguments and debate positions for and against the legalization of gambling in Hawaii, with each student making a final decision on the question and supporting this decision with at least three pieces of evidence.

Materials and Lesson Aids

1. Set of advertisements scanned into a computer program

2. Equipment needed to project scanned advertisements

3. Hand-outs summarizing survey data related to legalized gambling in Hawaii

Enactment

Time Estimate	Main Ideas/Concepts, Questions, and Teaching Methods
8–10 minutes	*Hook* Dozens of times every day, we're exposed to ads like this (flash first example on screen) in which a company makes a *statistical claim*. What do you notice about this ad? What are they trying to tell us by making this claim? Do you tend to believe these statistical statements? Why/why not? Where would the advertisers *get* the data they're referring to? (Flash other examples; ask similar questions, compare contrast; note that many

of the claims involve data from surveys, questionnaires, opinion polls.)
What concerns would you have about the *validity* of any of these claims?
(Possible responses: sample size, nature of questions asked, bias of interviewers, selective use of data)

2–3 minutes	*Student Aim* An understanding of math can help you to make sense of the things that people are trying to tell you, whether we're talking about ads or about other claims that someone might make. Today, we're going to apply our understanding of statistics to a real issue. For the next thirty minutes, you are all going to become citizens of Hawaii. We're here to debate an important issue that is soon to come before the legislature: *Should the state of Hawaii pass a new law that would allow for legalized gambling?*
25–30 minutes	*Development* Explain debate procedure: • Class will be split in half; pro and con positions chosen randomly • Sides will have ten minutes to prepare an argument, using data on handout, which provides info on projected costs/revenues, public opinions on the issues, gambling addiction figures Emphasize that each side should carefully analyze the sometimes conflicting, contradictory, outrageous claims made within the data. • Each side will prepare a three-minute argument, to be presented by four chosen spokespersons. • Each side will have a ninety-second official rebuttal opportunity. • Debate will be followed by an open discussion and a vote. • Teacher's role: answer questions about the material, moderate the debate, then facilitate the discussion. Debate, with teacher moderation. Open discussion—return to structuring device, allow students to step away from assigned debate positions.

Potential questions:
Which side seemed to have the stronger case? Why?
Which claims seemed most believable? Why?
How might pollsters/others gather data like this?
What concerns do you have about the validity of the data?
Did any of the statistics seem contradictory? How would you explain this?
What else might citizens need to know to make a decision like this?
Can a decision like this be made based on statistical information only? What other factors come into play?

5 minutes

Culmination
If you really were a member of the Hawaiian legislature, how would you vote on this issue (show of hands)?
Why did you vote the way that you did (sample opinions)?

Wrap-Up
Today, we've seen that statistical data and the claims that people make based on them play a major role in all of our lives. Some of your major concerns regarding these issues were (provide summary).

Leap
Over the next few days, I'd like you to look for examples of claims that people in the real world are making, using statistics.

Look Ahead
On Friday, I'd like everyone to bring three examples in print to class. Look especially for examples of claims that you're skeptical about, based on what we did today (Assessment and Evaluation will come through this related assignment).

Assessment and Evaluation

Did the list of concerns directly relate to the claims of the advertisements?

Was each argument justified logically?

Was each argument justified with at least three pieces of concrete evidence?

Points: 1–5 for each assessment question. Minimum number of combined points for acceptable achievement: 12

■ HANDS-ON PRACTICE ■

Plan a Reflective Discussion by using the following template. Refer to Module Three for a look at the Core Components of a lesson, and review Module Eleven for detail on this type of discussion.

Prelude (for teacher reference)

- Rationale (with connection to national/state standards)
- Performance Objective (remember to be specific about what your students should be able to *do* to show you what they've learned)
- Materials and Lesson Aids

Enactment (Student engagement: What might you say/do/ask at each stage of the lesson?)

- Hook
- Student Aim

  Structuring device preface (How will you set up/contextualize your main question?)

  Posing the structuring device as a question (How will you *phrase* this main question?)

- Development

  Students debate/share and challenge each other's opinions in response to the structuring device. (What techniques—e.g., a role-play, debate—will you use to promote this?)

  Teacher facilitates interaction with Trigger questions. (How will you phrase questions that you *might* ask?)

  List Pros and cons.

- Culmination

  Wrap-Up: What will you say/do/ask to help students *reach a final resolution on the structuring device?*

  Leap: How could students use/apply these ideas in the future?

Assessment and Evaluation

What will you ask students to produce during/after the lesson to show what they've learned?

How will you evaluate this product?

ENDNOTES

1. Thanks to Rebecca Ayers, Augustana College Class of 1999, for contributing this suggestion.
2. Thanks to Nick Polyak, Augustana College Class of 1999, for contributing this suggestion.
3. Thanks to Carissa Rojanasumaphong, Augustana College Class of 2001, for her contributions to this scenario.
4. Thanks to Charles Haben, Augustana College Class of 1999, for his contributions to this lesson plan.

Module 12

The Interactive Presentation Method

■ OVERVIEW: A VIGNETTE DEPICTING AN INTERACTIVE PRESENTATION

Lights out, PowerPoint on. Nutrition is the topic and a balanced diet is the theme. Mr. Singh projects slides of fish, chicken, beef, and soy; vegetables; fruits; grains; milk and cheese and smiling kids with terrific strong teeth. Double click and other slides portray overweight people, underweight people, advertisements of children gobbling down doughnuts and french fries and soda pop. Double click again and obese kids of every color fill the screen. Double click and there's a video of a grandmother hiking in some hills; she's svelte, strong, biting into an apple on the sound track.

Not a single student is falling asleep in the dark as Mr. Singh talks about each slide. Occasionally he asks a question, but he has his ten minutes and he's going full steam ahead, trying to impress on the teenagers in his classroom that their eating habits today will shape them tomorrow. Even in the dimmed room, even in the back, all of the candy-craving, potato-chip kids are alert, hanging on to every word. They're even scribbling.

Are these adolescents concerned with their old age? Is that the reason they're listening closely, jotting down notes, even drawing a thing or two—not doodles?

Mr. Singh's secret is the Interactive Presentation.

Before his first mini-talk and lights out, Mr. Singh gave instructions with Advance Organizer #1: During the mini-talk, pretend you've transformed into one of the people in the slides or video. Choose either a junk-food eater or a healthful eater. Jot down three to five reasons that your new self would give for eating the way "you" do. Then pretend you're a nutritionist and analyze the diet of the new you. As a nutritionist, give at least three reasons the new you should or should not change "your" diet based on the mini-talk. Next, the "nutritionist" draws a concept map for the new you, interrelating at least three concepts, which the "nutritionist" would inductively define (based on the facts in the mini-talk) about nutrition and health.

Then Mr. Singh gives his second mini-talk and Advance Organizer #2: Pairs of students will alternate roles as nutritionist and junk-food addict. The nutritionist explains and analyzes his concept map to the wayward eater.

So you see, those junk-food lovers are taking up the challenge about fish and kale, about teeth and bones, about health, yeah, and as Mr. Singh double clicks, he hopes that at lunch at least they'll eye soda pop warily and drink orange juice with their pizza.

Discussion

This scenario partly demonstrates that the Interactive Presentation (IP) method combines all of our methods into one. Another advantage is that all techniques apply as well. You can see that the Interactive Presentation method meets various learning styles in one lesson. This method also helps you "catch up" with your teaching agenda should you fall behind. The IP helps give you an edge on time because it calls for small chunks of teacher presentations, which we call "mini-talks." In these ways, the Interactive Presentation method permits endless flexibility along with focus and rigor.

■ FOCAL POINTS AND DISCUSSIONS

Focal Point 1 **What Makes the Interactive Presentation Method Distinctive?**

We'll begin with a global view or schema of the IP in Figure 12.1. Briefly, the IP features or method markers consist of what we call *parcels*. Each parcel contains (1) a teacher minipresentation, which we call a *mini-talk,* and (2) a student product, which we call a *mini-task*. An IP lesson may have as many or as few parcels as you prefer. Time and content guide that decision. Finally, a *minidiscussion* brings the key points into focus. In Focal Point #2, we describe each method marker in detail.

Focal Point 2 **The Interactive Presentation Method Markers**

We know you love to talk about your subject. Well, here's your chance. But as a constructivist teacher, even as you're expounding full force, you need to remember this ancient Chinese proverb:

> *I hear and I forget.*
> *I see and I remember.*
> *I do and I understand.*

Method Markers for the Interactive Presentation Method
Parcel One   • *Mini-talk #1*   • *Mini-task #1*   *Parcel Two*   • *Mini-talk #2*   • *Mini-task #2*   *Minidiscussion*

FIGURE 12.1 Interactive Presentation Planning Template

In keeping with this time-honored proverb, the Interactive Presentation method lets you talk about your subject—while alternating with student input. As we move through the Interactive Presentation method, we'll remind you of the Chinese proverb now and then as a preventative against turning the IP into a lecture, reducing your students to passive listeners.

Discussion 2 The Interactive Presentation Method Markers

As you consider these method markers, imagine yourself in the classroom, incorporating various methods and techniques.

Teacher Mini-Talk

The *mini-talk* may take five or ten minutes. Longer presentations tend to lose students' attention. This method marker enables you to introduce or review concentrated chunks of information along with concepts, principles, and themes with complementary textual, visual, and/or auditory materials. In the vignette, Mr. Singh used PowerPoint to display video as well as still images that functioned as focal points for comprehension, analysis, and synthesis. The mini-talk is most effective when it is clearly structured by a deductive or inductive framework (Module Four, Figure 4.9). A clear and focused structure is especially important for effective impact within the brief amount of time allotted to you.

Student Mini-Task

The *mini-task* may take five to twenty minutes or longer in a block program. The mini-task segment consists of a well-structured and focused activity or activities, which are carried out by a condensed method and techniques employed in longer lessons. Students work on each task as they listen to the mini-talk, applying the information as directed. In this way, your students become active listeners, thinking as you present.

In Mr. Singh's class, the students role-played and took notes, interpreting and analyzing the information in the mini-talk in keeping with their roles. Through a role-play perspective, Mr. Singh's students also drew concept maps that became a focal point in dyadic peer exchange. Finally, the students had to define the concepts themselves, briefly calling upon the Inductive Concept method (Module Eight, Part 2).

Altogether, Mr. Singh employed three techniques (role-playing, concept mapping, and peer-group learning—PGL) and one embedded method (Inductive Concept definition), not to mention the teacher mini-talk itself as a complementary method.

Notice the integration of the concept definition method with the concept mapping technique as well as the integration of role-playing with concept building. Mr. Singh could have decided on two methods with one technique each, or two or three techniques without a method in addition to the mini-talk. He planned according to his knowledge of how his students work within a given time frame.

Advance Organizers

The Interactive Presentation calls upon the *advance organizer*, a technique described with examples in Module Four. An advance organizer briefly describes or anticipates for the students what's just ahead and what they will be expected to do; it literally organizes your students' focus in advance of a task. In the IP, the teacher mini-talk contains one advance organizer for each task in the student mini-task segment.

EXAMPLES OF ADVANCE ORGANIZERS

- "During the mini-talk, try to identify all four concepts and jot them down for reference. Choose three of the four to interrelate in a concept map."

- "As you listen, apply the heuristic (see Module Four) *who, what, when, where, why, and how* to each of three principles that I will define and discuss."

- "In the simulation you will see about the Mississippi River, pretend that you're the boat captain. In this role, jot down at least three cause-and-effect relationships affecting your ability to navigate the river and deliver goods.

- "Before I begin, take a look at your activity sheet and notice the headings for filling in the table. After you fill in the table during the mini-talk, you'll apply the data to a controlled experiment that you design yourself."

- "As you watch the video, jot down at least four ways in which the main character fools himself. Based on the dialogue in the video, jot down what you think his motives may be and *why.*"

- (Written on board or handout): "As you listen to Dr. Martin Luther King, Jr.'s speech, jot down what you consider to be two or three of his most forceful arguments. Briefly describe your feelings about each. Phrases OK."

- "As you listen to this folk song about the American Revolution, write at least two arguments each for the colonists and the loyalists. Compare and contrast these arguments to those of the French Revolution. Exchange your ideas with a partner after the mini-talk."

- (Written on board or activity sheet): "During the mini-talk, identify at least three categories on the graph that demonstrate the concept of *X.* Write down at least one reason for each category. Be prepared to compare categories and defend your interpretation with your neighbor."

- (Written on board or activity sheet): "Fill in the first two main ideas with two supporting facts each as you listen to the second mini-talk. Anticipate in writing at least one other main idea in the third mini-talk that follows. Be able to justify your anticipated main idea. Relate to the theme of this lesson on your activity sheet."

- (Place an unhealthy plant on your desk.): "Write down three to five reasons for the plant's unhealthy state based on the mini-talk matched to the plant's appearance."[1]

- (Written or oral): "In any way you like, draw a representation of the relationship for the two events described in the upcoming mini-talk. Try to anticipate how this relationship connects to the theme."

- "Choose a partner near you now. According to your birthdays, the older will take the role of R, described in the mini-talk. The younger will take the role of M. After the mini-talk, R and M will debate, citing at least four supporting reasons for their stands. Be ready to challenge each other respectfully. So take good notes!"

Parcel

As you've seen in the template, a *parcel* consists of one mini-talk followed by one mini-task. Depending on the time frame, an Interactive Presentation may include one, two, or even three parcels. The complete parcel elements look like this:

Parcel One

- Mini-Talk #1 with advance organizers
- Mini-Task #1 with method(s) and technique(s)

Parcel Two

- Mini-Talk #2 with advance organizers
- Mini-Task #2 with method(s) and technique(s)

If you're able to plan two or more parcels, each parcel either develops ideas from the previous parcel(s) or adds related ideas, all governed by the lesson Rationale. *Parcels must relate to one another.*

Minidiscussion

At the end of the last parcel, your students will need feedback on the quality of their completed tasks and insights. Feedback helps students process their ideas against those of their peers. They also need your input. Feedback can be accomplished in a *minidiscussion* in various forms, condensed versions of the Directed, Exploratory, and Re-

flective Discussion methods (see Modules Nine through Eleven). The Interactive Presentation method may peak (e.g., express the overriding principles or theme) in the minidiscussion or in the Culmination, the final Core Component that directly follows the minidiscussion.

Cognitive Frameworks

Cohesion—Don't teach without it! An intentional deductive or inductive framework or a combination of both integrates the parcels—both internally and in concert with each other. These cognitive frameworks help you to interrelate facts, concepts, and so on aided by Bloom's Taxonomy (Module Five, Part 1). Mini-task segments need such a well-stoked engine to take full advantage of the limited time frame, a constraint that helps your students focus quickly—if you plan well. *Try to keep in mind that one parcel may be deductive and the other inductive or vice versa in the same lesson.*

Focal Point 3 Integrating Core Components and Method Markers: A Template

IP method markers appear in the Development just as do method markers in all the other methods. Our suggested template for integrating the IP method with Core Components appears in Figure 12.2. At your discretion, the *minidiscussion* can serve as the Culmination.

Focal Point 4 When Should You Use the Interactive Presentation Method in Your Classroom?

There are several situations that may call for the Interactive Presentation method. One is when you might be tempted to lecture, to "cover" a "lot of material." The mini-talk of the IP lets you "deliver" information while your students are active learners, kept mentally alert by the various tasks you assign them. In a constructivist approach, your students apply the small bundles of information from the mini-talk in ways that make them *think*—analyzing, synthesizing, and evaluating—rather than parrot back what you've said. (*Repeating what you've said is no indication of the depth of their understanding, if any.*) Breaking up teacher talk into small bundles rather than giving one long lecture enhances student absorption of the information.

Another situation for the IP is one in which you want to add variety, a mosaic of techniques and methods in a single lesson that keeps your students thinking every minute. All our methods have the potential to do this, but the Interactive Presentation moves from one technique and minimethod to another quickly. The assortment of

Prelude (for teacher reference)

- Rationale (What are you teaching?; Why are you teaching this?; Justification)
- Performance Objective (Preparation, Product, and Criteria; unfolds in Development)
- Materials

Enactment (student engagement)

- Aim
- Hook
- Development (with IP method markers)
  Parcel One (may be deductive or inductive)
  Mini-Talk #1 (with advance organizers)
  Mini-Task #1 (includes Performance Objective)
  Parcel Two (may be inductive or deductive)
  Mini-Talk #2 (with advance organizers)
  Mini-Task #2 (includes Performance Objective)
  Minidiscussion
- Culmination (Wrap-Up and Leap)

Assessment and Evaluation

- Assessment products:
- Evaluation rubric categories and point scale:

FIGURE 12.2 Template for Integrating Core Components with IP Method Markers

tasks helps meet different learning styles in one lesson. The rapid pace helps to concentrate the mind.

Discussion 4 When Should You Use the Interactive Presentation Method in Your Classroom?

The Interactive Presentation—along with the other methods—carries out the wisdom of the Chinese proverb:

They see and they remember. They do and they understand.

This positive learning experience builds students' self-esteem, which in turn builds a positive attitude toward learning with you.

Pitfall

The trap for you, enthusiastic about your subject, is to talk too much during the mini-talk. The result? Your students are thrown back into the role of passive listeners. Most of your students will tune out in little time; you will wonder why they haven't learned what you *so clearly explained*. The fault lies not with the students. Remember the warning of the Chinese proverb: *They hear and they forget*. Especially if they're not challenged *to think*. If you

talk too much, your students will not have enough time to process the mini-tasks in a minidiscussion or even to complete their tasks.

Imagine yourself in this all-too-familiar situation. You're sinking into your seat, listening to a lecture in a subject that does not inspire you. How often do you watch the clock? How much do you retain after each lecture? How much enthusiasm do you feel during such a lecture? Most important, how much do you retain after each test for which you memorized what the teacher had said?

While you love your subject and *just know* that your students will catch the contagion by exposure to your enthusiasm, the truth is that, like yourself as a student in many other subject lessons, your typical student will be bored—yes, *completely uninterested*—in lengthy teacher talk, even in *your* subject. Most students are not inspired by the subject that any one of us teaches. Except for charismatic speakers, teacher talk alone will not light the torch. In case *you* should be one of those rarely gifted charismatic speakers, you may enthrall your students as an entertainer might, but what will they retain one week later as passive listeners, trying to repeat what you said?

The Interactive Presentation offers a motivating alternative to the traditional lecture as a time-efficient method. So rehearse your mini-talks to be sure they fit into the appropriate time frame. See Figure 12.3 for a comparison of the lecture and Interactive Presentation.

Focal Point 5 Up Close: Planning and Conducting an Interactive Presentation Lesson

It's time to put flesh on the bones. What follows is a sample Interactive Presentation, an inductive framework that facilitates student expression of a theme based on the concept of bigotry. The lesson is designed for a block program with a ninety-minute time frame. We describe this lesson one Core Component at a time. Time prescriptions are approximations.

■ INTERACTIVE PRESENTATION SAMPLE LESSON PLAN ■

Subject: The Benefits of Bigotry (history)

Prelude

Rationale

1. *What?:* To build on the concept of bigotry introduced yesterday, arriving at a unifying theme. This is a lead-in to the unit on Nazi Germany.

Characteristics	Lecture	Interactive Presentation
1. Teacher role	1. Dispenser of information; primary thinker in the classroom	1. Facilitator of student thinking using small bundles of information.
2. Student role	2. Passive listeners; only occasional responders if at all.	2. Active thinkers; active responders.
3. Materials	3. Mostly orally delivered information; overhead transparencies; occasional graphics or other media are considered bonus attractions; mostly, materials are employed to emphasize the teacher's points, not to stimulate critical thinking.	3. Visual and auditory media are requisite materials designed to prompt student interpretation and critical thinking.
4. Method markers (broadly described)	4a. Mostly teacher talk.	4a. *Parcels* comprised of (1) teacher mini-talk(s), with visual and auditory materials used as prompts for critical thinking, and (2) active student input in the form of mini-tasks.
	4b. Teacher develops major concepts and themes.	4b. Students develop major concepts and themes in a minidiscussion based on mini-talk(s) and mini-tasks.

FIGURE 12.3 Comparison of the Lecture and the Interactive Presentation

2. *Why?:* Students will interpret and analyze examples of bigotry to establish the psychological need of bigotry in some individuals. Learners will synthesize examples to establish a theme.

3. *Justification:* INTASC Standards 1, 2, 3, 5, 6.

Performance Objective

1. *Preparation:* Two mini-talks and two mini-tasks will establish the psychological appeal of bigotry regardless of the targeted group. An activity sheet establishes a knowledge base and also prompts original interpretations.

2. *Product:* Students will be able to develop a theme in writing that synthesizes the two major concepts in their own original words.

3. *Criteria:* Students will be able to answer at least ten questions on activity sheets following two mini-talks. See prompts on activity sheet. A standard five-paragraph essay will develop the theme.

Materials

1. Photograph of KKK
2. Overhead transparencies as prompts for discussion
3. Activity sheets for mini-tasks
4. Video footage

Enactment

Hook (5 Minutes)

1. Display picture of the KKK and a burning cross.
2. Say: "Let's brainstorm your ideas in response to this image."
3. Write responses on board: Introduce the concept of bigotry.
4. Project transparency (Figure 12.4) with quotation of American Japanese during WWII: "The constitution is just a piece of paper." Review bigotry against obesity and homosexuality from yesterday's concept lesson.

Aim

(On transparency, Figure 12.4): What is bigotry's political value? What is bigotry's allure to the individual?

Development (with Method Markers and Performance Objective)

Parcel One (Inductive)

• *Mini-Talk 1* (10 minutes):

Advance Organizer (a): "Take notes on all seven key points during my talk about the KKK and Japanese

Big Questions:

1. What is bigotry's political value?
2. What is bigotry's allure to the individual?

* * * * * * *

A. KKK burning a cross: How does this act, using the ultimate Christian symbol, fit with Christian teachings?
B. Japanese Americans incarcerated in camps during WWII.
  1. Forced to sell homes and businesses in just one week.
  2. Distrusted because of their origins and Pearl Harbor attack. Yet many were citizens. Older Japanese despondent. Suicides. Japanese regiment received the highest number of honors in the war.
  3. "The constitution is just a piece of paper."
C. Compare and contrast racial prejudice against the Japanese in WWII with rejection of obese and gay people discussed yesterday.

FIGURE 12.4 Overhead Transparency for Mini-Talk #1

internment during WWII. You'll be asked to relate these to your first mini-task."

The Talk: The mini-talk relates the KKK in the Hook to the origins, rise, and present situation of the KKK. It also discusses the history of Japanese American citizens' internment during WWII.

Advance Organizer (b): "Now we're going to take a look at colonial bigotry and figure out the benefits to the Pilgrims. As you watch this video, you'll answer some questions on the handout. Then you'll discuss other questions with a partner. Be prepared to relate the colonial history to the KKK and Japanese internment in WWII. Let's quickly read the directions out loud beforehand in case you have any questions about them.

- *Mini-Task 1* (25 minutes): Students watch five-minute video segment and respond to activity sheet (Figure 12.5). Activity sheet includes culminating question to establish a principle.

Parcel Two (Deductive)

- *Mini-Talk 2* (10 minutes): Project transparency with Sartre's quotation about anti-Semitism (Figure 12.6).

Advance Organizer (a): "Now I'm going to talk about Jean-Paul Sartre's book *Anti-Semite and Jew.* As you listen, I'd like you to make a list of the four major points and at least two examples of each major point. Later on, we'll discuss how or if Sartre's theory applies to an infamous trial."

The Talk: The minipresentation first refers to the transparency. Then it outlines a summary of the main arguments in Sartre's book.

Advance Organizer (b): "Now we're going to watch a seven-minute videoclip about a murder trial that took place in the South in the early twentieth century.

As you watch, answer the questions on your second activity sheet (Figure 12.7). The last question asks you to consider Sartre's theory. Read the directions and ask any questions you may have before we begin."

- *Mini-Task 2* (25 minutes): Students watch video about the trial of Leo Frank and answer the questions on the activity sheet.

MINIDISCUSSION (10 minutes): Directed Discussion brings together concepts and principles, establishing anti-Semitism as the "ultimate evidence" and as personal empowerment and political weapon.

Culmination (5 minutes)

Wrap-Up: Recap with the Big Questions on first transparency (Figure 12.4). Ask: "Who benefits from bigotry and how?"

Leap: Students establish theme—something like *bigotry as a means of power.* Ask: "What is the underlying relationship between the two Big Questions?" "Tomorrow we'll begin to apply these ideas to the rise of the Nazis before WWII."

Assessment and Evaluation

Assessment products

Evaluation rubric and point scale

We invite you to outline the assessment products, including what you think are the key features for each product. Then design an evaluation rubric with (1) criteria for each task and (2) a point scale for this sample Interactive Presentation lesson. Remember to specify a minimum number of total points for acceptable achievement. Refer to Figures 12.4–12.7.

Figures 12.4–12.7 represent transparencies and activity sheets for this lesson.

Mini-Task #1

Question: Can you predict how Pilgrims in power would behave today?

Your Job

A. As you watch the video, *The Shadow of Hate,*[2] answer questions 1–3 on your own.
B. After you watch the video, work with a partner and together discuss questions 4–6. Each of you write down the answers for 4–6. If you disagree, write down the answers you prefer. Support your reasons.

Questions

1. Why did the first Europeans come to North America?
2. How would they describe freedom?
3. List the indicated number and type of persecutions they inflicted on the following groups.
   a. Native American Indians (1)
   b. Africans (1)
   c. Quakers (2–3)
   d. Baptists (2–3)

Discuss and answer with a partner

4. How might the early Europeans (Pilgrims) have justified their cruelty toward the groups they persecuted?
5. How could the reasons the Pilgrims searched for religious freedom apply to their treatment of other racial and religious groups?
6. Compare and contrast the ideology of the KKK and Japanese American internment during WWII with Pilgrim bigotry.
7. What limited judgments can you make about the psychological relationship between bigots and their victims? Support your viewpoint.
8. Predict how Pilgrims in political power might behave today. What groups might they join? What activities might they participate in? Would they hide their bigotry? Why?

Defend each viewpoint with at least three documented reasons.

FIGURE 12.5 Interactive Presentation Activity Sheet for Mini-Task #1

■ TIP FOR TECHNOLOGY INTEGRATION

Here's an idea for incorporating technology into the Interactive Presentation method.

During an inductive mini-talk on photosynthesis in a science class, students watch a computer simulation of photosynthesis that parallels the talk. The coupling of a verbal description with animation addresses different learning styles—linguistic, auditory, and visual. During the mini-task, students experiment with the simulation (e.g., altering the variables or omitting steps of the process of photosynthesis) and observe the simulated outcomes. An original student analysis of the importance of each variable and step in photosynthesis follows, resulting in a student table, graphic representation, and so on along with a student definition of photosynthesis.

> "If there were no Jews,
> the anti-Semite would make them."
> —*Anti-Semite and Jew,* Jean-Paul Sartre

FIGURE 12.6 Transparency for Mini-Talk #2

■ ROUNDUP ■

The Interactive Presentation method is a medley of mini-talks and student products with various methods, techniques, and materials. The variety addresses a range of learning styles in a single lesson. Another advantage of the Interactive Presentation is that, like the lecture, it's

---

Mini-Task #2

Question: What was the ultimate piece of evidence against Leo Frank?

Your Job

1. As you watch the video about Leo Frank, list one to three examples of anti-Semitism.
2. List as many pieces of concrete evidence as you can that supported Frank's guilt in the murder.
3. What was Tom Watson's motive in "convicting" Leo Frank in Watson's own publication?
4. Why was Watson elected to the U.S. Senate?
5. Compare and contrast the predominant gentile behavior in the Frank case with the Pilgrims' behavior in North America.
6. In this event, what role does anti-Semitism play for the public onlookers?
7. How does Sartre's theory about anti-Semitism apply to the Leo Frank trial? Be specific with at least four substantiated reasons.

FIGURE 12.7 Interactive Presentation Activity Sheet for Mini-Task #2

time efficient, allowing your students to consider a substantial amount of information. Finally, if you follow the time constraints, the IP does not let teacher talk be excessive and guides your students to be critical thinkers, applying, analyzing, and synthesizing the information with a wide range of prompts. See the Interactive Presentation method Flowchart in Figure 12.8 for a graphic representation.

■ HANDS-ON PRACTICE ■

With the template, flowchart, and Bloom's Taxonomy in hand, try planning your own Interactive Presentation. We're providing the template here. You may want to continue to develop the same topic as in previous Hands-On Practices or choose another topic altogether.

Planning Tip

For two parcels, decide on two major, related concepts, principles, and/or themes that capture the heart of the Rationale. Assign one of those distinct ideas as the focus for each mini-talk. Also keep in mind that the overarching concept(s), principle(s), or theme may peak in either the minidiscussion or the Culmination.

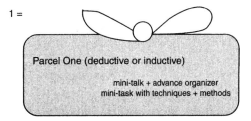

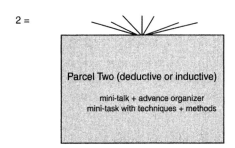

1 =

Parcel One (deductive or inductive)

mini-talk + advance organizer
mini-task with techniques + methods

2 =

Parcel Two (deductive or inductive)

mini-talk + advance organizer
mini-task with techniques + methods

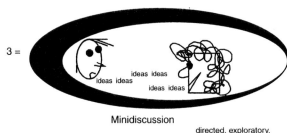

3 =

Minidiscussion

directed, exploratory, reflective discussions

© 2001 Ina Claire Gabler

FIGURE 12.8 Interactive Presentation Method Flowchart

Self-Instruct Planner for the Interactive Presentation Method

Subject _____ Topic _____
(Work on a separate piece of paper.)

Prelude (for teacher reference)

- Rationale (What two concepts, principles, and/or themes will capture the heart of this Rationale in the two mini-talks?)

  What are you teaching?

  Why are you teaching this?

  Justification

- Performance Objective

  Preparation

  Product

  Criteria

- Materials

Enactment (student engagement)

- Aim
- Hook
- Development (with IP method markers)

  Parcel One (may be deductive or inductive)

  Mini-Talk 1: (with one or more advance organizers)

  Mini-Task 1: (includes Performance Objective)

  Parcel Two (may be inductive or deductive)

  Mini-Talk 2: (with one or more advance organizers)

  Mini-Task 2: (includes Performance Objective)

  Minidiscussion (Include sample Trigger, Probe, and Redirect questions)

- Culmination

  Wrap-Up

  Leap

Assessment and Evaluation

- Assessment products:
- Evaluation rubric categories with point scale:

ENDNOTES

1. Based on a lesson by Cyndie Morain when she was a preservice teacher at the University of Illinois in Urbana-Champaign.
2. *The Shadow of Hate* is a video available from the "Teaching Tolerance" program of the Southern Poverty Law Center, 400 Washington Avenue, Montgomery, AL 36104.

SUGGESTED READING

Atwell, N. (1987). In the middle: Writing, reading and learning with adolescents. Portsmouth, New Hampshire: Boynton/Cook Publishers.

Eisner, E. (1985). *Educational imagination* (2nd ed.). Upper Saddle River, NJ: Merrill/Prentice Hall.

Middendorf, J., & Kalish, A. (1996). The "change-up" in lectures. *The National Teaching & Learning Forum, 5*(2), 1–5.

Shostar, R. (1990). Lesson presentation skills. In Cooper, J. M. (Ed.). *Classroom teaching skills,* 4th ed. Lexington, MA: D.C. Heath.

METHODS FINALE:
Integrating Methods

Here are two examples of combining methods and various techniques for unit planning. The first example is a template. The second example is a scenario entitled *Fishy Mystery*.

EXAMPLE #1   *Sample Combination for a Wide-Ranging Unit*

1. Field-test your students' schema of a unit's Rationales with an ILPE.

2. Employ Directed Discussions and/or Inductive and Deductive Concept lessons to introduce major concepts, principles, and themes.

3. Develop further substance with an Interactive Presentation.

4. Explore concepts, principles, and/or themes further with an Exploratory Discussion.

5. Assign focused research on the concepts.

6. Enable students to evaluate and synthesize various aspects of major concepts, principles, and themes with a Reflective Discussion, applying their research findings and achieving high cognitive levels.

7. Incorporate peer-group learning (PGL) techniques so that students can apply the concepts, principles, and themes introduced with the preceding methods, discovering new facts and insights with guided independence, using instructional materials.

EXAMPLE #2   *Example of A Unit with Methods And Technology*

A Scenario: Fishy Mystery*

Katie and Daryl, tenth- through twelfth-grade earth science and social studies teachers, respectively, are team-teaching a unit around an authentic student inquiry into a local water quality problem. The unit emphasizes students' problem-solving and critical-thinking skills. Entitled "What's Killing the Fish Downstream?," the unit comprises five block lessons.

* © 2001 David Curtis

A decidedly "low-tech" Hook, a dead fish on ice, will kick off the unit, which will be held in one of the school's computer labs. After holding up the fish, smelling it, and grimacing with disgust, Katie will present a short, local TV newsclip about summer fish kills in a nearby lake. Katie and Daryl will then investigate students' prior exposure to and knowledge of key concepts and information technology (ILPE Method) while laying groundwork for a guided student investigation. Their insights into the students' understandings will be applied during the ensuing lesson, which will integrate Inductive Concept and Exploratory Discussion methods. Twice during the Exploratory Discussion section, the students will break away in pairs to their assigned computers.

Guided by activity sheets (Module Six, Part 2) embedded in their digital notebooks, students will use digital geographic mapping software accessible via the Web to investigate spatial relationships between the lake and nearby features. Such features might include streams, drainage basins, roads, land cover, farm fields, a sewage treatment plant, a large shopping mall, and outlying subdivisions. Through a simple-to-use Web interface, the mapping software tool enables the students to zoom, overlay, and identify distinct features. In doing so, Katie will introduce the students to Geographic Information Systems (GIS), a powerful visualization and database technology with which to integrate data collection, visualization, and analysis.

During the discussion, Katie and Daryl will moderate student–student dialogues about possible factors linked to weather, climate, and land use that could affect water quality of the downstream lake. The class will collectively articulate a list of closely related questions to guide the investigation. Is runoff from the farm fields along streams that feed into the lake causing the fish to die, and if so, how? Might all those fertilizers have something to do with it? Could runoff from the shopping mall alongside the lake be the cause of the fish dying? Or might that sewage plant further north be the culprit? What is happening to the nitrogen and oxygen levels in the lake? Is there a connection with broiling summer temperatures that coincided with the fish kill? How were other lake creatures faring during this time? Were they also suffering ill effects, even dying? Using software for concept mapping, the class will also develop an initial schema of factors thought to affect water quality and related social issues.

The initial schema file will be saved and uploaded to the unit Website specially created to document the students' investigations for later assessment and presentation to peers. For homework, students will be required to access the Web from home, the public library, or the community technology center. They will read and evaluate information on water quality at an authoritative educational Website, then individually propose a tentative causal hypothesis to explain the fish kills, together with supporting arguments and ways to test it. They will write and upload their conjectures in their individually assigned digital notebook spaces and refer to them in upcoming class discussions.

Over the next one-and-one-half block lessons, Exploratory Discussions will be combined with peer-group learning techniques to sift through the varying hypotheses and pursue the most promising ones. Katie will guide the students as they develop strategies to gather and analyze data to test their theories. To accomplish this, they will utilize a variety of tools and datasets. These will include the Web-based mapping tool, which is linked to environmental datasets accessible via a statewide natural resources information Website; a graphing tool to investigate quantitative relationships between putative water quality factors; and an educational, Web-based computer simulator to invoke and examine various "what-if" scenarios. In one scenario, for instance, selected factors such as land use are changed while others (such as the amount of rainfall) are held constant, and the impacts on third factors, such as nitrogen levels, are viewed graphically.

The students' simulation experiments will be structured via carefully layered, open-ended question prompts that Katie is developing via email correspondence with the cooperating teachers. By the middle of the third lesson, through class and group work and individual homework assignments, the students will have refined their earlier schema or concept map to include causal interrelationships thought to account for the fish kill. Their theory will be that farm field runoff containing excessive fertilizer is the leading suspect. In stimulating overgrowth of algae, whose subsequent dying and decay depletes dissolved lake oxygen, the nutrient-enriched runoff is thought to bring about a precipitous decline in oxygen, aided by the high summer temperatures. So the fish can't breathe and die off in droves.

Next will come the tougher part: figuring out how to reduce or eliminate the problem. Working in small groups, students will run the Web simulator again and test alternative mitigation strategies that are most likely to prevent or reduce algae overgrowth, as judged by how well each strategy would diminish or remove the mediating causes leading to the fish kill. Again, the students will be guided by teacher prompts embedded in the students' digital notebooks. Students will then write up their findings and recommendations with justifications in their notebooks. The scene will be set for the final lesson.

Daryl will begin by using the Inductive Concept method. Students will generate a concept map of the social costs and issues with which to evaluate the alternative strategies, drawing upon their digital notebook entries from the previous lesson and incorporating the concept map refined in the third lesson. Employing peer-group techniques, Daryl will then moderate a Reflective Discussion of potential solutions to the runoff problem. Pairs of students will take on distinct roles—farmer, land-use planner, wildlife manager, suburban developer, citizen group, and so forth—to evaluate the proposed solutions and weigh their social costs and impacts. In a summative assessment to be carried out during an extended period, individual students, using multimedia authoring software, will create a final Web report. They will be required to propose and justify, with evidence (charts, graphs, and maps "captured" in their digital notebook during the unit) and reasoning, a cost-conscious plan that addresses the fish-kill problem while balancing different stakeholders' interests and concerns.

In the final block class, students will present their reports to the class and receive peer and teacher feedback, after which they will be able to fine-tune and edit their reports. Their reports will be compiled into a class Web project that will be posted on the school's Website. Parents, the local media, stakeholder groups, city and regional planning authorities, and other interested parties will be notified of the address and invited to comment via an electronic discussion board linked to the site.

Behind the Scenes

Chances are that if you're participating in an inservice workshop using *Invisible Teaching,* you have the administrative and collegial support that you need to either experiment with constructivism for the first time or to expand your present efforts and skills in that vein. Some colleagues or even supervisors, however, might think that as a student-centered teacher, you become too "invisible" in the classroom. Some of them may be skeptical about giving students the freedom—and responsibility—to make so many important decisions.

How can you respond to some of the skepticism among your professional peers?

Before we address that question, let's assume that you've implemented some of the methods in *Invisible Teaching.* Based on your ongoing assessments and evaluations, you know that your students are learning in greater depth; at-risk and once-disinterested students are beginning to participate with newfound interest. They tell you that for the first time, they enjoy your subject. There are even lessons that end with your students still talking about the ideas as they leave the classroom. Many of your students stop by before and after school to ask you questions related to these ideas, even to do additional activities or to finish something that they've started in class. Obviously, there is a disparity between your constructivist practice and the perception that some (but definitely not all) educators may have of it.

Why do so many teachers and educational administrators mistrust a student-centered, constructivist approach?

We believe that a primary reason is the classroom setting. The teacher is not always at the front of the room talking at students sitting quietly in neat rows (perhaps too quietly). A constructivist classroom may appear to lack structure. When students are exchanging their ideas in a lively hum, it seems as if they're socializing, not learning what they "need to know."

Such appearances may raise some of your colleagues' eyebrows. They may sincerely question the value of such "permissive" methods—or they may even be threatened if they've heard your students talking enthusiastically; perhaps those colleagues have not been able to engage their own students in the same way. Or they may earnestly believe that you are not keeping up with the curriculum and imposing disciplined standards on your students.

So to return to the original question, How do you meet professional criticism of a constructivist approach?

We believe that it is important to address the misconceptions. First, you can allay their concerns by informing the professional skeptics that a constructivist lesson is even more structured and thoroughly planned than a typical traditional lesson. For the most part, traditional lessons structure only the content. Even questions in a didactic context usually address lower-level comprehension skills and are content-driven, rarely facilitating critical thinking. Constructivist lessons structure both the content and the *thinking process,* providing prompts (questions and tasks) that guide active student engagement. Substance is related to students' frames of reference and motivates learners. Students not only learn content and develop higher cognitive skills, they learn how to learn.

Behind the scenes in this process, a constructivist educator must be well informed in order to facilitate effectively; she must apply knowledge of students' various learning styles for maximum advantage; she must constantly be assessing and evaluating throughout the learning to catch gaps of learning or loss of interest. In short, a constructivist teacher is a well prepared, intellectually rigorous teacher who challenges his students to think about significant ideas at the highest levels (Brooks & Brooks, 1999; Newmann, 1997; Wiggins & McTighe, 1998).

Motivated students working conceptually retain more of the curriculum—which is the compass of your syllabus. In fact, the students may examine that syllabus and in time design a learning plan. They retain more because their learning *matters* to them.

As for the bottom line: Research has shown that "diverse, active, and intellectually provocative forms of instruction" result in the best test scores (Wiggins & McTighe, 1998, p. 132). Not only that, but "constructivist students" develop a greater ability than their traditionally taught counterparts to think deeply as they use knowledge outside the classroom: These students experience learning as part of their lives and personal enrichment.

At this point we'd like to remind you to revisit the "Fishy Mystery" scenario in "Methods Finale." You may recall that this scenario depicts ideal constructivist teaching and learning, integrating student-centered methods in a way that is instructively rigorous and also motivating. As ideal as this picture may seem, it demonstrates authentic learning that motivates students, and not only the already successful students. Authentic learning can motivate those students who are bored, disinterested, or lacking the necessary skills—the very students you might think could "never do this." From our experience, such students are often the ones to become the most engaged in authentic learning, seeing relevance in school for the first time. This motivation prompts them to learn the necessary skills in a meaningful context.

Chances are that there may be one or more teachers in your school employing student-centered methods also. We suggest that you work with them. Exchange ideas and plan interdisciplinary units and projects. In this way, the more teachers in your school who are committed to engaging students and challenging them with in-depth learning, the more the numbers of those teachers will grow. In this way, you and your colleagues can build a vibrant learning community.

Remember that constructivist teachers care deeply about their students, about their interests, about the development of their thinking abilities, about their joy in learning. Constructivist teachers continuously try to create classroom experiences that will prepare their students for a brighter future. If you are seeking ways to expand your teaching skills, we know that you care about your students. Let them know that, in everything you do. Teach with high expectations, even if you are doubtful at first; your students—and you—will find yourselves on new and enriching paths. Be among those who have "the courage to be constructivist" (Brooks & Brooks, 1999).

REFERENCES

Brooks, M. G., & Brooks, J. G. (1999, November). The courage to be constructivist. *Educational Leadership*, 18–24.

Newmann, F. N., & Associates (1997). *Authentic achievement: Restructuring schools for intellectual quality.* San Francisco: Jossey-Bass.

Wiggins, G., & McTighe, J. (1998). *Understanding by design.* Alexandria, VA: Association for Supervision and Curriculum Development.